On Being Old

Contemporary Psychology Series

Series Editor: Professor Raymond Cochrane
School of Psychology
The University of Birmingham
Birmingham B15 2TT
United Kingdom

This series of books on contemporary psychological issues is aimed primarily at 'A' Level students and those beginning their undergraduate degree. All of these volumes are introductory in the sense that they assume no, or very little, previous acquaintance with the subject, while aiming to take the reader through to the end of his or her first course on the topic they cover. For this reason the series will also appeal to those who encounter psychology in the course of their professional work: nurses, social workers, police and probation officers, speech therapists and medical students. Written in a clear and jargon-free style, each book generally includes a full (and in some cases annotated) bibliography and points the way explicitly to further reading on the subject covered.

Psychology and Social Issues:
A Tutorial Text
Edited by Raymond Cochrane, *University of Birmingham* and Douglas Carroll, *Glasgow Polytechnic*

Families: A Context for Development
David White and Anne Woollett, *Polytechnic of East London*

The Psychology of Childhood
Peter Mitchell, *The University of Wales College at Swansea*

On Being Old: The Psychology of Later Life
Graham Stokes, Gulson Hospital, Coventry

Forthcoming titles:

Health Psychology: Stress, Behaviour and Disease
Douglas Carroll, *Glasgow Polytechnic*

Food and Drink: The Psychology of Nutrition
David Booth, *University of Birmingham*

Contemporary Psychology Series: 6

On Being Old:
The Psychology of Later Life

Graham Stokes

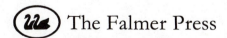 The Falmer Press

(a member of the Taylor & Francis Group)
London • Washington, DC

UK   The Falmer Press, 4 John Street, London WC1N 2ET
USA   The Falmer Press, Taylor & Francis Inc., 1900 Frost Road, Suite 101,
       Bristol, PA 19007

© Graham Stokes 1992

First published 1992

A catalogue record for this book is available from the British Library

Library of Congress Cataloging-in-Publication Data are available on request

ISBN 1 85000 839 6
ISBN 1 85000 840 X(pbk)

Jacket design by Benedict Evans

Typeset in 10/11.5pt Garamond
by Graphicraft Typesetters Ltd., Hong Kong.

Printed in Great Britain by Burgess Science Press, Basingstoke on paper which has a specified pH value on final paper manufacture of not less than 7.5 and is therefore 'acid free'.

Contents

Contents

To Jayne, for her patience, support and kind words, and to Liam and Rebecca who will enjoy later life in the 2060s.

Acknowledgments

Particular thanks are due to Professor Raymond Cochrane who read the earlier drafts and provided helpful suggestions which improved the final version immensely, and to Lesley Bradshaw who typed several versions of the manuscript with unerring accuracy and was kind enough not to complain about my handwriting.

Series Editor's Preface

> For Age, with stealing steps,
> Hath clawed me with his clutch.

Lord Thomas penned these unhappy words in about 1550, and a few years later William Shakespeare was even more explicit when he wrote, 'Age, I do abhor thee, youth, I do adore thee'. Why? Well — 'Youth is full of pleasance, age is full of care'. Before and since the sixteenth century it is not hard to find negative references to ageing and old age in literature, science and popular culture. Even basically positive reference such as Wordsworth's advice to a Young Lady has a sting in the tail:

> But an old age, serene and bright,
> And lovely as a Lapland night,
> Shall lead thee to thy grave.

It must be the association of old age with impending death that makes it frightening, sad and even repulsive to so many people. Psychologists too have been guilty of studying old age and the ageing process as a deviation from the happy norm of youth. So we ask questions about the rate of cognitive decline with age, study the process of social withdrawal, examine the aetiology of dementia.

Graham Stokes, an experienced psychogeriatrician clinical geropsychologist, does all these things in this book, but also considers the positive aspects of ageing and challenges the stereotype that age invariably means decline, degeneration and disengagement.

The startling facts of demographic trends mean that the size of the old and very old population of Britain and other post-industrial societies is set to escalate over the next few decades in both absolute and relative levels. It is important, both for those who will form part of this population boom and those who will live alongside it, to be aware of the psychological as well as physical aspects of the ageing process and be prepared to adapt to the changes, for good and ill, that ageing brings. We can take some comfort from the research evidence reviewed in this book that the vast majority of even very old people continue to function perfectly normally in all psychological domains.

As with all the other authors of books in this series, Graham Stokes has written with the person beginning their encounter with scientific psychology in mind. The book is pitched at a level designed to be accessible to students in the first year of their courses, be they studying 'A' level, for a degree, or for a professional or vocational qualification. No compromises are made with the quality of evidence used to support the conclusions drawn, and no apologies are offered for challenging well known 'facts' where the research evidence does not support them.

Old age is a territory we will all enter, and we can journey there with more knowledge and more confidence after reading this book.

Raymond Cochrane
Birmingham
December 1991

Preface

The purpose of this book is to communicate the rapidly expanding knowledge of the psychology of later life to students in a form which is readily comprehensible to people new to the field of gerontology — the interdisciplinary scientific study of ageing and old age. It is aimed at students at either 'A' level or beginning their undergraduate degree, and is not intended to be used as an advanced text in geropsychology. The book will also appeal to those who work with older people in the course of their professional work: nurses, social workers, speech and language therapists and medical students.

The organization of the book commences with an appreciation of the dramatic demographic changes that have occurred in the elderly population this century. We are now experiencing what has been called a 'gerontological boom'; a great increase in the numbers of older people, especially those who are very old. This has led to speculation about what it will be like to grow old in years to come, and the consequences for society of increased numbers of dependent, aged adults. To address these issues, Chapter 1 examines the phenomenon of ageing populations from a demographic perspective.

Thereafter, the position is adopted that human ageing is not a single process, but is a complex interaction of developmental phenomena that operate throughout the lifespan and which can be studied from a variety of perspectives. To cover the different aspects of the ageing processes, the text reflects biological, psychological and social considerations of ageing.

Taken as a whole, this book moves from the processes of ageing to the psychological and psychosocial aspects of later life. Looking at the effects of old age on intellectual performance and memory functioning we examine the evidence for and against fundamental changes in later life. Aside from a consideration of basic cognitive processes and products, Chapter 8 reviews the topic of creativity, wisdom and later life achievement.

The experience of old age is not solely a product of internal biological and psychological processes, but also represents the relationship between the aged individual and society. The section on social adaptation investigates old age within the context of society, and appreciates the behaviour of elderly people within the framework of their intimate social networks. The first chapter deals with the question of personality and adjustment. Do people retain the same personality as they age or is each stage of the life cycle characterized by a personality type that is appropriate for that age span? After a theoretical discussion on adaptation, which examines the relationship between patterns of personality, personal competence and environmental factors, chapters on family life and friendship, retirement, sexuality and bereavement consider the major life transitions in old age.

Finally, the book ends with a consideration of the psychological problems encountered in later life. We therefore move from an appreciation of 'normal' ageing in the absence of disease and disability, to an understanding of later life pathology which is either of psychological origin or has significant psychological sequelae. The epidemiology and behavioural characteristics of disease states and emotional disorder, most notably dementia and depression, are discussed both from a biomedical perspective and within the framework of psychological models of causation and intervention.

My hope is that the fundamental matters of ageing and old age covered in this book will provide a firm foundation on which to build a greater understanding of the psychology of later life, as well as helping students to appreciate the contribution other disciplines, such as biology, medicine and sociology, make to the development of the new science of gerontology. I find working with older people stimulating and rewarding, and at times a deeply humbling experience. I hope my enjoyment and interest is conveyed in these forthcoming pages, and that it serves to fire the enthusiasm of students and professional workers alike who one day may share the same impressions of older people and later life as I currently hold.

Graham Stokes
September 1991

Part One

Age and Ageing

Chapter 1

An Ageing Society

A great achievement of the twentieth century has been to add over twenty years to the average life expectancy at birth of British people. To survive into old age is no longer an unanticipated privilege for a small minority of people but an experience shared by the majority. However, it is uneasily suspected that most elderly people endure poor health in deprived circumstances, neglected by their children and such family as they have left. Abandoned within their communities, solitary and ignored, as they grow to be really aged, intellectual decline and advancing physical disability inevitably leads to a miserable existence within an institution.

Public debate on policy issues which affect elderly people reflect concern that ageing populations sap the economic lifeblood of nations. At the very least, the rapid increase in the numbers of older people is viewed as a major contemporary economic and social challenge. For example, as the prevalence of morbidity and disability increases in later life, National Health Service (NHS) expenditure on adults rises steeply with age. For people of working age (i.e. between 16 and 64 years), the 1983 per capita annual NHS expenditure was approximately £125 for younger adults, rising to £200 for those in late middle age. However, for people over 75 the annual expenditure per person was around £1,000 (Grundy, 1989). It is understandable, therefore, that the cost of providing adequate health care, housing, social services and income maintenance exercises the minds of those concerned with the formulation of policy and its implementation in practice.

However, if we are to respond to the needs of elderly people, action must be based on a secure foundation of knowledge of old age. To what extent is physical and mental infirmity a feature of later life? Do elderly people find themselves in a position of social neglect alienated from the mainstream of society? Medical, psychological and social studies have loosened the grip of some of the mythology surrounding the ageing process and the elderly as a social group. Improved demographic statistics enable us to identify more clearly the numbers of older people, where they live and future population trends. As a consequence, priorities for intervention can be established based not on stereotypes and prejudice, but on empirically determined assumptions.

1

Who is Old?

The challenge of defining old age is more complex than might appear at first sight. The phenomenon of ageing can be considered from a number of perspectives. The biologist is often concerned with 'longevity and the antecedents of death' (Cunningham and Brookbank, 1988), the sociologist tends to focus on social roles and the relationship the aged have with society, while the psychologist is concerned with individual adaptability and adjustment. Birren and Renner (1977a) define ageing as referring to 'the regular changes that occur in mature genetically representative organisms living under representative environmental conditions as they advance in chronological age'. Thus, ageing is far more complex than the assumption that it is indexed solely by advancing chronological age.

The issues surrounding ageing, such as 'how old is old' and who decides upon a person's age status, will be discussed in the rest of Part One on the processes of ageing. While such discussion and examination is essential, for this book to have meaning a point in the lifespan must be chosen after which we can talk about adults having entered 'old age'. Despite chronological age often not being the optimal indicator in all situations or for all individuals, I will arbitrarily restrict myself to an understanding of the group who, in advanced industrial nations (for much depends on the demographic context in which the person lives), live beyond the age of 65 years. Such people cannot, however, be regarded as a homogeneous social group. Taylor and Ford (1983) examined age, sex and social class differences and established substantial variation across sub-groups in their income, health, psychological functioning and social support. Victor (1989), in an examination of income inequality in later life, concluded that old age is not a leveller, but represents 'the continuance and culmination of differentials established during working life'.

As many elderly people are now living into extreme old age, to add precision to the investigation of later life, it is wise to make a distinction between the age groups 65–74 years (the 'young-old') and those over 75 years (the 'old-old'). This is justified on the grounds, for example, of health and economic status. Seventy-five is the age after which notable disability, whether it be mental or physical or both, becomes prevalent (Pitt, 1982). Gilbert *et al.* (1989) found that only 5 per cent of people under 70 were severely disabled, while 40 per cent of those over 85 were so classified. Hunt (1979) observed that 17 per cent of men over 85 were either bedfast or housebound, while his corresponding figure for women was 21 per cent. The old elderly are also more likely to live in poor housing and have incomes below the official poverty line. Gilbert *et al.* (1989) offer different explanations for the economic impoverishment of the very aged, one of which sees the relationship between income and age as being the result of a cohort effect. Older people are poorer because they were born and spent their working lives during a different historical period compared with the 'young-old' and thus have less chance, for example, of being in receipt of an occupational pension.

Ageing Populations

Demographers often classify populations on the basis of the percentage of people beyond the age of 65 (Hendricks and Hendricks, 1977). Thus, a young population is usually considered to be one in which those 65 and over constitute less than 4 per cent of the total population. Similarly, a mature population has between 4 to 7 per cent of its members in this age group, while an aged population has over 7 per cent in the age group 65 or older.

To date, only the advanced industrial societies of North and Western Europe and North America can be classified as countries with aged populations. In the United Kingdom the proportion of the population over 65 has trebled since the beginning of the century. Whereas roughly 5 per cent of people were in this age group in 1900, by 1987 over 15 per cent of the UK population was over 65, and by 2025 it is predicted that the figure will be 18.7 per cent.

Within this broad age band interesting and significant demographic changes are taking place. The numbers of elderly people are stabilizing at around 9 million, although the size of this age group is expected to increase to 11.3 million by the year 2025. However, within the 65 and over age band, a dramatic change in the age distribution is taking place with the population aged 85 years and over growing most rapidly (Social Trends, 1989). According to the Central Office of Information (1977), by the year 2001 while there will have been a 4 per cent increase in those over 65, within this age population there will have been a 20 per cent increase in those between 75–79, a 31 per cent increase in those 80–84 and an increase in those still older of 46 per cent. In order to get a concrete appreciation of this 'gerontology boom' (Cunningham and Brookbank, 1988), Grundy (1989) reports that in England and Wales in 1986 there were 639,000 people aged over 85, accounting for 1.3 per cent of the population as a whole. By the year 2006 the numbers will have reached 1,116,000 and constitute 2.1 per cent of the total population.

The ageing of populations is a relatively recent phenomenon associated primarily with the growth of industrialization and the facilities available in technologically advanced societies. Although rapid expansion of the proportion of the population aged over 65 began in the middle of the nineteenth century for Sweden and France, other contemporary industrial nations, such as Canada, Germany, Japan, the United Kingdom and the United States, did not display such patterns until the present century (Hendricks and Hendricks, 1977).

The numbers of people living into late life in North America has multiplied dramatically since the turn of the century. In the United States the elderly population has increased from 3 million in 1900, to 26 million in 1980. Cunningham and Brookbank (1988) report that by the year 2000 the figure will increase to over 30 million, and by 2020 a further increase to 40 million is projected. Currently, 11 per cent of the population is over 65. Depending on assumptions regarding fertility and mortality, it is projected that between 13 and 18 per cent of the United States population in the year 2020 will be elderly. In Canada, while the population is four times greater than in 1901, the number

Table 1.1: Type of household arrangement in which elderly people live by age (%)

Type of Household	65–69	70–74	75–79	80–84	85+	All
Alone	23.7	31.8	41.8	51.3	48.2	33.6
Elderly Married Couple	37.0	44.1	36.7	23.8	12.5	36.2
Married Couple — One Spouse < 65	19.6	7.1	1.9	0.9	—	9.6
Two or more single elderly	2.7	4.4	4.6	6.0	10.5	4.3
Single elderly with single non-elderly(s)	5.0	4.7	6.1	8.0	14.7	6.0
Elderly couple with single non-elderly(s)	9.2	5.6	3.7	3.1	2.7	6.1
Elderly person or couple with non-elderly couple	2.8	2.5	5.2	6.9	11.3	4.1
	100.0	100.2	100.0	100.0	99.9	99.9

Source: Gilbert *et al.*, 1989

of people over 65 has increased seven times and accounts for nearly 9 per cent of the population.

Generally speaking, all these countries demonstrate the lowest birth rates, lower death rates and greater longevity than the rest of the world. While popular opinion assumes that declining mortality is sufficient to bring about an aged population, the critical variable is, in fact, a declining fertility rate. Populations do not necessarily age simply because of declining death rates.

Before moving on from this aspect of demography, it is of interest to note that throughout the industrial world there appears to be a trend for women to live longer than men. At birth the differences in expected longevity are in the range of two to eight years depending on such variables as local circumstances and racial background (Hendricks and Hendricks, 1977). Data for England and Wales indicate that at 65, men can expect to live another 13.5 years, women another 17.4 years (OPCS, 1989). As a consequence, women form the majority of elderly people. There are around 4.7 million elderly women in England and Wales which constitutes 60 per cent of the total aged population (OPCS, 1989). For those people aged 75 and over there are twice as many women as there are men.

Where Are 'the Elderly'?

United Kingdom demographic data clearly reveals that it is not the fate of most elderly people to pass their final years in institutional care. The vast majority of older people, around 94 per cent, do not live in either hospitals, nursing homes or residential accommodation. However, the kind of household in which older adults live varies greatly according to age (Gilbert *et al.*, 1989). Table 1.1 shows household arrangements by age.

In the two youngest age groups (65–74 years) most older adults live with their spouse. With advancing age, however, the proportion of elderly people living alone steadily increases. This is a recent phenomenon for as Dale *et al.* (1987) identified the proportion of elderly people living by themselves grew from around 10 per cent in 1945, to over one-third in 1980. The reasons for this demographic change are varied. Of significance is the trend for children when marrying to leave the family home to set up their own independent households. In addition, as more retired people are able to afford to keep homes of their own, on the death of a spouse there are greater numbers of older adults left living alone. As a consequence the most common living arrangement after the age of 75 is one of elderly people living by themselves. For older adults over 80 around half live alone, most of whom (may be as many as 85 per cent) are widows spending their last years of life unaccompanied by their spouse. However it is not possible to regard single living arrangements as representing a forced choice shrouded in sadness and anticipated neglect or to indicate a tendency for younger relatives to abandon their older kin, for Thompson and West (1984) report the strong desire of many elderly people to live alone rather than live with relatives or in care. There is often expressed anxiety about becoming dependent, either financially or physically on others, especially their grown children (Fiske, 1980).

Despite the preference of many elderly people to live by themselves, as the years pass an increasing proportion of the 'old-elderly' do live with younger adults. While there has been a major decrease in the proportion living with others over the past forty-five years (Dale *et al.*, 1987) in the 85-and-over age range 29 per cent continue to live with younger people, with a further 11 per cent residing with elderly people who are not their spouse (e.g. an ageing child who is in his or her late 60s).

The increasing dependency of older adults as indexed, for example by changes in their living arrangements, has led demographers to examine the overall impact on society of greater numbers of aged dependants. The relationship is examined by the 'old age dependency ratio' which is obtained by dividing the number of people over 65 by the number of adults who are in the working age range of approximately 16 to 64. This crude measure of dependants to producers has established a dependency ratio which has been rising for decades and is expected to rise sharply as we enter the next century as a result of cohort fertility and greater longevity (Cunningham and Brookbank, 1988). However, increased dependency does not inevitably lead to a high usage of statutory services. While the state has gradually assumed greater responsibility for supporting elderly people (Wroe, 1973), Gilbert *et al.* (1989), following an examination of specific disabilities, argue that the 'provision of support services is, for most services, not substantial....' (p. 106). They conclude that statutory services are provided to a much greater extent to those who live alone than to those who live with others. Overall, the use of statutory support services depends on a combination of the effects of disability, the type of living arrangement and whether the service can be provided by informal carers (e.g. family, friends or neighbours).

Despite the fragmented nature of the modern nuclear family in industrial societies and the effects urban developments have exercised on neighbourhood communities, as we shall see in Chapter 10 most care, help and support comes from informal sources. While a reduction in family support may have occurred (e.g. Wroe, 1973), in large part because of the numbers of middle-aged women (the traditional family supporters of the 'elderly') who now go out to work (Moroney, 1976), Lebowitz (1980) disputes the view that family support is not available, either because of geographical distance or lack of concern. For instance, it is not typical for elderly people to be isolated from their children. Abrams (1978) reported that approximately 60 per cent of older adults with at least one surviving child had a child living within six miles of them. As many as a third lived in the same street or neighbourhood. In addition the majority of elderly people were satisfied with the frequency with which their children visited. Thus, it would appear to be the case that many of the elderly who live by themselves, are not alone in the literal sense but reside instead in a state of 'supported independence' (Townsend, 1963). Of interest, Townsend (1963) found in his research at the end of the 1950s in Bethnal Green, London, that the supportive relationship was reciprocal, with old people caring for grand-children, preparing midday meals, etc.

It needs to be appreciated, however, that around 30 per cent of elderly people never had any children, and that the children of the 'old-old' will them-selves be elderly and possibly less fit and active (Woods and Britton, 1985). Are these aged adults destined to find themselves isolated and neglected within their communities? Recent studies (e.g. Wenger, 1989) have examined the support offered not only by relatives but also by 'non-kin'. Looking at who provides the help and what kinds of help are forthcoming, Wenger (1989) has developed a typology of support networks in old age. These networks consist of all those who are available to an elderly person to provide companionship, support or personal care in a regular way. On average, elderly people have five to seven members in their support networks, most of whom are family and a high proportion are middle-aged or older (Wenger, 1986). Different network types based on differences in membership and proximity results in different expectations and obligations in terms of the provision of help and support. Undoubtedly, understanding the variety of support networks and their distri-bution in the community is critical for policy-makers when discussing the nature and cost of predicted changes in the old age dependency ratio.

Living Conditions of Older People

While many older people live capably in independent household arrangements it must be recognized that much of the housing is either inappropriate to current need or inadequate. There is the disturbing problem of elderly women in receipt of very low incomes living on their own in accommodation which had previously been the family home. It is not just a question of too much living space so that only part of the home is lived in and the rest is neglected. Difficulties also arise where living arrangements are no longer compatible with remaining physical ability. For example, when the toilet and bedroom are located upstairs, the staircase may be an insurmountable obstacle. Similarly, steep steps to the garden or the street can result in frail, elderly persons becom-ing prisoners in their own homes.

Problems are compounded when elderly people live not only in inappropriate housing but also in inadequate conditions. Fox (1981) notes that elderly people are more likely than young people to live in inadequate housing. Woods and Britton (1985), reporting 1976 survey data, state that over 10 per cent of older adults have only an outside toilet, and in a quarter of households headed by a person over the age of 65 at least one of the basic amenities of hot water supply, a bath or an inside toilet is lacking.

Overall, the effects of the built environment on functional behaviour cannot be underestimated. Impaired performance and disturbed behaviour in old age can just as easily be the outcome of 'unhealthy buildings' as the consequence of 'unhealthy bodies'.

Progress toward overcoming the perils of impoverished housing has been achieved in the development of 'sheltered' housing. Such living arrangements remain true to the desire of many elderly people to live independently, for while such accommodation is warden supervised, occupants have the status of tenants. Independence is fostered by the prosthetic design of the buildings and interior layout which compensate for certain abilities and skills which have been lost or damaged. While sheltered housing is not suitable accommodation for elderly people with major dependency needs, unless they become considerably disabled there is a low propensity for tenants to leave sheltered housing to enter residential care (Boldy *et al.*, 1973; Coleman, 1986). If they do, few survive the transition more than a few months.

Conclusion

Ageing and aged people rightly provide us with areas of both concern and interest. The growing proportion of older adults in the population raises many important issues for society and focuses our attention on the personal, social, health and economic problems associated with later life.

These potential problems need to be placed in perspective, however. Evidence does not support the view that elderly people are in the main neglected by relatives and rejected by their communities. Even when poor health and disability become a feature of life most are supported in the community, often in their own homes by an informal network of relatives, friends and neighbours. Thus, while the 'old age dependency ratio' is set to rise sharply, state expenditure on the increasing health and social needs of aged people will, in part, be offset by the support networks available in old age. Strain will therefore, be confined not just to the public purse, but the ability and willingness of the community to continue caring may also be severely tested. Yet, old age can also be about achievement and contribution, for as has already been noted, the provision of support can be a reciprocal relationship.

It is possible that the sheer magnitude of the increase in numbers of elderly people will produce many changes in society, among which may be the view society has of older adults. There are already signs of a changing climate of opinion. Groups representing elderly people are becoming more assertive,

Chapter 2

The Biology of Ageing

What are the physical changes associated with ageing, and if, as expected, they are indexed by bodily decay and deterioration can they be prevented or reversed? Can the lifespan of humankind be extended? What determines a person's life expectancy?

To answer these and related questions, the reality of ageing has to be discussed from a biological standpoint. As noted earlier (p. 2), ageing can be distinguished along three dimensions: biological age, psychological age and social age. While these 'ages of mankind' undoubtedly interact and influence each other they 'are not necessarily in close synchrony' (Birren and Renner, 1980). It is, therefore, possible and advised when discussing the process (or more accurately, processes) of ageing to investigate independently those factors which contribute to the developmental changes which occur after maturity. However, the temptation to indulge in pointless debate on whether intrinsic or extrinsic influences are the sole cause of ageing is to be avoided. The overwhelming evidence is that both contribute to human ageing, although their relative contribution may vary over time, environment and culture.

Methodological Issues

The examination of ageing from a biological perspective is based upon the twin pillars of laboratory animal experimentation and the study of people either as they age (longitudinal research) or the observation of groups of people at different stages of human development (cross-sectional methodology).

All animal studies, because of species differences, may be of questionable relevance. More meaningful data are obtained from observing people directly. Longitudinal studies are desirable for they involve the recruitment of a group of subjects who are observed throughout their life spans. Thus, age-related changes in an individual can be tracked in that individual. However, such studies are expensive, suffer from the problem of subject attrition as people move away, die or are unwilling to be assessed continually, and as Woods and Britton (1985) comment, are 'beyond the stamina of most researchers'. The relative scarcity of longitudinal studies confirms this viewpoint.

In age research cross-sectional studies have surface appeal for they are relatively easy to set up and yield accessible data with little delay. However, they can be difficult to interpret. In this methodology, groups of people of different ages are compared on the basis of data collected at a single point in time. While the groups are matched on significant socio-economic and demographic variables, such studies can only establish age differences, not age changes. The identification of group differences cannot be taken as evidence that a younger age group will, over time, develop the same characteristics observed in older populations. It is easy to attribute erroneously later life qualities and changes to the maturational process of biological ageing, when they are in part the consequence of, for example, nutrition and medical care when young, educational experiences, early life influences and prevailing cultural expectations. Such cohort effects will not be shared by younger people, and so the characteristics they ultimately display in old age may be markedly different.

While longitudinal research mitigates cohort influences it cannot eliminate them. As already noted, ageing possesses a social dimension which not only directly affects how people age, but can also influence how an ageing person adjusts to later life and regards the future (psychological ageing). Furthermore, environmental effects may obscure biological age changes. Biomedical advances designed to replace or compensate for the failure of bodily organs and sensory systems have in some ways transformed the quality of life available to many of today's older people. As we continue to strive for greater longevity who can tell what biomedical advances await us in the future and the consequences they will have for future generations of aged people? Thus, when making comparisons between different populations, especially across time, cohort influences always remain. Longitudinal research needs to be interpreted wisely, causal effects need to be attributed accurately, and attempts to extrapolate findings to other ageing populations need to be treated with caution.

Biological Ageing

The definition of ageing already presented (p. 2), is favoured by several authors for it 'allows for expansion of function with age as well as decrement' (Birren and Renner, 1980). Other biological definitions are limited in their outlook focusing on the accumulated changes in living organisms which result in decreased power of adjustment and an increased probability of natural death. Such interpretations of biological ageing give primacy to the corrosive, ultimately destructive nature of changes in later life, thereby supporting and perpetuating the sense of foreboding which often accompanies impending old age.

Senescence

The general decline of physical well-being in later years is known as senescence. Unlike other species humans have a high rate of survival during the period of growth and maturation leading to years of declining survival in old age. Senescence has two elements: those negative organic alterations which have a strong genetic component, and those which are the consequence of 'unpredictable, accumulative, environmental' factors (Cunningham and Brookbank, 1988). The age-dependent changes which occur in senescence may result in an increased susceptibility to certain infections, cancers and diseases such as arteriosclerosis, diabetes, hypertension and Alzheimer's disease. Debate centres over whether the common diseases associated with advancing years are intrinsic, genetically determined phenomena inseparable from the process of ageing, or are primarily attributable to 'accidental', environmental factors.

The whole area of biological ageing is complex with no consensus of opinion. No single cause has been identified which can account for all the age-dependent changes which occur. Theories include that biological ageing may be at the cellular level which raises the prospect that cells of the body are genetically programmed for eventual senescence and death. Hayflick (1982) proposes a 'biological clock' which results in the functional loss and ageing of cells. 'Natural' death is therefore equated with 'genetic' death. Non-genetic theories of cellular ageing have also been developed, although Cunningham and Brookbank (1988) contend that 'genetic themes are the most promising'. Those theories concerned with levels of organization above the cellular level are known as physiological theories. These focus on age changes in organ systems. Negative alterations occur in all bodily systems, yet these are likely to be the result of an underlying process of ageing rather than the primary cause of senescence.

The Nature of Physical Decline

With advancing years, even in the absence of disease, changes in the structure and function of bodily systems are inevitable. Yet the progress of senescence is slow and varies according to the systems affected and from person to person. Cunningham and Brookbank (1988) describe the age-related changes which can occur in the major organ systems:

Brain
It is the brain as the seat of arousal, motivation, emotion/personality and higher intellectual abilities which makes us what we are. It carries out many of its functions at the subconscious and unconscious levels, most of these being concerned with the maintenance of life. However, with age obvious anatomical and physiological changes occur (Habot and Libow, 1980).

Studies of the age*ing* brain are notoriously difficult, whereas investigation of the age*d* brain is relatively simple, although interpretation remains difficult (Bondareff, 1980). Degenerative changes in the aged brain include gross atrophy with a parallel loss in weight (Cunningham and Brookbank, 1988). It normally decreases by about 10 per cent from its maximum weight in early adulthood to that observed in the ninth decade of life (Corsellis, 1976). This reduction in weight may be due to cell loss or a deterioration in the 'white matter' (myelin) that surrounds the nerve fibres. Neuronal loss in senescence was first described at the end of the last century. In the cerebral cortex generalized atrophy is not seen, but is selective instead, although the degree of selectivity is not known. In certain areas as many as 50 per cent of cortical neurons are lost. The number of changes in the structure and composition of the brain do not correlate with behavioural or intellectual change (Bondareff, 1980). As we shall see in Part Two, while functional decrements do occur they are not usually disruptive or incapacitating.

Sense organs
Taste, smell, vision and hearing all deteriorate (Marsh, 1980). The decline in the sense of smell may be due to the loss of brain cells in the olfactory bulb of the brain, as well as to the long-term inhalation of noxious substances such as tobacco smoke.

Changes in the visual apparatus are manifold and may result in perceptual alterations. Response to illumination and colour discrimination declines in old age. The increased time needed for the recognition of visual information may not be the product of deterioration in the sensory system, but may result from slower information-processing activity (see Chapter 6). Woods and Britton (1985) note that interpreting findings on hearing ability is difficult. However, it would appear that high-frequency acuity and sound localization are affected by ageing. Tinnitus increases in incidence with age.

Skeletal muscle
The age-related changes observed in striated muscle are similar to those iden-tified following long-term muscle inactivity. The degree of wastage is more apparent in the lower part of the body than in the upper half. With advancing age there is a decrease in the size and number of muscle fibres in some human muscle.

Bone
Bone mass in both males and females decreases with age, although this occurs more slowly in men. The thinning of bones may, in extreme cases, bring about a condition known as osteoporosis, wherein the bones become exceedingly brittle.

Skin
The permanent wrinkling of the skin with age results from a loss of elasticity. Wounds take longer to heal in aged people and there is an increased likelihood of skin cancers with age.

Hair
The death of hair-forming cells in the hair follicles results in baldness and loss of body hair, especially in men. Hair that is not lost becomes grey due to the loss of the pigment-forming cells.

Immunity

Impaired functioning of the immune system with senescence results in reduced protection against viral infections and diminished surveillance for cancer cells.

The phenomenon of autoimmunity, wherein the immune system attacks as alien the cells of the body that houses it, increases with age. The consequences of this are varied, but can result in pathological conditions such as arthritis, multiple sclerosis and sterility.

Cardiovascular system

It does not appear to be the case that the human heart does truly atrophy with advancing years. The appearance of coronary heart disease in middle age is strongly influenced by genetic factors.

Respiratory system

Respiration becomes progressively difficult for those people over the age of 40.

Kidneys and bladder

Renal function has declined by about 50 per cent by the age of 65 years. A decrease by 20 to 30 per cent in the weight and volume of the kidney with ageing results in impaired kidney filtration. As a consequence the process of eliminating nitrogenous waste is less efficient in later life.

Many changes in bladder function occur with advancing age. These include lower bladder capacity and a higher volume of residual urine after micturition. This leads to frequent filling of the bladder and an increased need to urinate. It is not known whether age-related abnormalities of the autonomic nervous system contributes to the deterioration in bladder function with age (Everitt and Huang, 1980).

Gastrointestinal system

With age the surface epithelium of the mouth atrophies, and the underlying connective tissue degenerates. For some elderly people loosening of the teeth occurs.

In the stomach, ageing results in chronic gastritis. This condition results in decreased absorption of vitamin B_{12} and iron through the stomach. Furthermore, in 16 per cent of people in later life, an autoantibody directed against the factor responsible for B_{12} transport is found.

Liver functions decline which results in reduced capacity for the metabolism of drugs and hormones. As a consequence certain medications remain for a longer time in the body of elderly people compared with younger adults. This has major implications for the practice of prescribing medicines for older people. If drug dosage data established during trials with younger people is applied to those in later life, over-prescribing with attendant adverse health effects is possible.

Tolerance for alcohol, which is metabolized in the liver, is reduced markedly in old age.

Alterations in the function of the large bowel (colon) results in more frequent constipation with advancing age. Cancer of the colon is an increasing health risk in later life.

Sex hormones and sexual function

In women reproductive functions cease relatively abruptly at menopause. Men, however, continue with reduced fertility until advanced old age. Conversely while sex drive may increase in post-menopausal women (female libido is dependent on the hormone testosterone, levels of which are essentially unaltered following the menopause), it persists in somewhat diminished fashion in ageing men. While physiological changes do alter sexual capacity in later life, their effects are greatly exaggerated (Hendricks and Hendricks, 1977). The loss of a man's capacity for erection is not a natural accompaniment of ageing. Changes do occur in penile erection, but only in so much as the response takes longer for men aged over 50 years as compared with younger males. However, once achieved it is normally maintained for extended periods of time without ejaculation. Following ejaculation older men experience a refractory period much longer than that displayed by younger men before erection can be reattained. If an elderly man becomes impotent there is often no underlying physical cause, and such periods often end as abruptly as they appeared.

Temperature regulation

There is a decline in heat storage with age, so that in older people cold environmental conditions result in a more rapid reduction in skin temperature.

Summary

Overall, from early middle age all body systems show anatomical alterations with a corresponding decline in function. While none shut down completely, defects at the cellular level accumulate and ultimately lead to diminished viability.

Lifespan

Lifespan represents the maximum recorded age attained by the longest surviving member of a species, and is a genetic characteristic of a given species. The fact that lifespan is a species trait strongly indicates that it is genetically controlled.

While the current life span of the human race is estimated to be 116 years, this has not always been so. The maximum lifespan of primitive humans was approximately 77 years. There has, therefore, been a slow evolution in human longevity from the early Stone Age to the present day.

It is likely that the change in longevity which has occurred since the beginnings of time is related to changes in the size and structure of the human brain. 'The larger the brain is in relation to body size, the longer the life span is' (Cunningham and Brookbank, 1988). From primitive humans to present day *Homo sapiens* the number of neurons in the cerebral cortex has increased by a factor of nearly one hundred over lower primates (Cutler, 1976). This greater number of cortical neurons is sometimes referred to as 'biological intelligence'. This term relates to the fact that the increase which has occurred during the course of human evolution exceeds the number required to control bodily functions necessary for life. As some of the increase in cortical neurons is implicated in the development of the speech centre in the left cerebral cortex, an association between the evolution of speech and greater human longevity is indicated. Speech enables younger members of a species to benefit from instruction given by experienced, older members during the period of biological maturation. The teaching and communication of ideas necessary for intellectual and social development is clearly facilitated and enhanced by language and likely to result in definite survival advantages. The unanswered question is, however, what came first, the growth in the size of the cerebral cortex and the development of speech, or increased longevity which enables young members of a species to have access to the wisdom of aged adults.

Life Expectancy

The genetic constitution of the human race determines its *lifespan*. Individual *life expectancy* varies according to personal genetic make-up, environmental conditions and personal lifestyle within the maximum allowed by the lifespan of the species. Average life expectancy is conventionally defined by the age at which 50 per cent of a population born on the same date are found as survivors (Cunningham and Brookbank, 1988).

In considering life expectancy, while the genes of individual members of a species vary in a relatively small way when compared with the genetic differences between species, it is this smaller genetic variability that primarily accounts for variability in life expectancy between genetically unrelated members of the same species (Cunningham and Brookbank, 1988). Tragically, as a result of habit and hazard only a small proportion of people live to realize their personal life span to which their genes may have entitled them.

Support for the primary status of genetic determination comes from a study of fifty-eight pairs of identical twins (Kallman and Sander, 1949). These investigators found an average intrapair difference in age at death of approximately thirty-seven months. This contrasts with an age difference of seventy-eight months for fraternal twins who, of course, are not genetically identical. Further support is demonstrated by the work of Murphy (1978) who demonstrated that the longevity of parents and grandparents exerts a notable influence on the life expectancy of their progeny. Thus, family history is a powerful predictor of life expectancy.

The already noted difference in longevity between the sexes (p. xx) may arise for a number of presumed reasons. Possibilities such as hormonal or chromosome differences or different social roles are suggested, but overall there is likely to be a strong genetic component (Cunningham and Brookbank, 1988). Huyck (1990), reporting United States data, considers that the sex difference in life expectancy seems to be increasing even though social role changes are enabling women to enter areas of activity previously the sole or major preserve of men.

In many areas of the world today people possess a life expectancy that approaches the genetically determined lifespan of humans. While changes in the genetics of the human race are responsible for changes in lifespan since the pre-history of humankind, it is the transformation in environmental circumstances over the same period which has resulted in an increase in average life expectancy from approximately thirty years to more than seventy years in modern industrial societies. In earlier times life expectancy was markedly affected by infant mortality and a period of increased health risk after weaning. Throughout adolescence and adulthood infectious diseases, famine, warfare and accident exerted a heavy toll on human life. Survival beyond the age of 50 was rare. In today's advanced societies the mortality rate declines until about the age of 12 and then increases throughout life as an exponential function of age.

Survival into old age is no longer dependent on physical strength and resistance to disease. The development of public health policies and biomedical advances have dramatically transformed the profile of morbidity and mortality. Many diseases which were feared at the turn of this century are no longer of major concern. Principal causes of death in the United States in 1900 were pneumonia and influenza, tuberculosis, diarrhoea and enteritis and heart disease. As we approach the end of the twentieth century medical advances, especially in the treatment of infectious diseases, have removed the threat of most of these ailments. Today the leading causes of death in industrial societies are heart disease and cancer.

Reports about great longevity must be treated with caution as many of the claims are unsubstantiated (Mazess and Foreman, 1979). Leaf (1973) identified Abkhasia in Georgia, the Hunza Valley in the Himalayas and the Valley of Vileabamba in Ecuador as places on earth where exceptional longevity occurs with greatest frequency. In such areas, and also in random individual cases of longevity, a significant question to ask is whether life expectancy is advanced by the absence of environmental stressors leading to a genetically programmed life expectancy which approaches maximal lifespan, or whether longevity is actively promoted by specific environmental conditions and living habits. For example, in those high altitude areas of Ecuador and Himalayas where average life expectancy is great, diets are low in fat and high in vegetable protein, the people are low in body fat (among the Abkhasians being fat is equated with ill health), and partake in physical labour, while an absence of competition and a stoic approach to life may result in minimal stress levels.

If environmental conditions and diet have a positive effect on life expectancy can they be incorporated into lifestyle recommendations? In brief, eating 'correctly', exercise and not engaging in hazardous habits (e.g. smoking, alcohol misuse) will go a long way toward enabling a person to fulfil their genetic potential. Cunningham and Brookbank (1988) note that certain physiological processes, such as cardiac efficiency and lung function, which decline during senescence, benefit from exercise and suitable diets.

For the past twenty years it has been recognized that physically active older people are healthier than their sedentary peers. Those who are physically fit and active perform better than those who are inactive on a range of tests that measure the behavioural slowdown that accompanies senescence. Unfortunately, less than 20 per cent of people in their 60s exercise to a degree required to improve cardiovascular function.

Eating 'correctly' in later life is essential in the pursuit of longevity. While, the nutritional needs of both younger and older adults are basically the same, as activity levels tend to decline with age and the rate of body metabolism slows down fewer calories are needed to maintain lean body weight. An excess of caloric intake will lead to an increase in the amount of body fat, and in extreme cases obesity can accompany old age. This not only affects mobility (e.g. walking, climbing stairs, getting in and out of chairs or the bath), it is also associated with hypertension, adult onset diabetes, breathing difficulties and heart disease. The outcome is likely to be premature death.

The long-term effects of smoking are all bad resulting in emphysema, lung and mouth cancer and heart disease. The biological effects of alcohol are greater for older than for younger adults. Recent studies (e.g. Mishara and Kastenbaum, 1980; Barnes, 1982; James, 1983) have highlighted the problems of heavy drinking and alcoholism in old age, and its association with poor health.

Conclusion

While chronological age is 'one of the most useful single items of information about an individual if not the most useful' (Birren, 1959), the concept of physical time does not correspond to the reality of biological ageing (Schroots and Birren, 1990). A more sensitive indicator of ageing and residual lifespan which accounts for individual differences among people of the same chronological age is biological age. This can be defined as 'an estimate of the individual's present position with respect to his or her potential life span' (Schroots and Birren, 1990).

Attempts to measure the rate of biological ageing has led some investigators to employ the concept of biological markers of ageing. However, efforts to establish markers of biological age and ageing have been criticized on grounds that there is, for example, no unitary measure of biological age as the ageing of functions within the body varies considerably. For instance thermoregulation, which is a complex homeostatic function, can become unreliable and unstable with age thereby increasing the risk of accidental hypothermia. A more simple bodily function can show much less susceptibility to ageing effects. Everitt and Huang (1980) propose an 'ageing clock', probably located in the hypothalamus, which precisely schedules an underlying sequence of ageing changes. However, it is hypothesized that each bodily function may be controlled by separate clocks resulting in variable ageing effects.

Thus, while the pursuit of identifying biomarkers has appeal, the goal remains not only unfulfilled at present, but may ultimately reveal itself to be an uncertain objective. As a consequence, Schroots and Birren (1990) can safely affirm that 'there is no evidence of a better predictor of length of life, residual life span...than plain chronological age'.

Although there is no way at present in which the process of senescence can be slowed down or reversed, the ability to compensate for and accept our ageing bodies and functional losses is often the key to whether later life is regarded as a period of continued usefulness, recreation and productivity. Appropriate personal adjustment to senescence can result in a lifestyle which mitigates biological ageing effects and enables the aged person to benefit from the richness of their experience and their accumulated wisdom. Unfortunately, a reluctance or inability to adapt to inevitable bodily decline can result in old age being a time of depression and despair. Clearly, the point has been reached when the process of ageing needs to be considered from a psychological perspective.

Chapter 3

The Psychology of Ageing

Movement through the life cycle is a gradual and imprecise process which cannot be anchored to specific chronological ages at which people pass from one stage of life to another. In exactly the same way as 'one may be older or younger than one's chronological age, in both a biological and (biomedical) functional sense, one may also be older or younger psychologically' (Birren, 1959). Does a 60-year-old man who marries a woman half his age and starts a family regard himself as being in late middle age, soon to be labelled as 'old'?

Psychological ageing is a complex and unique phenomenon. It requires an understanding of psychological time experience which Schroots and Birren (1990) define as the perception, subjective judgment and estimation of the duration of events and the amount of elapsed time. These perceptions result in individual interpretations of the past, present and future, and can influence whether age-graded behaviour, expected by society, is displayed. Rakowski (1984) notes that individual differences in time perspective increase with age, as does the complexity of the individual's time perspective.

Yet, regardless of the age at which individuals consider themselves to be 'old', old age is often characterized by 'bewitchment by expectation' (Pitt, 1982). A set of attitudes come into play which are often based on myth and ill-informed stereotype. Reduction in enthusiasm for life, withdrawal from activity and lowering of morale may be less often the effect of physical ageing than an attitude to oneself as aged and without value. Later life is not viewed as a time for growth and achievement. As will be seen in the next chapter such self-appraisal is significantly influenced by society not having a positive conception of old age. The life of the individual appears increasingly without meaning, and their contribution to society negligible (Harrison, 1973). After a lifetime of productivity and involvement older people often wish to be of continuing use to somebody. It is their misfortune that modern society's expectations are at variance with this desire.

Later life cannot be viewed as either the only life stage which allocates people social roles and status which produces conflict, however, or the only phase of the life cycle which is characterized by the need to adjust and negotiate crisis. Throughout the life course there is a need to adapt to environmental demands, the successful or unsuccessful negotiation of which may

Table 3.1:   A developmental stage model of psychosocial change

Developmental Stage	Life Crisis to be Resolved
1 Infancy	Basic trust v. Basic mistrust
2 Childhood (1)	Autonomy v. Shame or doubt
3 Childhood (2)	Initiative v. Guilt
4 Childhood (3)	Industry v. Inferiority
5 Adolescence	Ego identity v. Role confusion
6 Young adulthood	Intimacy v. Isolation
7 Adulthood	Generativity v. Stagnation
8 Old age	Integrity v. Despair

Source: Erikson, 1963

markedly affect personal development. Our understanding of the trials and triumphs of the life cycle has been aided by normative models of human development which have proposed a structure within which life events are experienced. Probably the most influential theory of life course changes which extends beyond middle age to include a psychology of old age is that developed by Erikson (1963).

A Normative Model of Human Development

Erik Erikson's analytical theory of human psychological development extends from infancy to old age. While the eight developmental stages are sequential, those of adulthood are not assigned to specific ages. As a person progresses through their life cycle they will negotiate significant crises, undertake life tasks and aspire to developmental goals specific to each of the life stages. Resolution of each stage facilitates adaptation to the next developmental stage. The eight stages of development with the associated life crises to be resolved are detailed in Table 3.1.

For those working in the field of gerontology (i.e. the study of ageing and people in old age), it is the penultimate stage of generativity versus stagnation (or rejectivity, wherein the person continues to grow but does not share their experience), and the final stage of integrity versus despair (or disdain, including self-disdain) which hold the greatest interest. It is unfortunate, therefore, that Erikson's stages of personality development have not been subject to extensive empirical analysis. For example, it is not known whether the achievement of integrity in later life is dependent on the prior attainment of generativity in midlife. That the outcome of each stage affects the experience of those which follow is not in doubt. As Erikson himself has said, 'Each life task is interrelated. The experience of earlier stages comes to fruition in old age' (communication cited by Feil, 1985). However, the exact nature of the relationships between the stages are unknown, and the mechanics of change remain uncertain.

Empirical research into human development is difficult to conduct for data on progression through the life cycle is dependent, for example, upon subjective reports which can be unreliable (Cunningham and Brookbank,

1988). Furthermore, many investigators hold the opinion that the concepts developed by Erikson are difficult to operationalize. This view is challenged by Kogan (1990) who cites research that has successfully achieved this objective. For example, Ryff and Heincke (1983) constructed developmental personality scales to assess generativity and integrity, and while the cross-sectional nature of their research precludes a developmental stage analysis, the results support Erikson's theories of mid- and later life. However, in general it may well be that our efforts to confirm the concepts of developmental stage theories are frustrated by the inadequacy of the methods and means of assessment available.

An alternative, apparently antithetical approach to the life course is proposed by Bromley (1990). The complex sequence model views 'adult life as a somewhat disorderly and unpredictable affair in which there are wide differences between individuals and their circumstances, and into which a large element of chance intrudes'.

The Psychology of Old Age

Erikson *et al.* (1986) have recently described the characteristics of the stage associated with old age. The achievement of ego-integrity represents a feeling that life's major goals have been attained, acceptance of one's life without regret, harmony between past, present and anticipated future, and a loss of fear of death. It will come as little surprise that integrity is rarely achieved. As Fiske (1980) notes, although some people portray wisdom, possess effective means of coping and adjustment, and gain a sense of fulfilment as they grow older, this is not the prevailing pattern.

Successful adaptation in later life is not simply a matter of coming to terms with the loss of family and friends, and the erosion of health and vitality. While adjustment to such deprivation can be fraught with strain, losses that older people expect as inevitable may be well negotiated. For some the anticipated losses of later life may be experienced with a pleasant sense of relief (Fiske, 1980), or be regarded as not having been as traumatic as feared. It is for these reasons that the observation of loss and privation may not be associated with emotional upset. A significant 'protector' may be the false anticipations which accompany people into old age. Life may be difficult, but not as tough as anticipated, so the emotions associated with presumed stressful life events may be positive, not negative. Events that are unexpected, however, such as the death of a child, require major adaptive abilities.

At a more fundamental level, society can actively work against the final life task of achieving integrity. Growing old with dignity and a sense of personal and social worth can be difficult. As the values in society change and a new structure of ideals and expectations develop, an aged person's interpretation of their past life can be threatened, and a positive redefinition of previous tasks and lifestyles made increasingly improbable. In a century as progressive as the twentieth century, wherein technological advance has revolutionized travel, communication and routines of daily living within a lifetime, adaptation may only be achieved through a continuing series of 'identity crises' (Fiske, 1980).

McCulloch (1985, cited by Coleman, 1986), in his study of how elderly people adjust to the discontinuities between past and present, reports that some enter a state of 'moral siege'. Such psychological action enables older adults to cope at a time of dramatic social upheaval by allowing them to remain satisfied with their own lives. They value the past and denigrate the present, for to accept the 'values of modern society is tantamount to denying meaning to their own lives as they have led them'.

McCulloch observed another group who were also unable to transcend the differences between past and present, but unfortunately for them they were unable to shelter within a state of 'moral siege'. These people were in an alienated state of 'questioning' unable to accept either the past or present.

One of the many critical aspects of the psychological circumstances of old age 'is the perception of time left' (Cunningham and Brookbank, 1988). When younger, activity can be delayed, frustrations and failures dismissed with the intention 'to try again' and goals deferred until later. In old age such 'futurism' is obsolete. Unfulfilled dreams and hopes will remain just that, unfulfilled. Thus, one of the major losses in later life is the loss of a psychological future.

Related to this concept of 'time left' is the heightened appreciation of one's own mortality. Realization that life will end is not solely the product of declining health and the tendency to tire more quickly, but a consequence of seeing close relatives and life-long friends of a similar age to oneself die. A feeling in later life 'that there is more that has gone by than is yet to be' (Cunningham and Brookbank, 1988), leads to a pervasive sense of finality.

As many elderly people, even those who appear to be functioning well, do not escape unhappiness and self-disdain (Busse, 1985), depression can be viewed not as a pathological condition but as 'one of the "normal" characteristics of old age, at least in western society' (Coleman, 1986). For example, Coleman (1986) found one-third of his sample were significantly demoralized. However, it is likely to be more accurate to assume that it is not the syndrome of depression (i.e. a major or mild depressive disorder) which is 'normal' but symptoms of depression (Bucks, 1990). Confusion surrounds the term depression for it is 'equated with an illness, viewed as a syndrome, thought to be a symptom, or discussed as a normal affect' (Penfold and Walker, 1984). Support for the view that it is possible to discriminate between symptoms of depression and the presence of a coherent syndrome is widespread (e.g. Blazer, 1980; Zemore and Eames, 1979). Blazer (1980) found that 25 per cent of his sample showed symptoms, but only 3.7 per cent satisfied the criteria for major depression. Thus, it is the former which can be the 'normal' consequence of ageing, not the latter.

'Differential Gerontology'

It would be misguided to assume, however, that negative effect in later life is the direct and inevitable consequence of deprived and threatening circumstances experienced during these years. Events encountered in old age are responded to according to personal history. To focus solely on observable and present features of older people's lives 'denies the historical roots of personal "needs" and circumstances and implies an unrealistic homogeneity in the face of knowledge that as humans get older they become more idiosyncratic' (Johnson, 1978). Similar sentiments regarding lifespan effects are expressed by Harrison (1973) who regards later life not simply as a stage but a continuation of an intricate pattern of life careers. Coleman (1986) acknowledges the idiosyncrasy of old age by noting that the diversity of experience over time means that ageing maximizes psychosocial differences.

Thus, the psychology of old age requires not just an appreciation of the current life situation, but an understanding of the lifespan as well. This construction of ageing has generated the term 'differential gerontology' (Thomae, 1976) which holds that as different historical experiences yield different expectations and patterns of behaviour in old age, a lifespan perspective on ageing is the only means by which understanding can be achieved. For some elderly people the past may represent a platform which may give them strength to continue; for others their past may bring little comfort and even less stability in later life. With recognition of the importance of a biographical perspective to the psychology of ageing, lifespan psychology is becoming increasingly popular. While normative theories of human development continue to hold their attraction, the uniqueness of human behaviour means that if gerontology is to contribute to our understanding of individual differences in ageing and reveal the rich and varied fabric of old age, biographical and autobiographical data cannot be neglected. A normative division of the life cycle into segmental stages remains useful only in the most general sense.

Lifespan Satisfaction and Morale

A degree of resilience is needed to cope with the potential hardships of old age and it is possible that a sense of fulfilment, based on value judgments on one's own past, is crucial to late life adjustment. The ability to be flexible in the face of inevitable age-related changes, and to avoid them dominating the final years of life, may be fostered by a favourable review of life.

Neugarten *et al.* (1961) queried whether satisfaction with past life is a constituent of morale in later life. The question is whether lifespan satisfaction provides not only the ability to withstand and accept the losses of later life, but serves to promote happiness and morale in the present. Erikson's concept of ego integrity asserts that satisfaction with past life has a positive influence on adjustment in so much as those who possess a sense of fulfilment will be happier in the present as well. Thus, life satisfaction is an index of successful ageing.

Empirical research reveal that lifespan satisfaction is a psychosocial phenomenon which increases with age and is relatively impervious to negative changes in later years. It is related to morale in old age, although predictors of morale in aged people are complex (Thomae, 1980). It is possible that having a satisfactory life to look back on provides the older person with the psychological strength to sustain optimism and confidence in the face of adversity.

An alternative explanation for a linkage between past and present life satisfaction sees a relationship between the material, emotional and social benefits (e.g. income, marriage and friendship network) obtained during the life course which carry over into the present where they continue to provide favourable experiences and circumstances (e.g. savings, companionship and social integration). A further interpretation is offered by the observation that current mood influences recall (e.g. Tobin and Etigson, 1968; Beck, 1976; Sherman, 1981). For example, if loss is a current feature of later life, an elderly person may focus on loss themes in their past. Similarly, if a depressed, pessimistic perception of life prevails, then the life cycle may also be viewed negatively even if it was not experienced as so. The outcome of such re-interpretation is cognitive consistency which is a significant psychological need for most people.

Whatever the causal mechanism (and there is unlikely to be a single explanation) it is clear that 'looking back' is related to current emotional status and as such serves to offer further support to a lifespan interpretation of ageing and old age.

The Functions of Reminiscence

It is evident that recalling experiences and events from one's past life is neither the panacea for losses and trouble to be faced in later life, nor is it the unhealthy preoccupation it was once considered to be. Only thirty years ago elderly people were advised not to reminisce about their past lives for fear it could create misery and distress (e.g. Havighurst, 1959). At worst, it was regarded as a symptom of intellectual deterioration, suggestive of senility. Aside from mental infirmity it was also taken as evidence of regression so to defend oneself against the trauma of declining function and social neglect; denial of the passage of time when confronted with a bleak future and imminent death; and symptomatic of depression.

Cummings and Henry (1961) saw reminiscence as an aspect of the interiority and withdrawal from external activity common among aged people. An understandable effort to seek comfort from the joys of a life well-lived. As 'disengagement' is seen by many investigators (although not by Cummings and Henry) as representing unsuccessful adjustment to old age, by association reminiscence was also viewed unfavourably.

A departure from this negative view of reminiscence occurred when Butler (1963) wrote a seminal paper on the function of life review. Rather than seeing reminiscence as a pathological feature of ageing, Butler regarded it as a 'normal' activity of old age enabling elderly people to come to terms with their lives. Life review remained a psychologically positive act, even when recalling distressing memories, if it resulted in reconciliation and acceptance. Overall, life review is not only a 'normal' activity, but a psychological pursuit not exclusive to older people (Molinari and Reichlin, 1985).

McMahon and Rhudick (1964) identified a group of well-adjusted war veterans who were enthusiastic reminiscers. However, the process and purpose of reminiscence observed by these investigators differed from that proposed by Butler (1963). While Butler saw life review as a rigorous examination of the past involving a 'resurgence of unresolved conflicts' (Coleman, 1986) with the prospect of achieving Erikson's final life task of 'ego integrity', McMahon and Rhudick (1964) viewed reminiscence as primarily having a storytelling function. The storyteller entertains and informs in the manner of an oral historian, the traditional means by which culture, custom and values have been handed down from one generation to the next. However, reminiscers in this study reminisced not only for social ends, but by creating meaningful myths and exaggerating the centrality and significance of their role, the veterans compensated for loss of function and status in old age. They preserved their self-concept by investing in an image of oneself as one had been. Interestingly the investigators found that their 'best-adjusted' group did not denigrate the present or glorify the past. They were satisfied simply to recount past experiences and pleasure, and gain satisfaction from doing so.

The defensive role of reminiscence in protecting self-worth at a time when people can feel undervalued in an increasingly estranged lifestyle (McMahon and Rhudick, 1964) was also identified by Lewis (1971). Similarly, Lieberman and Tobin (1983) interpret life review as a means by which an ageing person can maintain identity, rather than regarding it as the process by which somebody can be reconciled with their past. However, such an approach to reminiscence can still be incorporated into the life cycle theory of Erikson (1963), for as McMahon and Rhudick (1964) state, 'the adaptational significance of reminiscence can best be understood in the light of Erikson's view that identity formation is a lifelong task'.

Thus, there is no single function of reminiscence. Rabbitt (1988) regards it as a gradual, healthy adaptation to fading social demands, so 'when the theatre of the mind becomes the only show in town archival memories begin to be actively explored'. In support of this, Holland and Rabbitt (1991) established that it is current life situations and not old age *per se* which encourages elderly people to recall memories from their lives and ostensibly 'live in the past'. Reminiscence may be the process by which ego-integrity is achieved, a way to maintain self-identity and promote self-esteem in later life, an opportunity to change dominance relationships and highlight uniqueness as elderly people talk about subjects they know more about (Goudie and Stokes, 1990), or the means by which older adults can be seen as valued members of society by communicating wisdom through storytelling. It is probable, however, that the latter function is of decreasing utility. In contemporary western society older people are no longer widely respected as oral historians. There is no single reason for this circumstance but it is likely to involve the greater availability and accessibility of the media, and in this century of rapid technological and social developments, a prevailing opinion that the recollection of past values and habits is an archaic and obsolete pursuit.

Whatever the motivations are to reminisce, people are not invariable. We have changing needs, so reminiscence may be used at different times for differing reasons. When moving from one living arrangement to another an elderly person may indulge in storytelling about the past, at another time recalling past achievements may be used to protect self-image, while on other occasions it may be more important to reconcile past conflicts, and so on.

Reminiscence and Adjustment

Many studies have found reminiscence not to be related to adjustment. Butler (1963) noted that the outcome of life review may be negative for those people who cannot achieve a satisfactory resolution of past conflicts and accept their life cycle: 'Success is by no means guaranteed' (Coleman, 1986). Failure may result in various unpleasant emotional reactions. For example, a morbid preoccupation with the past as people 'compulsively' reminisce but find no relief in the activity, a wish to 'flee' from the past by 'blocking' the life review process because it is too painful to cope with the feelings it arouses or the onset of guilt, regret and despair.

In a major study of reminiscence and reminiscing, Coleman (1986) developed a four-fold typology of attitudes to reminiscence and related morale. In this study, 42 per cent of the sample valued memories of their past and enjoyed high morale. In contrast, a further 30 per cent also displayed high morale but saw *no* point in reminiscing as they had 'better things to do'. Low morale was associated with being troubled by unhappy and disturbing memories (16 per cent of the sample) and the avoidance of reminiscence because the elderly subjects (12 per cent of the sample) could not tolerate the sense of loss experienced when contrasting the past with the present. This last finding shows that it is simplistic to assume that 'past' life satisfaction is in all instances equated with morale in old age. Coleman concludes that 'neither the tendency to reminisce or not to reminisce is likely to be associated with morale. Both reminiscence and non-reminiscence can be expressed positively or negatively'.

Gender Differences

Do sex differences (i.e. physiological differentiation between males and females), and gender differences (i.e. social prescriptions associated with each sex) affect experience and functioning in later life? Consideration of biological ageing has established that females are hardier insomuch as their life expectancy is greater. At the level of a psychosocial analysis as men and women traditionally occupy different positions and adopt different roles in society, their ageing experiences also differ. In many ways a double standard of ageing exists which results in ageing being in general a more difficult experience for women (Sontag, 1978). This is not only because, as they live longer, they are more likely to live alone and experience financial hardship in old age, but also because women 'are defined more narrowly' (Cunningham and Brookbank, 1988). A woman is presumed to lose her sexual value at an earlier age than man (Sontag, 1978) while the period of greatest responsibilities and accomplishments for women draws to a close between the ages of 40 to 45 (see Neugarten *et al.*, 1968a). Even though the age norms are continually shifting, so long as women are viewed as having principal responsibility for child rearing, men will continue to have an age-related advantage when considering such issues as the timing of 'greatest responsibilities' and 'greatest accomplishments'. Neugarten *et al.* (1968a) report, for example, that men are often viewed as not having moved into their top job until they are 50. Consideration needs to be given to the fact that women have several decades of life after motherhood and will probably experience years of widowhood. Can it be said that contemporary society is finding ways to meet the needs of women by providing meaningful role options?

While growing old for both men and women requires psychological adjustment and social redefinition, men, to their advantage, are 'allowed' to age without penalty in several ways that women are not. For example, being physically attractive is far more significant in a woman's life than in a man's, but beauty is associated with relative youthfulness (the study by Neugarten *et al.*, 1968a, identified an age range of 20–35 for 'good looks' in women), and thus does not stand up well to ageing. Sontag (1978) considers that the traits of competence, autonomy and self-control which constitute 'masculinity' are not threatened by the disappearance of youth. However, those which index 'femininity', namely attractiveness, sensuality, grace and passivity do not improve with age. For many women a task of ageing is to maintain a physical image, unchanged, for as long as possible. It is of interest to note that some researchers (e.g. Sinnott, 1986) believe that the characteristics which define masculinity and femininity become less apparent with age. Men and women seem most divergent in late adolescence and young adulthood, and become more similar as they age. While some investigators believe that the reported decrease in sex-typed qualities which distinguish men from women does not represent a significant late-life shift in behaviour and attitudes, Sinnott sees the drift away from sex-linked characteristics as a genuine release from the constraints of gender roles toward an androgynous identity.

Emotional development also appears to be subject to gender differences. In a study of older women who had little or no experience of the world beyond the parental family, school and their own families it was observed that the emotional trauma of early childhood was perpetuated in their relationships with their husbands and children (Fiske, 1980). Among elderly men the effects of emotional deprivation in early life had dissipated by middle age. This gender difference was explained by Fiske in terms of the cohort of elderly women having experienced adult life 'generally at one remove, at first via their husbands, later through their adolescent and adult children'.

While the finding from this research is consistent with the psychoanalytic view that women remain fundamentally attached to the emotional roots of childhood and find in early adulthood 'no paths open to further development' (Freud, 1973), Fiske notes that ongoing longitudinal research reveals that women are beginning to expand their psychological horizons as society's norms and expectations relating to 'a woman's place' change. The role and significance of social prescription clearly needs to be understood when investigating the ageing process and it is to this dimension that we now turn.

Chapter 4

Social Age and Social Ageing

'Later life' is socially prescribed in so much as society has an entry boundary, albeit an ambiguous one, for old age and identifies social roles and patterns of behaviour which are consistent with the attitudes and norms which prevail toward later life. Thus, old age can be seen as a social construction. While 'physiological phenomena set limits on social definitions of position and role' (Moore, 1963), they cannot account for the norms and prescriptions associated with later life. These in themselves are not static social phenomena but vary historically. Since the turn of the century our perception and experience of old age has been transformed by immense social change, yet it is true to say that throughout this time social prescription has invariably reflected a negative view of being 'aged'.

Goudie (1990a) notes that as long ago as the ancient Romans, old age was seen as a disease to be cured. Despite the development of scientific explanations of ageing over the past 200 years the idea of rejuvenation persists to the present day. People do not easily accept the reality of ageing, nor the advancing prospect of death; although what people often fear are the myths and distortions which surround the processes of ageing.

In modern society honours are heaped on the benefits and joys of youth. Sontag (1978) believes, however, that the emphasis placed on youth is not to be taken as a literal description but a metaphor for 'energy', 'enthusiasm', 'a restless search for change' and 'a state of wanting'. A consequence of these dominant values is an aversion to ageing and the appearance of aged people.

Keeping elderly people at a social distance in order to avoid unrewarding interaction means that many younger people have little direct contact with older adults. This deprives them of opportunities for learning about, and understanding, the reality of ageing, thereby enabling half-truths and inaccuracies to be promulgated. However, bridging the 'generation gap' is not easy, for people of similar chronological age share a value system and cultural expectations which means that people of different age groups react differently to the same social phenomena. Common social ground is therefore difficult to achieve, and social distance is thereby maintained.

Ageism

Ageism is a pejorative image of a person in later life simply because of their age. As Woods and Britton (1985) state, elderly people are the victims of discrimination based 'on the accumulation of birthdays and not on any rational basis'. Such age-related expectations develop early, for pronounced negative attitudes about older people have been observed in young children. While there is evidence that we are becoming more sensitive to ageism, negative opinions toward old age remain prevalent in society. Thomae (1980) comments on surveys in the United States and Germany which found that old people were regarded as 'stubborn', 'touchy', 'bossy', 'incompetent', 'dependent', 'passive', 'rigid', 'irritable', 'inactive', 'withdrawn', 'suspicious' and 'indolent'. Not surprisingly, research has also shown that older adults share this negative image of themselves as an age group (Kuypers and Bengtson, 1973).

Negative stereotypes have been bolstered by media which often present an image of elderly people as sad, decrepit and cantankerous. It is rare to see the benefits and psychological assets of old age portrayed. When they are it is often in the guise of 'how amusing these old folks are, getting up to "pranks" and indulging in age-inappropriate behaviour'.

Although stereotypic images are often not malicious, prejudiced attitudes can have very real consequences. Some elderly people do have negative characteristics, but the inference that they are shared by all older adults is unsound and can lead to overt acts of prejudice. Thus, age discrimination is an unfortunate feature of daily life for many aged people.

Ageism has much in common with racism and sexism (Palmore and Manton, 1973). However, the unique peculiarity of ageism is that the majority of people who hold such prejudices will eventually become aged, and thus are destined to find themselves victims of the very discrimination they served to encourage. Explanations for this seemingly absurd behaviour are varied. It is possible that extremely negative views of ageing are a psychological defence against a person's own ageing (Butler and Lewis, 1977). Busse and Blazer (1980) consider we are confronted with a 'gerontophobia' as older people remind us of our own ageing and mortality. Hendricks and Hendricks (1977) state that ageism is facilitated by a belief that elderly people 'are somehow different from our present and future selves and therefore not subject to the same desires, concerns and fears'.

A negative perception of ageing and later life, and the associated attribution of value to youthfulness may, in part, be related to there being no biological 'task' for old age. People now outlive their biological utility in so much as we survive for many years beyond child bearing and active parenting. As a consequence there ceases to be a 'natural' process to guide the life course. While such a narrow perception of human behaviour denies the diverse richness of the life cycle, it is evident that for many people there is limited opportunity to develop alternative goals in later life.

It is probable that the increased longevity of humankind is also responsible for the decline in respect and admiration for older people in modern society. In ancient times it was unusual, and a source of interest, for people to live beyond the age of 50 (Cunningham and Brookbank, 1988). When survival into old age represented physical strength, cunning and wisdom, elders were respected and admired. As exceptional physical and psychological qualities are no longer necessary prerequisites for survival, aged people no longer merit the reverence once offered to them. The negative perceptions of ageing and accompanying decline in esteem for older people can therefore be seen as the product of the historical process of modernization (e.g. Coleman, 1986).

However, it is a simplistic image to assume that all old people are stigmatized *per se* (Ragan and Wales, 1980). For example, respect and deference is observed in everyday social interaction with aged family members, while outrage characterizes public opinion when confronted with reports of abuse of an elderly person. Overall, it is reassuring to find that extreme prejudice is held by only a minority of people, and is unlikely to occur if people have close relationships with old people, such as grandparents. Negative stereotyping also appears to be related to low educational attainment, with extreme opinions less likely to be held by better educated people.

The Myth of Social Ageing

Hendricks and Hendricks (1977) describe some of the myths of later life:

Elderly people live alone, abandoned by others, beset by serious health problems;

Elderly women experience profound psychological trauma as their maternal role is gradually eroded;

Occupational retirement leads to a dramatic decline in morale for men;

Older adults are not only sexually inactive, but sexually disinterested.

These widely held views are misconceptions unsupported by fact. While some of these circumstances, attitudes and emotions are observed in older people they can also be found in other age groups as well (Palmore, 1969; Maddox, 1970). Despite an absence of empirical support the oft-quoted stereotypes of old age continue to thrive. It is even the case that older people who do not experience the trauma and disability erroneously attributed to old age see themselves as exceptions.

In an attitude survey in the United States (Harris *et al.*, 1975), only 2 per cent of the respondents considered the years after the age of 60 as the best in life, while approximately 33 per cent of those aged between 18 to 64 years, and an even greater proportion of those over 65 saw retirement age as the least desirable. The survey also revealed however the significant prejudices and mistaken views the general public hold toward old age. For example, younger people consistently hold more negative views about later life than those who are actually over the age of 65. They expected the problems encountered in old age to be far more serious than they are for those who actually experience them. For example, less than 25 per cent of older people in the survey reported fear of crime to be one of their most serious concerns, yet 50 per cent of the general public thought crime constituted one of the biggest worries in the lives of older people. While over half of the respondents felt that most elderly people had very serious problems of poor health, poverty and loneliness, only 21 per cent, 15 per cent and 12 per cent respectively of elderly people reported such profound concerns. Overall, Harris *et al.* (1975) found that for every elderly person who felt their life was worse than they thought it was going to be, 'there are at least three age mates who claim they are pleasantly surprised — it is better'. However, these observations did not prevent many older adults in this survey from viewing later life as the least desirable age. Yet to what extent was their disenchantment the consequence of having to confront stereotypical perceptions of elderly people and a denial of opportunity in later life?

Too great reliance on 'accepted opinion', and a belief that the views and judgments of elderly people are of no account, inevitably leads to the imposition of values onto aged adults and the construction of stereotypes. Meaningful contributions to the improvement of life quality in later years can only occur if we take note of what older people are reporting as being areas of need and concern. Failure to do so means that the accompaniment to increasing longevity will continue to be deprivation and discrimination.

Social Roles

Social Age and 'Eldering'

Role changes have been described as the central elements of late life adjustment. Yet, while the transitions of old age are profound, they are a continuation of the transformations and adjustments that occur in the relationship between the individual and society throughout the life cycle (see Figure 4.1).

Movement through the life course has been termed 'age mobility'. As people age they encounter a sequence of role entrances and exits, the process of role adaptation being 'accomplished by socialization, regulated by social institutions and accompanied by shared meanings and values' (Ragen and Wales, 1980). Birren (1959) introduced the term 'social age', which 'refers to acquired social habits and status, to the individual's filling the many social roles or expectancies of a person of his or her age in his or her culture and social group' (Schroots and Birren, 1990). Social age is obviously related to chronological age, in part to psychological age and to a lesser degree to biological age. The dynamic process of social ageing is enshrined in the concept of 'eldering' (Schroots and Birren, 1990), which is defined as the processes of social role change through the social institutions of which the individual is a member in the direction expected by society.

Neugarten *et al.* (1968a) consider that when age-graded behaviour occurs outside the accepted span of chronological years it is deemed inappropriate and sanctioned. If the person is 'on-time', adjustment is usually not traumatic as

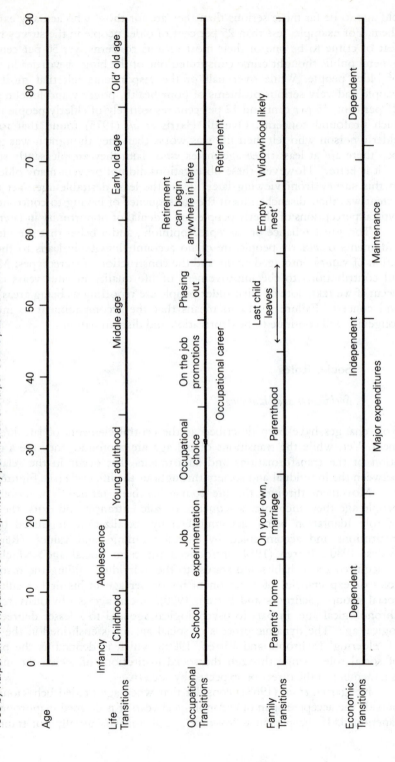

Figure 4.1: Table from Gerontology: The Psychology, Biology and Sociology of Aging by Walter R. Cunningham and John W. Brookbank, Copyright © 1988 by Harper and Row, publishers Inc. Reprinted by permission of Harper Collins publishers Inc.

events and changes have been anticipated and have society's approval. Behaviour is seen as typical for that part of the life cycle. However, a person is 'off-time' if their behaviour is not consistent with the 'expected sequences and rhythms of life' (Neugarten and Hagestad, 1976). People feel good about themselves if they are 'on-time', but if they are either early or late they will experience emotional discomfort. The greater the degree of temporal desynchronization the greater will be the stress experienced. Neugarten and Datan (1973) believe that identifying 'a social time clock that can be superimposed upon the biological clock' is a useful way of understanding the life cycle. McGrath and Kelly (1986) offer a similar explanation for the temporal rhythms which underlie social role change.

This discussion on 'eldering' must not leave us with a rigid conceptualization of social ageing. Although the life course can be interpreted as having a beginning, middle and end, not everyone will experience the same life events in the same order or at the same time. As people grow and develop they take many different paths as alternative routes open up. For example, Bengston *et al.* (1977) describe how the patterns and pace of ageing vary according to gender, socio-economic status and race. As stated earlier (p. 23), normative models of human behaviour can only possess general utility.

Role Changes in Later Life

The transition between middle and old age is sometimes characterized by ineffective socialization and inadequate preparation for the roles of later life (Rosow, 1974). 'Age mobility' may result in a disturbance of social interaction as the ageing person and their 'significant others' attempt to adapt to the new age-graded expectations. As new attitudes and interaction patterns emerge with the mutual acceptance that the person is no longer middle aged but old, equilibrium is restored. At this point of restored homeostasis, expectations and norms from the previous age status dissipate and those which define the older status are prominent. However, 'there is little guidance for these transitions in role except for common sense admonitions to "act your age"' (Cunningham and Brookbank, 1988).

For most people, later life tends to be the stage of life when 'careers' (a sociological concept referring to sustained involvement in a circumscribed area of social activity) are shed, either voluntarily or compulsorily. As a consequence, the new social realities can be harsh. Children grow up and leave home, resulting in what has been called the 'empty-nest' phenomenon. Retirement terminates the major occupational career which at the very least provided financial security, if not significant psychosocial benefits such as identity, self-worth and companionship. Growing physical limitations and sensory deterioration might put an end to strenuous activity and leisure pursuits which had been a source of personal enjoyment. While an advantage of old age is that people have a greater share of discretionary time when compared with other age groups, limited finances and declining health often means they are disadvantaged in their ability to exploit recreational opportunities.

Accompanying these life changes, 'careers' end not through personal choice or compulsion, but because stereotypical images dictate that certain roles and behaviours are no longer appropriate in later life. This is evidenced in such telling phrases as, 'mutton dressed as lamb', 'dirty old man', and 'you can't teach an old dog new tricks'. Informal norms dictate standards of dress, leisure and sexual behaviour expected of aged adults. Formal sanctions are not necessary to 'enforce' compliance, for as Ragan and Wales (1980) comment, 'the informal but powerful negative sanction of making older people feel ridiculous if caught in inappropriate behaviour is effective in distributing prescribed and proscribed behaviours by age group'. The outcome is that many aged people are socially oppressed, and denied both status and the opportunity to expand their personal horizons or contribute to community life (Johnson, 1975). For some this can mean a need to adjust not to unsatisfactory roles but to a state of 'rolelessness'.

However, to conclude on a more encouraging note, it is important to note that late life roles and norms are not that well researched. Although some investigators maintain that age-graded norms direct behaviour (e.g. Ragan and Wales, 1980), the extent to which normative prescriptions actually modify the behaviour of older adults is open to debate. Do they succumb to expectations, or do they attempt to pursue their preferred lifestyles regardless?

Age-Stratification

The roles which are available to older people are not associated with either high status or monetary gain. The unequal distribution of power, prestige and wealth in later life is the product of age-stratification (Ragan and Wales, 1980). As people progress through the life course they undergo changes in power and prestige depending on their age group. For example, while middle-aged people command influence and control resources, by and large aged adults do not. The life course can be regarded as a succession of statuses people are called upon to occupy as a consequence of ageing, those associated with childhood and old age being ranked lowest. Rather than the knowledge and experience of advanced years being placed in high regard, the contribution of old people to society is disregarded and poorly rewarded.

Models of age-stratification also identify interaction effects between age, social class, sex and race (e.g. Riley, 1976; Jeffries and Ransford, 1979; Ragan and Wales, 1980). This has unwelcome implications for status in later life. As women predominate among the elderly population, the lower relative status of women in society is likely to have contributed to the negative social image of older adults.

Cross-Cultural Ageing

The vast majority of research on ageing and old age is concerned with people living in modern urban society in advanced industrial nations, representing a consideration of the processes of ageing within a specific culture characterized by particular norms and circumstances. We cannot observe ageing 'in its pristine biological form' immune from the effects of 'human invention' (Clark and Anderson, 1967), and thus ageing must be discussed in terms of an age × culture interaction.

Investigating the variety of psychosocial outcomes to the biological process of ageing in the thousands of societies documented by social anthropologists therefore requires a rigorous examination of the effects of human culture and associated systems of norms, values and customs. For example, Ragan and Wales (1980) note that in the USSR where labour shortages were common, workers were encouraged to continue working rather than to retire. As a consequence, older workers were valued for their experience and a positive image was thereby promoted. In the United States and Britain, where there are the contrasting problems of unemployment, a view that older workers are less alert and more inefficient prevails, with the accompanying norm that they deserve relief from work and should make room for younger workers.

While there are certain similarities in role transition across cultures which may reflect biological communalities, there are also strong heterogeneous features in 'eldering' which indicate that cross-cultural research holds considerable promise for improving our understanding of the phenomena of ageing. Ultimately, however, regardless of the nature of such phenomena, we need to identify the consequences of the biological, psychological and social processes of ageing on performance and behaviour in later life, and it is to these issues that we now turn.

Part Two

Psychological Products and Processes

Chapter 5

Intellectual Products in Old Age

The stereotypic image of intellectual ageing is one of an inevitable decline in competence as a person advances in age. This common assumption appears to be confirmed by some of the degenerative changes observed in the ageing brain. However, a growing body of research in intelligence allows us to challenge existing opinions of psychological competence in later life.

While increased research activity tends to be descriptive rather than experimental, empirical work on cognitive functioning has been successful in raising, and in part answering a range of significant questions. How is age related to intelligence? At what age does intellectual development peak? Is there general intellectual stability or deterioration? If there is decline, what is the rate, practical significance and pattern of deterioration? Are there mental abilities which remain stable and others which decline, and if this is the case what distinguishes the former from the latter? The literature reviewed in this chapter suggests that the prospect of inevitable and dramatic intellectual decay which troubles many people as they age is in all probability based upon a misplaced assumption. Although my intention is to deliberate upon the empirical outcomes of adult intelligence research, the initial focus of attention needs to be on the basic issues of how do we conceptualize and measure intellectual functioning.

The Concept of Intelligence

While 'the existence of intelligence seems to be one of the certainties of psychological life' (Howe, 1990) debate continues as to whether intelligence is a legitimate theoretical construct. Spearman (1904) introduced the idea of a general dimension of intelligence which underlies all purposeful intellectual products. This unidimensional view of intelligence was challenged by the works of Thurstone (1938) and others which described multidimensional models that conceptualized intellectual functioning in terms of multiple faculties rather than a unitary construct.

Howe (1990) concludes that there are strong grounds for believing that the notion of general intelligence (the so-called 'g' factor) is 'obsolete and counterproductive'. Theorists who adopt this position contend that measured intelligence is a description of an individual's performance on the tasks which form intelligence tests, and not an explanatory concept offering a reason for what has been observed.

A contrasting viewpoint to that proposed by Howe argues that 'the existence of relatively separate abilities does not mean that a "g" factor is an empty construct' (Nettlebeck, 1990). The nature of intelligence can be understood in terms of a hierarchical model wherein an underlying general cognitive factor influences intellectual ability across a broad range of tasks and problems.

Cunningham and Brookbank (1988) regard general intelligence to be at the top of the hierarchy with increasingly specific abilities being represented as we progress toward the base of the organizational model. While it is possible to study intelligence at any of the levels of the hierarchical structure, the level of common or primary mental factors is considered by most psychologists to be optimal for the investigation of age relationships with intelligence. This level focuses upon mental abilities such as word fluency, memory span, visual memory, general reasoning, spatial orientation and verbal comprehension. Schaie (1990) states that a person's ability to perform on a set of primary mental factor tasks is our operational definition of the expression of intellectual ability. This intellectual product can be termed psychometric intelligence. Primary mental abilities are intercorrelated and can be organized into higher-order factors such as the concepts of fluid intelligence and crystallized intelligence. Higher forms of intelligence, which are uniquely human characteristics, include the ability to abstract, comprehend complex relationships, apply logical thought to problem solutions and communicate insight.

Methodological Issues

An understanding of intelligence requires not only an appreciation of hypothetical constructs and concepts, but also a knowledge of the methodological issues pertaining to the assessment of intellectual products.

Test Construction

Since the time of Sir Francis Galton, there have been attempts to measure intelligence. Early efforts focused upon sensory acuity and reaction time, and were not particularly successful in predicting future performance outside the test setting. The first tests which were predictive were developed by Binet and Simon and represented an empirical development of the theory proposed by Spearman (1904, 1927). Refinement of these assessment measures led to the development of the intelligence quotient (IQ), which represents a division of mental age by chronological age (set at arbitrary maximum of fifteen years) and is analogous to general intelligence. An individual's IQ can predict school performance, level of educational achievement and is also related to occupational status. Thus the measurement of intelligence has traditionally been concerned with creating in the test setting, activities which would represent and predict intelligent behaviour in the real world.

Nowadays, the most commonly used global intellectual measure is the Wechsler Adult Intelligence Scale (or WAIS; Wechsler, 1955) which adheres to the multidimensional view of intelligence. The WAIS consists of eleven operationally distinct sub-tests which sample a range of intellectual functions. These are aggregated into two broad dimensions: verbal IQ and performance IQ. These in turn are combined into a full-scale intelligence quotient. However, as with the vast majority of measurement instruments it was developed for children and young adults to predict educational attainment at school and occupational aptitude among the general population. Thus, a pertinent question to ask is how does the WAIS and other measures of intelligence relate to older adults? Kendrick (1982) has questioned the use of such tests with elderly people, reporting that they are not relevant to the everyday life of older adults. In other words they lack 'ecological validity', and so reduce motivation and cooperation, and produce deficits of statistical, but not practical significance. Woods and Britton (1985) consider the WAIS to be of 'dubious validity' when used with elderly people. What are clearly required are measures that are indigenous to elderly people (Schaie, 1980).

It is not simply that the tests are age-inappropriate in terms of their content, but the overall length of many intelligence measures such as the WAIS can also lead to performance decrements. For example, Furry and Baltes (1973) noted that fatigue adversely affects test outcome. The complexity and difficulty of test material also exercises a negative effect on the ability of elderly people to perform. Thus by causing tiredness and reducing motivation, test construction may be a critical reason for impoverished psychometric performance in old age.

The confounding effects of test material also arise when the sensory deficits and physical decrements of aged people are not taken into account. For example, the typefaces of tests are often inappropriate for work with elderly people. A related concern is whether we are actually measuring the same intellectual function in the young and old in the same way. For example, time-limited numeracy tests may not be assessing numerical skills in later life, but instead may be an examination of perceptual speed. Cunningham and Brookbank (1988) assert that 'many such shifts in meaning of a test score are conceivable'. In light of these observations it cannot be assumed that assessment measures have equivalence over wide age ranges. This concern with the internal validity of test instruments means we must always be aware of alternative explanations for the data of studies which examine intellectual products and ageing.

While test design can result in older people not doing as well as their younger counterparts, it is difficult to argue that this factor is a complete explanation for observed age-related differences. Nor can it be said that the criticisms levelled against test construction are beyond dispute. Some investigators assert that while most intelligence tests were developed originally for children or young adults, the reliability and validity of these instruments remain reasonably adequate into old age (e.g. Savage *et al.*, 1973). Furthermore, the view that elderly people do not try as hard or care as much in test conditions was not confirmed in studies by Botwinick *et al.* (1958) and Ganzler

(1964). Cunningham and Brookbank concluded that the lowered motivation hypothesis 'has precious little research support'. It is even possible that the poorer performance by elderly people may in part be the consequence of over-arousal and an excess of motivation.

The belief that older people may tire more easily has face validity, but as Cunningham *et al.* (1978) demonstrated, 'there were no significant effects of fatigue on ability performance' even in very lengthy test sessions. Cunningham and Brookbank (1988) conclude that motivation, tiredness and the meaningfulness of material are unimportant biasing effects on psychometric intelligence. Thus, the case for contending that the construction of intelligence tests exerts a significant adverse effect on the ability performance of aged people remains unproven.

Research Design

In an overview of research on intellectual change during the first half of this century, Wechsler (1958) identified a pattern of change which revealed that intellectual ability declined from a peak in early adult life (Figure 5.1). From around the age of 30 years to the mid-60s the rate of decline was gradual and then from young-old age onwards deterioration accelerated. Matarazzo (1972) suggested that by the age of 75 years the decline represented an erosion of one-third of peak intellectual capacity. Thus, intelligence test performance data as a function of age are in accord with the expectation that as people age, intellectual ability declines.

It is certain, however, that methodological factors mean this trend is spurious; an artefact of inadequate research design and deficient interpretation. The outcomes of research on intellectual abilities in old age must be treated cautiously, to an extent that some conclusions can be largely dismissed (Schaie, 1980). Intellectual changes over time cannot be established by averaging the results of samples at different age levels and then comparing their relative performance. The various age points on the curve of decline reported in Figure 5.1 were established by the use of such cross-sectional data. As already noted (pp. 9–10) cross-sectional methodology can only establish age differences, and so the data are only adequate to illustrate to what extent adults at different ages differ in intellectual performance at a particular moment in time (Schaie, 1990). Cross-sectional data are unsuitable to answer the question as to how intelligence changes with age within individuals.

When age is associated with a particular level of intellectual ability, it could imply a true association reflecting the consequence of the biological ageing process, or it could also mean there are significant cohort differences in cross-sectional comparisons of individuals at various ages (Miller, 1977). Cohort influences involve a variety of different early experiences relevant to intellectual development and intelligence test performance, such as educational opportunity, nutrition and medical care all of which will differ across generations. As younger and older people are not comparable with regard to a range

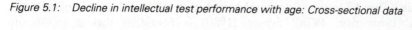

Figure 5.1:   *Decline in intellectual test performance with age: Cross-sectional data*

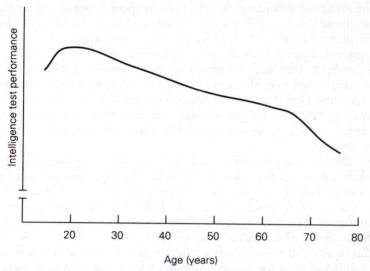

Source: Derived from Wechsler (1955); reproduced from Woods (1982, p. 69), in Levy, R. and Post, F. (eds), The Psychiatry of Late Life, *with permission of Blackwell Scientific Publications, Oxford.*

of important environmental influences it is facile to assume that the age differences established on psychometric intelligence are the product of biological degeneration. Also at the time of assessment age-related sociocultural influences may exert a differential effect on performance. For example, the self-appraisal by elderly subjects that they will perform badly because of cultural stereotyping may result in a self-fulfilling prophecy. Prohaska *et al.* (1984) implicated a lack of confidence in one's ability to succeed in the poor performance of some elderly people. Assessing older people in unfamiliar test settings may also lead to performance decrements as strange and stressful circumstances can account for much of the loss in competence in advanced old age.

Overall, it is generally felt that cross-sectional methodology exaggerates the decline in intellectual functioning that occurs as a consequence of 'normal' ageing. While it is difficult to separate cohort differences and age effects, Schaie (1983) believes that cohort differences are a major source of variance in intellectual functioning. The development of cross-sequential methodology (e.g. Schaie, 1967), which in essence involves a series of cross-sectional studies at different points in time with both independent random samples and as many as possible of the people tested on earlier occasions, attempts to identify and distinguish between age effects, cohort influences and time of measurement effects (Woods and Britton, 1985). The cross-sequential study by, for example, Schaie and Labouvie-Vief (1974) demonstrates the extent of cohort influences. While cross-sectional data identified age-related decline, longitudinal data revealed gradients which were less marked with the exception of the oldest age group (over 67 years of age). Although this methodology is not without criticism (Botwinick, 1978), Schaie (1980) is confident that a significant 'proportion of observed differences in test performances between young and old must be attributed to their difference in experiential backgrounds and other population characteristics which have changed across generations'.

With greater educational opportunity, improved nutrition and lifestyle changes it is probable that age differences in psychometric intelligence will become more compressed over the next decade. For example, as most intellectual abilities are more closely related to educational achievement than age and as each succeeding generation has, on average, attended school longer than the preceding generation then we should expect a levelling off of cohort effects, at least for some abilities.

Evidence that people are well placed to do better on intelligence tests when they reach old age, is provided by research which has revealed marked generational shifts in levels of psychometric performance (e.g. Flynn, 1984; Willis, 1985). The point at which intellectual 'decline' is observed is moving up the chronological age scale generation by generation so that later-born cohorts perform better than earlier-born cohorts at the same age (Schaie, 1990). The consequence of these cohort changes may not only be to reduce the large ability differences between young and older adults, but on certain mental abilities such as numeracy it may well be that in the future elderly people will be advantaged compared with younger adults (Schaie, 1990).

It is possible, however, that the level reached by recent cohorts as a consequence of educational improvements and lifestyle developments may represent the maximum limit of growth potential which can be realistically achieved given that the resources society can dedicate to educational advancement and welfare provision are not infinite. Therefore, 'the positive shifts in potential experienced in early old age by successive cohorts may consequently come to a halt by the end of this century' (Schaie, 1990).

In light of these cohort change data it is legitimate to ask whether there can be any reasonable permanence in age norms for psychometric intelligence at times of rapid alterations in population characteristics. As cross-sectional data are typically used for the development of age norms, 'one cannot be sure that the next age bracket in the table of norms will indeed perform at the same level as did the former cohort' (Schaie, 1980). Once this is acknowledged we are obliged to appraise accurately the competences of contemporary older people and appreciate how cohort differences have led to erroneous conclusions from age comparative cross-sectional methodology.

To avoid the problems endemic in cross-sectional data, longitudinal research design can appear attractive. As noted earlier (pp. 9–10), however, longitudinal studies also suffer from methodological and logistical problems. In the area of adult intelligence research what is of critical concern is that findings are unlikely to be representative of the general population. The problems are twofold. First, the repeat presentation of material can produce a learning effect. Thus, practice effects may mask an age-related decline and result instead in evidence of improved performance. As certain mental abilities may be particularly susceptible to practice, outcome data may be difficult to interpret.

The second, and most serious, methodological weakness is that some people are not available to be reassessed. As attrition is not random, but selective, in so much as it is the less healthy and able subjects who are lost, this has profound implications for data interpretation. Given that poor health is, for example, related to poor psychometric performance, longitudinal studies may be biased against identifying intellectual decline. Siegler and Botwinick (1979), supporting the view that it is the intellectually and physically superior who are represented throughout longitudinal studies, observed that at each reassessment those subjects still available to the study recorded higher mean intelligence test scores on the first occasion of testing than those who participated in the preceding assessment. That selective attrition is not simply a marginal concern is revealed by the fact that in a study by Savage *et al.* (1973) only one-sixth of their sample were retested after seven years.

The conclusion must be that psychometric intelligence in old age can be crucially affected by methodology. While it cannot be assumed that all age-related alterations can be explained by methodological artefacts, knowledge of the different methodologies and their respective strengths and weaknesses allows us to avoid the simplistic notion that ageing produces inevitable intellectual decline. We need to know what method of research was employed in any particular study and also recognize that existing methodology, to a large extent inadequately addresses the issue of age-changes in functioning.

Intellectual Change

The previous section illustrates that a review of the literature on intelligence in older age-groups must proceed cautiously so to avoid unsafe interpretations and conclusions. However, we can be forceful in stating that in the absence of pathology, a general decline in intellectual functioning is not a feature of the life course from early adulthood into old age. Any diminution in intellectual competence which may occur is not global in nature, but a highly specific event. Schaie (1990) reports that virtually no people show deterioration on all mental abilities even by the time they are in their 80s. These data reveal that at age 60, 75 per cent of subjects maintained their level of functioning over seven years on at least 80 per cent of the mental abilities tested, and this was so for slightly more than 50 per cent of the sample aged 81 years. There is no evidence that men and women differ on general intelligence or the extent of intellectual decline with age (Huyck, 1990).

Although these are encouraging results, there is clearly some reduction in intellectual ability in later life. To establish what precisely is happening we need to identify those abilities which are sensitive to ageing, at what age we can expect to observe the onset of decline and whether such changes are inevitable or subject to individual differences. We therefore need to move away from the 'blunderbuss' approach of global intellectual measures to an examination of the conceptual components and cognitive abilities which constitute intelligence. Unfortunately, there are no useful cross-cultural comparisons of intellectual ageing in other societies, so the data to be reviewed will be confined to research conducted in advanced industrial western society.

Verbal and Performance IQ

If we look beyond the full-scale IQ of the WAIS, to the verbal and performance components, how do these relate to ageing? Wechsler (1955; 1958), on the basis of cross-sectional data, documented a differential 'decline' in verbal and performance abilities insomuch as verbal sub-test scores showed less of an age trend than did performance scores. Performance IQ decrements were reported by Wechsler to be apparent in middle age, with verbal ability deficits becoming increasingly noticeable around the age of 60. Norms for the recently revised form of the WAIS for people aged to 75 show significant age differences on performance measures which involve perceptual speed, while there is relative stability on the verbal sub-tests. Evidence for the continuation for this pattern into advanced old age has been documented by Field *et al.* (1988). The discrepancy between verbal and performance measures is well replicated (cf. Jarvik, 1973) and found across both sexes, racial groups and socioeconomic levels (Eisdorfer *et al.*, 1959).

Woods and Britton (1985) summarize WAIS research findings from longitudinal studies as revealing intellectual stability to age 60, and then if negative alterations do occur they are initially in the realm of performance skills, until a person ages beyond 70 when verbal ability shows some decline. They reject the view, once commonly held, that age-related intellectual change starts in middle age, although cross-sectional comparisons invariably identify speed-related decrements while people are still in their fifties.

Explanations for the differential ageing effects on WAIS data range from hypothesized intellectual processes to methodological considerations. Those items of the WAIS which 'hold' (i.e. verbal abilities) are considered to reflect the stored or accumulated experience of adults, while those sub-tests which 'don't hold' (i.e. performance IQ) involve abilities which require speed of information processing or problem-solving skills (Woods and Britton, 1985).

Methodological variables are implicated in the inconsistent findings of longitudinal studies which have reported changes in WAIS scores in older people. Problems of selective attrition, different frequencies of assessment and different age profiles across studies may well be responsible for the inconsistencies reported, and thus make comparisons between longitudinal data difficult.

Primary Mental Abilities

Although the WAIS remains a popular measurement instrument, Schaie (1990) considers 'its factorial complexity makes it less attractive for assessing intellectual changes across age and time'. As a consequence many recent studies of age-effects have employed test batteries measuring various combinations of primary mental abilities. Schaie (1980; 1983; 1990) reports a major cross-sequential study which began in 1956 and has tracked large numbers of people over the age range 25 to 81 years in seven-year age groups over seven-year intervals. Subjects are assessed on five measures of intellectual competence (see

Table 5.1:   Primary mental abilities

Verbal Meaning	— the ability to understand words.
Spatial Orientation	— the ability mentally to rotate objects in two-dimensional space.
Inductive Reasoning	— the ability to infer rules from examples that contain regular progressions of information.
Number	— the ability to manipulate number concepts.
Word Fluency	— the ability to recall words according to a lexical rule.

Source: Schaie, 1990

Table 5.1) which 'are prominently represented in virtually any meaningful activity of a person's daily living and work' (Schaie, 1990). The group data summarized by Schaie (1990) reveal that on average there is a gain in intellectual competence in early adult life. It peaks when people are in their late thirties or early forties. Stability in intellectual performance characterizes middle age until the mid-50s and early 60s are reached. The average decrements observed between the ages 53 to 60 years only reach statistical significance for 'number' and 'word fluency'. After the age of 60 decrements are statistically significant throughout thereby indicating that while some people in their mid-50s show a small decline in intellectual competence it is not until people approach their 70s that deterioration becomes prominent.

Although the prevalence of deterioration in primary mental abilities is reliably established for group data, controversy surrounds the pattern of individual differences that may exist. Not all elderly people of advanced age manifest intellectual deficits. Schaie (1990) reports that, depending on the age group, between 60 to 75 per cent of all subjects between the ages of 67 to 81 years remain stable or improve on specific primary mental abilities tests over the preceding 7-year period. After the age of 60 until age 74 significant deficits affect less than a third of the participants, and even by age 81 only between 30–40 per cent are manifesting similar changes.

As has already been described those aged adults who do display negative alterations do not manifest a global shutdown of intellectual competence. It is possible that in order to maintain an effective level of intellectual functioning in old age it is necessary selectively to maintain certain abilities but not others, and that this process is guided by individual strengths and needs. Theories of 'selective optimization' in old age, which will result in an altered cognitive style, have been proposed by several investigators (e.g. Hussain, 1981; Baltes and Willis, 1982).

Consistent reports from various studies show that word fluency, which is the most speeded task, is highly sensitive to age. Regardless of the psychometric measures employed, speed of response is negatively affected by ageing. Tasks involving the ability to make rapid comparisons of letters and figures reveal marked aged differences. While the tests can be completed, age sensitivity concerns the speed with which they are conducted. There is mounting evidence that perceptual speed may be the most age sensitive mental ability. Data supporting the variable relationship between age and speed requirements come from both cross-sectional and longitudinal methodology, as well as experimental manipulation. As we shall see in the next chapter on cognitive processes, 'intellectual speed' is often associated with the quality of thinking, and thus old age may well be characterized by poor quality intellectual competence.

In contrast to the findings on 'intellectual speed' those abilities which are well-practised in everyday life, such as verbal comprehension and numeracy, are not sensitive to age and thus most elderly people are perfectly able to carry out these over-learned skills. Cunningham and Brookbank (1988) propose a neurological explanation for these differential sensitivities. They hypothesize that many cells and cell systems can carry out the information transmission function underlying well-practised mental abilities and thus these abilities are relatively immune to cell death and decreased functioning unless a critical threshold of cellular degeneration is passed. However, when unfamiliar responses are needed or 'time-limited' performance is required, diminished neurological functioning results in impaired competence.

Debate centres on the age sensitivity of reasoning abilities, such as inductive reasoning, as studies have yielded markedly differing results. While Foulds and Raven (1948), drawing on cross-sectional data, observed strong age differences beginning before the age of 30, Cunningham and Brookbank (1988) report that longitudinal studies have not shown a decrement in inductive reasoning until people age beyond 50. Schaie (1980) describes how cross-sectional data reveal that the decline in inductive reasoning attains practical importance by age 53, while longitudinal methodology suggests this does not occur until age 81. It is possible that there are wide interindividual differences on this measure of psychological competence (Cunningham and Brookbank, 1988). As it is suggested that health is associated with inductive reasoning, this could be why longitudinal studies do not uncover major deficits in inductive reasoning.

Crystallized and Fluid Intelligence

Evidence of specific intellectual decline led to the formulation and continued popularity of a theoretical viewpoint which accounts for the resistance of some primary mental abilities to ageing and the age sensitivity of other factors. This is known as the theory of crystallized and fluid intelligence (e.g. Cattell, 1963; Horn, 1970). Crystallized intelligence (Gc) is the accumulation 'of the individual's informational resources including both specific knowledge (e.g. the meaning of a word) and methods of doing things or solving problems' (Cunningham and Brookbank, 1988). This aspect of intelligence increases with experience or at least remains stable throughout adulthood. It is thought that everyday abilities such as mechanical aptitude, and understanding social relationships also reflect crystallized intelligence. Fluid intelligence (Gf) involves the ability to reason, abstract, perceive relationships between objects, acquire new ideas and adapt to change. It is this dimension of intelligence which is prone to deteriorate with age.

Woods and Britton (1985) conclude that this structural theory of intellectual competence appears to have validity. However, such alterations are not to be regarded as inevitable, for what the theory is addressing is the *probability* that fluid intelligence is more likely to decline in later life, while crystallized intelligence is more likely to show no evidence of deterioration with age (Horn and Donaldson, 1976).

Problem-Solving

There is evidence that elderly people are less efficient at solving complex problems (e.g. Arenberg, 1974, 1982; Rabbitt, 1980). The reasons for this relative incompetence are varied. Older adults are less efficient in organizing their problem-solving strategies and find extreme difficulty in focusing on the task at hand when confronted with peripheral, inconsequential information (Rabbitt, 1965). Chown (1961) and Schaie (1958) found that older people are more rigid in their thinking and show greater perseveration, leading to the employment of previously learned strategies which interfere with the development of new concept formation. Rabbitt (1977) observed that when simple and more complex problem-solving strategies are available, older people tend to select the simpler solution even though this may be the less efficient approach.

As complex problem-solving involves learning and memory, any factors which interfere with the acquisition and retention of information will adversely affect the ability to resolve problematic situations. Woods and Britton (1985) note that elderly people are further disabled when new problems are to be faced because they are poor at implementing memory support strategies such as note-taking, and thus experience information overload.

Overall, the problem-solving capacity of elderly people is a relatively unexplored area which requires more investigation. Most of what we do know is based on cross-sectional comparisons, and so while there are significant generational differences these are, at least in part, the consequence of cohort influences such as the differential experience of formal education. Age differences are not reported until late midlife, although Schaie (1980) notes a need to take somewhat more time to achieve equal levels of accuracy before this age. However, what is possibly the most significant point to address is whether the problem-solving capacity of older people, while being different from that of younger adults, is sufficient for the demands of their current life-stage. Schaie believes that whereas complex problem-solving is a feature of middle age, this cannot be said for old age where problems are simpler and increasingly orientated towards much more egocentric goals. Thus while examination of problem-solving abilities in artificial settings reveal marked differences, these may have little practical significance for aged people.

Language

Woods and Britton (1985) report that 'remarkably little research indicates the effects of ageing on language abilities'. Enderby (1990) reports that older people have well-preserved semantic memory (i.e. memory for the meaning of words), and grammar, although there can be a delay in the access to vocabulary. There is reasonable evidence that elderly people tend to use longer, more complex sentences. Changes in vocal characteristics occur because factors such as smoking, posture and toothlessness can adversely affect articulation. Comprehension of spoken language may deteriorate because of poor hearing and difficulty with screening out competing stimuli.

Individual Differences

It is clear that there are some intellectual products which reveal little or no decrement. There is also a significant proportion of elderly people who show no change on most intellectual measures into very old age. Miller (1977) noted that on many measures the range of variability increases, so the average performance score 'must then reflect a proportion who show much larger changes and a proportion who show very little change'. Thus, individuals whose intellectual functions do not significantly decline are obscured in group data by those who deteriorate markedly.

Are there identifiable antecedents of age-related cognitive decline? Wilkie and Eisdorfer (1971) found that hypertension is associated with lower intelligence test performance, and Abrahams and Birren (1973) related serious cardiovascular disease to intellectual deficits. Similarly, Hertzog *et al.* (1978) found that people at risk from cardiovascular disease tend to decline earlier on all the measures of intellectual competence employed in their study. Overall, there is an inverse relationship between indicators of physical health and intellectual performance. Birren (1970) observed the possibility 'of little change in intellectual function in the years after 65, given good health'. However, sensory impairments, especially hearing, are also related to intellectual deficits. Conversely, Savage *et al.* (1973) identified a group of exceptionally physically well-preserved older adults, who the investigators labelled as 'supernormals' who obtained significantly higher WAIS IQs than their peers. They were more active and survived for longer than would have been expected. Further, Siegler (1980) noted that in most longitudinal studies higher intellectual performance at the start of the study is strongly associated with survival.

A related area of interest is the relationship between intellectual change and survival. As long ago as 1962, Kleemeier suggested an 'imminence of death' hypothesis which argued that the factors associated with approaching death may affect intellectual performance and be detected quite a time prior to death. Savage *et al.* (1973) identified a decline in psychometric intelligence some three years before death at whatever age. In the two years prior to death the decline in abilities seen in the previous years accelerated. However, in the immediate pre-death phase there was a sudden loss of WAIS verbal abilities which had previously been maintained.

The critical feature of the 'imminence of death' hypothesis is not the relationship between intellectual level and death, but the identification of an accelerated and generalized change in psychological competence in the years prior to death. Support for the hypothesis is equivocal, however. Some studies have failed to establish evidence of accelerated decline, while others have reported varying time periods, ranging from three months to ten years prior to death, during which an increased rate of decline occurs. Furthermore, we need to avoid intellectual decline being viewed simply as an indicator of imminent death, for such change may be the consequence of a potentially treatable illness, with performance improving after the restoration of health.

Schaie (1990) reported a number of structural variables that tend to inhibit the rate of intellectual decline. While age is not kinder to the more able *per se*, factors often associated with high ability, such as high levels of education, occupational status and income, as well as demographic variables such as intact marriage, lengthy marriage to an intelligent partner and exposure to stimulating environments, do appear to have positive effects on intellectual change. Retirement can have favourable cognitive sequelae for those who retire from routinized jobs, but may have a detrimental effect for those retiring from stimulating occupations (see Chapter 11).

Schaie (1990) notes that the antecedent status of the personality trait of rigidity/flexibility is reliably associated with intellectual performance. This trait can be separated into 'attitudinal flexibility' and 'motor-cognitive flexibility'. Schaie showed that those with flexible attitudes in midlife tend to experience less decline in intellectual competence with advancing age than those who were observed to be comparatively rigid in middle age. It was also demonstrated that high levels of motor-cognitive flexibility at the 'young-old' stage of life are highly predictive of a person's verbal and numerical skills in advanced old age.

In conclusion, empirical research on individual differences in intellectual competence in later life and the identification of antecedents for differential performance undermines the argument that intellectual decline in old age is inevitable for all people. Contextual variables which were once regarded as methodological confounds obstructing our understanding of ageing effects can now be regarded as potential indicators of intellectual decline or maintenance in later life.

Re-Training

To what extent can intellectual competence in later life be improved by systematic re-training of cognitive ability? If as Labouvie-Vief *et al.* (1974) maintain, most performance deficits reflect the impoverished social environments within which elderly people function, then intervention strategies which provide stimulation and reinforcement of intellectual behaviour may well lead to cognitive improvements. Schaie (1980), although not referring to the impoverishment of later life, considers the pace of socio-cultural change this century has generated a serious problem of intellectual obsolescence for many elderly people. As such, it is important to distinguish between age-related intellectual decrements that result from biological changes occurring within the individual (whether related to 'normal' ageing or pathology) and obsolescence effects, for it is likely to be the latter component of intellectual decline which is amenable to cognitive re-training. Support for the argument that elderly people, dis-advantaged because of cohort effects and understimulation rather than loss of intellectual capacity, can benefit from informal or formal education is offered by the concept of 'plasticity'. This emphasizes that intellectual performance is a growing and developing function even into old age and thus can be improved given sufficient practice and encouragement. In this way, intelligence is considered to be malleable or 'plastic' (e.g. Huyck, 1990).

Evidence of selective training improvement is becoming increasing abun-dant. Baltes and Willis (1982) report significant training gains for people over the age of 60 for the primary mental abilities of figural relations and induction. Schaie and Willis (1986) demonstrated similar gains in the areas of inductive reasoning and spatial orientation. However, in both studies there was no evidence of transfer effects to other primary abilities.

The improvements reported by Schaie and Willis (1986) are the product of longitudinal methodology and thus it was possible for the investigators to show that significant gains were apparent for people who had declined in intellectual competence as well as for those who had remained stable. Approximately 40 per cent of those people who had declined were restored to the level of functioning displayed fourteen years earlier. Willis (1989) notes that the availability of longitudinal data enables investigators to identify the antecedent factors which serve to predict the likelihood of training success or failure. Evidence suggests that health status is related to the outcome of train-ing interventions (Schaie, 1989). Schaie (1990) cites a long-term follow-up study of people exposed to cognitive training over a seven-year period which reveals a significantly lower decline for those trained compared with a control group. In contrast to these encouraging findings, Botwinick (1978) found no evidence that systematic re-training generates skill improvements in the area of problem-solving ability.

Schaie (1990) optimistically concludes that it is reasonable 'to assume that much of the cohort-related aspect of older person's intellectual disadvantage when compared with those at midlife may well be amenable to compensation by suitable education intervention'. More cautiously, Cunningham and Brook-bank (1988) acknowledge that while psychometric performance can improve with training, evidence of transfer effects to related abilities in conjunction with sustained behavioural improvement over time is limited.

Conclusion

Overall, research developments have challenged historical attitudes toward intelligence and ageing. Increasing awareness that global intellectual decline is not inevitable as people age, that when age-related decline does occur it is in general specific and not dramatic enough seriously to affect the adaptive ability of the majority of older people and that it may be possible to develop re-training interventions that maintain or improve certain intellectual functions, will hopefully encourage the emergence of a more realistic appraisal of intellec-tual ageing which focuses upon the maintenance of intellectual health in old age rather than emphasizing the prospect of deficit and decay. To this end it is to be hoped that age-appropriate 'educational' experiences compatible with the life space of older adults will become a feature of later life with the inter-related aims of reducing the risk of intellectual obsolescence and promoting competence in activities of daily living. We may then be able to maximize our human 'potential for creative adaptation' (Birren, 1973) to the environment during the entire lifespan.

Chapter 6

Cognitive Processes in Later Life

To understand late life changes in intellectual functioning in particular, and behavioural performance in general, we need to be acquainted with the effect ageing has on basic cognitive processes such as perception, attention and information processing. It is generally thought that older people experience an inevitable deterioration in the complex chain of cognitive processes which commences with sensory input and culminates in a behavioural output. It takes time for the nervous system to register incoming physical stimuli, organize and process the stimuli through the central nervous system, integrate the data with material from memory in order to provide meaning, use the information gained to choose a response and finally to execute the response by various effector organs (e.g. Welford, 1980). The onset of process decrements would inevitably lead to impaired outcome performance.

There is no doubt that a fundamental and pervasive change that occurs with age is a slowing of thought and behaviour. We have already seen that slowing is a significant feature in the decline of certain aspects of psychometric intelligence in later life. Changes in the speed of thought and action may be a fundamental explanatory variable to account for age differences in many aspects of psychological performance. With regard to the processing of information in old age if each component link of the chain is slowed, the complete response may take more time and so affect negatively the outcome either qualitatively or quantitatively. The conclusion may therefore be drawn that if an individual cannot think quickly, they cannot think well. Rabbitt (1968) made the analogy between an ageing person and an ageing computer in so much as they are slower to process information and do so with less efficiency. Thus, a major area of interest in the psychology of ageing is the extent and significance of cognitive slowing and a search for the locus (or loci) of this decrement. Is it at the level of perception or at the outcome stage of effector responses? Or is the retardation primarily focused in the central processes of decision making?

Furthermore, is it possible to relate the slowing of cognitive processes to a biological slowing, as proposed by several investigators? If the slowing is within the peripheral nervous system, at the level of visual input or motor output, this 'would not have such severe potential consequences for overall adaptation' (Woods and Britton, 1985). If it were to be primarily concentrated in the central nervous system, however, the implications would be far more serious.

Sensory and Perceptual Processes

Perception is the process by which a person organizes and makes sense of incoming stimuli, yet with the sensory changes which occur with advanced age in virtually all individuals, both the quantity and quality of sensory information available to elderly people may be reduced, resulting in a diminished perceptual system.

Vision and Visual Perception

While visual abnormalities such as glaucoma and cataracts are not inevitable in later life, ageing does result in losses of visual functioning. Poor visual acuity increases with chronological age, especially in conditions of insufficient lighting or low contrast between details and their background. This decline can be mitigated, though not entirely eliminated, by greater illumination (Welford, 1980). As changes in the eye reduce the quality and intensity of light reaching the retina, older people are effectively operating under conditions of poorer lighting at all times.

Tolerance of glare diminishes because of an increase in the opacity of the lens and dark adaptation is slower so that older people take longer to adapt to changes in the level of lighting when going from well-lit conditions into a semi-darkened environment. Welford also notes that the area of effective visual field diminishes so that the size or intensity of stimuli need to be increased if they are to be seen. Needless to say, events occurring away from the centre of the visual field may fail to be observed. Data identifying alterations in colour vision with age are equivocal (Kline and Schieber, 1985).

Welford believes that perceptual changes are to be understood not simply in terms of anatomical deterioration of the sense organs, but also arising as a result of increased neural activity in the sense organs, afferent pathways and brain with age. Thus, the problem is not only that sensory deficits reduce 'signal strength', but the weakened nerve impulses resulting from incoming stimuli have to be discriminated from heightened spontaneous background neural activity (known as 'neural noise'). This negative shift in the signal-to-noise ratio produces a reduction in signal discrimination thereby impairing performance.

Having considered the effects of ageing on vision, the changes in perceptual quality are many and varied. In general, older people are less sensitive to changes in the strength of visual stimuli. This can be measured by presenting a series of very weak stimuli and determining the physical level at which the subject can identify the stimuli 50 per cent of the time. An alternative method involves measuring the minimal difference in physical stimulation that is needed for a person to detect a just noticeable difference. Group data show that elderly people require a stronger signal in order to perceive, for example, a dim light or need greater physical change in stimulation before a difference is detected.

Perception cannot be regarded simply as a passive process of receiving stimuli and producing responses, however. A more complex concept of perception described by Cunningham and Brookbank (1988) is known as signal detection theory. This views the perceptual process as involving an appraisal of the nature of the stimulus before an individual decides whether to respond or not. Research has found that older people on some perceptual tasks tend to be more conservative in so much as they need to be more certain of the nature of the stimulus before they respond. However, the age differences are not great compared with the overall age-related decrements in perceptual sensitivity. The role of motivation in information-processing will be discussed at length later in this chapter.

Another recent development in the study of perception and ageing is the notion of stimulus persistence. As it may take longer for a stimulus to work its way through an aged nervous system, perceptions tend to persist longer thereby reducing the efficiency of the perceptual system. However the experimental support for this idea is equivocal.

Hearing and Auditory Perception

Both ageing and noise pollution contribute to the problems of hearing in later life, although whether the relationship is additive or interactive is currently being debated (Cunningham and Brookbank, 1988). The various changes in the ear have been described by Welford (1980). Generally, hearing losses are greater among men, yet sex differences are decreasing over time, most probably as a result of women being increasingly exposed to industrial and occupational noise pollution.

Although age-related decrements in auditory perception appear to be more gradual than in visual perception, 'the adaptation to the slower losses may be more difficult' (Cunningham and Brookbank, 1988). While this contention is clearly debatable, the rationale behind it relates to the critical role of auditory perception in communication with others. Deficits may introduce profound negative alterations in interpersonal behaviour, orientation and psychological adjustment in general. An essential aspect of speech intelligibility is the ability to appreciate differences in the physical stimulation of a tone. With age, pitch discrimination declines, especially for higher pitch. In conversation, problems of speech intelligibility are often more significant for consonants which are frequently of higher pitch than vowels.

Overview

While there are individual differences in performance, Kausler (1982) reported that perhaps as much as 90 per cent of perceptual ability remains substantially intact in the face of normal ageing, despite the evidence of, for example, age-related losses in visual functioning. Situational factors are also of importance as they can lead to markedly impaired outcomes. For example, circumstances which place an elderly person under strain or those which are unfamiliar do not aid perception. While this means that performance in later life may at times be deficient, the implication is also that we can create supportive prosthetic environments which compensate for those abilities which have been damaged. Not only might this involve reducing glare and improving illumination, but as irrelevant stimuli inhibit visual perception, then the careful design of signs and labels which provide only essential information and avoid excessive details or 'clutter' can only encourage adaptive behaviour.

Has it been established, therefore, that information processing decrements in old age are located within the sensory input processes? While there is inefficiency and consequent slowness in the peripheral nervous system when sensory losses are compensated for by, for example, the presentation of stimuli within the capabilities of elderly people, slowing of response time remains as a function of advancing age. Is the locus of slowing therefore at the level of effector response? It would seem not. Singleton (1955) found that deficits in experimental reaction time were not the product of actions slowing with age, while Murrell and Forsaith (1960) found that the slowness of older industrial workers was not the consequence of retarded motor responses but resulted from the increased time needed to plan and decide upon which actions were to be taken. If motor responses are held constant, but the complexity of decision is manipulated, it can be assumed 'that the bulk of the slowing is at higher cortical levels in the brain, involving decision time' (Cunningham and Brookbank, 1988).

Central Information Processing

It is the opinion of many psychologists that while the sensory and effector response stages of information processing show some slowing, changes in the peripheral nervous system are not of sufficient magnitude to account for the overall decline in response time with age. It is probable that the critical cause of cognitive slowing is the ageing of the central nervous system with respect to the central processing of information and decision-making. Although the evidence for this argument is both indirect and incomplete, CNS slow-down with a concomitant slowing of information-processing would have negative implications for behavioural performance. Birren (1965) views changes in the processing of information in the older CNS as accounting, at least partially, for a large number of cognitive alterations in later life.

Welford (1980) reports that until the 1940s it was assumed that changes in the sense organs, muscles, joints, heart and lungs, together with changes in the demands of later life, accounted directly or indirectly for virtually all normal changes in performance. It was thought that central nervous system processes remained virtually unchanged throughout life. The significance of central factors first became evident when studies were made of changes in sensory-motor performance with age. Many experiments have been conducted to investigate the speed with which people of varying ages can process information and perform simple tasks. One of the most commonly employed techniques in the study of sensory-motor performance is the reaction-time task wherein a person is required to make a simple error-free response as quickly as possible when presented with a stimulus. The task can be made more complex insomuch as subjects may be asked to make a choice when confronted with several signals and several possible responses.

The experimental design of reaction-time tasks minimizes extraneous influences and controls for major perceptual limitations among subjects. Visual stimuli are presented with sufficient illumination so subjects have no difficulty in perceiving the signal. Only simple behavioural reactions are required so to control for any motor response decrements. Similar procedures are adopted when auditory stimuli are used.

In comparison with younger people, the reaction times of aged adults are, on average, always slower (e.g. Welford, 1977a). When greater task complexity is introduced there is a corresponding increase in age-differences. If the burden of decision-making is minimal, there is usually little increase in reaction time until people reach their 70s. However, if a choice is required between two or more responses to different signals, and if signal presentation is unpredictable, the increase in reaction time with age is greater.

Attempts have been made to identify the central processes implicated in the slowing of performance. Botwinick (1978) examined the function of expectancy in reaction-time task. Both brief and long preparatory intervals between a warning signal and reaction time stimulus cause older adults difficulties. On the one hand they have problems with anticipation and learning how to 'get set' quickly, while on the other they are less able to maintain readiness for long periods. Gottsdanker (1982) demonstrated only a slight increase in reaction time with age when preparation for the reaction-time stimulus was easy. When a longer preparatory interval was introduced, however, a much larger age difference was recorded.

An age-related decrement in accuracy has also been noted under certain, but not all conditions (Rabbitt, 1968). For example, on relatively simple tasks older adults tend to be slower but more accurate. On more complex tests, until about age 50, people retain levels of accuracy but at the cost of increased time. However, by age 70, there is a tendency for older adults eventually to 'give up' at the expense of accuracy. Welford (1958) interpreted these findings as indicating that complex problem-solving tasks which require time interact with memory capacity. The longer a person spends on the task the greater the probability that essential information held in the memory may be forgotten, thus contributing to a loss of accuracy.

Increases in mean reaction times with age have been related to changes in the ability of elderly people to monitor the adequacy of their previous responses (Welford, 1977b). Older people have a greater tendency to monitor their reactions, and while monitoring is in progress immediate attention cannot be given to new signals and this will delay the decision to react to new stimuli.

Overall, tests designed to evaluate reaction time have revealed great individual variability among elderly people. While group data reveal consistent age-related decrements, individual performance outcomes are averaged so those elderly subjects who perform well within the normal range of younger people are merged into the group average. Antecedents associated with slower reaction time include raised blood pressure, cerebrovascular and cardiac disorders, and low levels of activity (e.g. Welford, 1977a, Birren *et al.*, 1979). Slowing is modified by personal history and prevailing circumstances. Task familiarity is important insomuch as age differences are lessened on familiar ones. Extensive experience makes a person more proficient and usually faster in performing that task. Thus, in reality, the consequences of cognitive slowing may only reach significance when aged people are faced with relatively unfamiliar and demanding activity. It is for this reason that reaction-time tasks, as a measure of information-processing in later life, have been criticized as inappropriate and lacking 'ecological validity' (Kendrick, 1982). As Cunningham and Brookbank (1988) comment, cognitive slowing in old age is a major concern only if it affects aspects of everyday living, and yet it would appear that highly practised, familiar tasks are least sensitive to ageing effects. Thus, it is clear that ageing *per se* is only one factor that affects the speed of information-processing and performance in later years.

Attention

While central information-processing in old age results in delayed performance, attention may be a further basic psychological factor in the overall process which needs to be taken into account, for attention decrements will also interfere with adaptive responses. Vigilance is the ability to detect stimulus change over a long period of time. Therefore it requires the motivation to persist with the task at hand in the face of increasing fatigue. Vigilance does not appear to be age-related unless the task is sustained over an extended period of time when beyond the age of 60 fatigue can result in notable performance loss. Decrements are also observed if memory requirements are implicated in the vigilance task. Overall, Cunningham and Brookbank (1988) conclude that with the exception of fatigue and memory-related dysfunction, 'there is little convincing evidence for age differences in vigilance'.

The information-processing system cannot respond to all the sensory stimuli it is exposed to. Selectivity is required so that irrelevant stimuli can be detected and discarded. Selective attention is the means by which a person actively filters incoming stimuli to determine whether or not they are relevant. There is evidence that elderly people are more distractible and cannot disregard the clutter of irrelevant information. Farkas and Hoyer (1980) showed that when older subjects have to scan irrelevant stimuli to locate the relevant stimulus, age differences appear. As it is not the case that elderly people are unable to perform the task, but rather they take an excessive amount of time to complete the task, Kausler (1982) concludes that this is due to a slower rate of information processing in elderly people as the number of stimuli processed increase.

Divided attention is the ability to dedicate finite attentional resources to competing relevant stimuli. An example of such behaviour would be the ability simultaneously to attend to a conversation while preparing a meal. Cunningham and Brookbank (1988) report that if the tasks are not demanding, older and younger people differ little in their ability to attend to simultaneous activity. If the tasks are complicated or demanding, however, elderly people appear less able. While this may reflect more limited attentional processing resources on the part of elderly people, an alternative explanation views the performance decrement as further evidence of a slowing down of information processing in older adults.

Overall, it would appear that attention is age-sensitive only when the tasks are demanding in terms of speed, sustained effort and memory. To minimize the possibility of confounding attentional factors, reaction-time tasks often employ a warning signal in advance of the experimental stimulus.

The Locus of Slowing

While attempts continue to isolate the age deficit it is clear that slowing is in evidence at each stage of information-processing. Age-related slowing in both the peripheral and central nervous systems has implications for all basic psychological processes. In light of these observations is there any merit in pursuing a 'focused' analysis of age deficits by engaging experimental subjects in tasks designed to identify the efficiency of particular information-processing stages? Cerella (1990) has recently rejected such an approach, maintaining that we need 'to replace the piecemeal explanations of the past'. The various sensory, central and motor processes operate not in isolation, but are components within a complex, interacting system. Recent theoretical work described by Cerella emphasizes that age-deficits are distributed throughout the information-processing system and not localized in particular stages. This interpretation is referred to as the generalized slowing hypothesis. Combining this work with the idea that cognition is 'a computation on a neural network', 'the new ageing theories view age deficits as defects of some sort distributed throughout a neural network of some sort' (Cerella, 1990).

The first theoretical development of these ideas was the 'reference model', which represented the brain as a neural network composed of links and nodes. Cerella describes information-processing as commencing with a signal from the input end of the network to the output end, with each step through the network taking a fixed amount of time. The time an individual takes to react is simply the time required for the signal to reach an output node, the length of time being determined 'by the number of links that must be traversed times the delay per link'. However, ageing is a destructive process which is conceptualized as breaking links at random. As a consequence a signal must circumvent broken links, each detour increasing the path length and increasing the time needed to process information (Figure 6.1). The accumulation of broken links and the detours they trigger lead to response latencies that increase exponentially over the lifespan.

Figure 6.1:   Schematic neural network

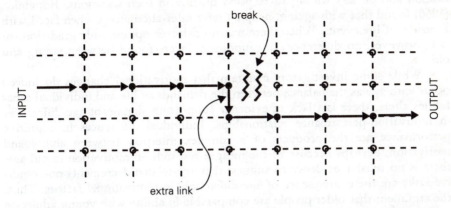

Nodes represent neurons and dotted lines axon connections between neurons. The illustrated network performs no computation, merely transmits signal from left to right. Latency is determined by the number of links, eight in the 'intact' network. However one link on the optimal route is broken, forcing the signal to detour and adding one more link to the path for a total of nine. Reproduced from Cerella (1990, p. 203), in Birren, J.E. & Schaie, K.W. (eds), Handbook of the Psychology of Ageing (3rd ed.), with permission of Academic Press, London.

The reference model and a second generation of models described by Cerella (1990) assume that the latency of the aged neural network reflects the status of the neural substrate, and that the limits of functioning are determined biologically. There is no place for psychological concepts such as attention or perception. Instead, cognitive ageing is located in the field of neurophysiology, although the nature and processes of the neural substrate remain unknown. For example, what is the relationship between deficits in the neural network and psychometric intelligence in old age?

These models present us with an economical and parsimonious explanation for a large body of data on ageing and cognitive processes, which replace the many task-specific explanations that have proliferated over the years. However, this body of recent theory, while sufficient to account for most of the age effects identified in the various experimental task conditions, cannot hope in a 'few broad strokes' to achieve a complete ageing equation. Yet, as Cerella (1990) notes, 'schematic neural networks are a rich modeling medium'.

Alternative Psychological Explanations

As has been already described under certain task conditions older people may sacrifice speed for accuracy, thereby leading to raised reaction times. Some supporters of this point of view argue that there are no age-related information-processing losses but that older people, because of their decreased tolerance of error, are more cautious. Thus increased response latencies need only be attributed to this motivational change. If an elderly person perceives a risk of failure (and it is quite probable that older adults tend to evaluate the probabilities of success differently from younger people), they will exercise caution and be less willing to respond quickly in such situations. Botwinick (1966) found that with ageing, people prefer safer alternatives when faced with a variety of life events. When there was no risk-free option, only gradations of risk, however, no differences in cautiousness were found between young and old.

While some investigators maintain that motivational changes do indeed occur with age as the balance between the demands of life and individual capabilities alters, there is a lack of evidence supporting significant age-differences in motivation-performance relationships. Individual differences in cognitive performance are the products of a complex interplay between ability and motivation. Perhaps because of the meagre research on motivation in old age, there is no reliable evidence to suggest that age-related decrements on cognitive tasks are the consequence of age-differences in motivational factors. Thus, the argument that older people are comparable in ability with young adults on a given task but they nevertheless perform at a lower level because of motivational processes which 'are less efficacious' (Kausler, 1990) is not confirmed by the experimental data.

Cerella (1990), in a review of motivation and reaction time, concludes that the response latencies of elderly people do not support the 'speed-accuracy shift hypothesis'. As a result of reviewing aggregate data from a number of information-processing studies, he observed that increased latency did not result in greater accuracy when compared with younger people. In fact when differences were apparent these were in the direction of a slight decrease in accuracy with age.

An alternative psychological explanation regards increased reaction time as a result of a decreased use of cognitive functions. The implication is that with sufficient task practice the initial performance decrements should dissipate, and the older person should achieve parity with younger subjects. However, the 'disuse hypothesis' is not supported by the findings reviewed by Cerella (1990), in which only 11 per cent of the initial deficit was eliminated over the course of practice. The remaining 89 per cent of the initial deficit proved irreversible, and this may represent a 'biological limit' which is not the produce of disuse and so remedial intervention would not be indicated.

Cerella suggests that reference to cautiousness, cognitive disuse, attentional deficits, perceptual insensitivity and other psychological factors are unnecessary, 'for the data are adequately predicted by declines in the neural substrate'. This does not mean that such factors are unimportant, but rather they function in the elderly as they do in the young, so that their particular effects do not alter during the ageing process and thus cannot account for age-related deficits.

Conclusions

Cognitive slowing clearly is an age-related phenomenon for some people, yet are such changes significant? Changes in the processing of information in the older nervous system are measured in fractions of a second. In everyday life this means that most old people continue to function adequately in most situations, especially in those which are familiar. Despite reliable evidence of partial decrements in basic psychological processes, elderly people can draw on experience, previous learning and semantic memory in order to compensate for reduced cognitive efficiency. While compensatory action and processes are less effective in complex and demanding circumstances, that some critical actions may be significantly influenced by changes of a fraction of a second, and that if a prolonged sequence of actions is required the slowing can accumulate, it remains the case that most aged people adjust and are able to accommodate to the demands of later life.

Chapter 7

Learning and Memory

Learning and remembering are concepts which are sometimes used interchangeably. When information is acquired, and a reorganization of cognition and behaviour occurs, learning is said to have taken place. Memory is normally employed when the focus is on the retention and retrieval of information which does not result in a restructuring of thought and action. Yet these definitions do not represent a sharp distinction between learning and memory. They have processes in common, for both registration and remembering occurs during learning, while subsequent performance is affected not only by the ability to remember, but also by the strength of original learning (Schonfield, 1980). For people of all ages it is clear that better learning produces better remembering. If a person reveals a 'memory deficit', can we be sure that acquisition ever took place? Performance deficits could be due to failure and inefficiency in acquisition, storage or retrieval. Thus, it is not surprising that what is known about learning helps us to also understand memory, and vice versa.

Learning in Later Life

Experimental Evidence

Can you teach an old dog new tricks? The common stereotype is that elderly people neither wish to learn new ways or skills, and for those few who are so inclined learning is both laborious and inefficient.

Schonfield (1980) defines learning as a relatively enduring change in behaviour resulting from experience. To understand the process in old age we want to know how elderly people learn, and what influences learning efficiency in later life. First, we will examine the results of experimental laboratory studies which have investigated the ability of older adults to learn new material in settings which are artificial and once again raise the previously detailed concern about 'ecological validity' and the need for naturalistic cognitive research.

Within the conceptual paradigm of traditional stimulus–response associationism it would appear that older people are much harder to condition, for example they have been found to be slow to learn on classical blink conditioning tasks (Braun and Geiselhart, 1959; Kimble and Pennybacker, 1963). Botwinick and Kornetsky (1960) using the classical conditioning of the galvanic skin response also found older people were slower to learn. While this is a real age-linked phenomenon, the spread of acquisition scores is great, indicating marked individual differences.

Although the average older person maintains their skill level at something already learned, the learning of new motor skills appears slightly more difficult for older adults insomuch as younger people learn more quickly (Cunningham and Brookbank, 1988). The more demanding and complex the skill to be learned the more substantial are the age differences. The reasons for this age-related decrement are not fully understood. Motor skills are a sequence of precise actions usually dependent upon perceptual feedback at various stages of the sequence. The deficit may be the consequence of a slowing of information processing, stimulus persistence in the perceptual system or because older people may have greater difficulty evaluating the accuracy of successive responses.

Verbal learning tasks, as measured by the acquisition of paired associates in which a subject must learn to associate a word or nonsense syllable with a similar verbal presentation, reveal age differences in the learning curve. Elderly people need more trials to achieve the same degree of learning as younger people. So as with other forms of learning in old age, learning still occurs but at a slower rate.

The reasons for the observed age-related difference in the rate of learning paired associates are varied. Monge and Hultsch (1971) showed that the rate of item presentation is critical, for under highly speeded conditions of responding age differences are more pronounced. Another factor is the strength of prior associative learning. For example, the power of the pre-experimental associative strength of the words BAT-BALL is greater than ZOO-TABLE. Research shows that age differences are large under conditions of weak associative strength and substantially reduced under medium or high associative strength. Finally, mediational instructions advising the use of mental images of the paired associate words often aids recall. However, while younger people are more likely to use mediators spontaneously, older adults await instruction to do so. Although learning often improves when older people use mediators, an interaction with speed is revealed for their effective use occurs when elderly subjects are provided with a relatively longer period of response time.

Learning and Retention

It is a common belief that older people forget new learning more rapidly than younger people. However, as we have seen, laboratory studies of learning in later life shows that older people do not learn as well as young adults do, so it is possible that the quantity and quality of original learning may account for differences in the rate of forgetting. Cunningham and Brookbank (1988) report that when older adults are given more learning trials so to achieve the same criteria of learning as younger subjects, comparable rates of forgetting are found. Thus, greater forgetting by elderly people appears to be at least in part a function of poor initial learning.

Enabling Learning to Occur

Schonfield (1980) and Welford (1958) believe the urge to succeed among ageing adults in experimental learning studies is strong. Poorer learning performance is therefore not the product of older people being less motivated to practise efficiently the various psychological processes which enhance learning. So are these real age-related learning decrements of practical everyday significance? It is difficult to say because of the type of artificial experimental activity employed. As Schonfield (1980) states, whether or not the findings of research studies can be applied to day-to-day life depends on the degree of similarity between laboratory and 'natural' conditions. Unfortunately, the artificial nature of the vast majority of learning research is only too clear to see.

While experimental data identify age differences in learning performance, the literature also thoroughly documents that elderly people can and do learn (Cunningham and Brookbank, 1988). Learning may be more effortful and slower, but it does take place. Thus, a healthy attitude to learning in later life is that acquisition is to be expected, but that age-related obstacles and impediments need to be overcome.

Later life is not a period of stagnation, but a time of great change. People are required to adapt to enforced limitations. Intellectual obsolescence can result in dependency and ineffectual behaviour unless ameliorated by fresh learning experiences. We have already discussed the evidence for the efficacy of cognitive re-training. Does the experimental study of learning offer any indication as to the type of remedial strategies and prosthetic conditions which would serve to enhance the prospects of a successful outcome to training and education?

Schonfield (1980) concludes that the tension of a strange learning environment is almost certainly greater for older adults. As excessive anxiety interferes with performance, any learning procedures with minimize stress and tension are to be advocated. Leech and Witte (1971) created a non-demanding 'teaching' environment and found learning efficiency on a paired associate task improved.

Research indicates that timing and pacing are also critical variables. Older people are slower to acquire skills, so fast, externally controlled learning situations are especially problematic for people as they grow older. Monge and Hultsch (1971) maintain that pacing difficulties can occur from about the age of 40. Botwinick (1978) raised the question of whether it is the speed with which the material to be learned is presented or the demand for a quick response which causes older adults difficulty. While the provision of extra time for responding benefits elderly subjects, the case for slowing the rate of presentation is not proved. However, Schonfield (1980) reports that the evidence is against recommending total self-pacing, for a point can be reached when older people are slower than is warranted by their level of potential efficiency. As discussed earlier, it is hypothesized by some investigators that motivational alterations may result in cautious behaviour in old age. This may produce overcaution and produce errors of omission, rather than errors of commission on learning tasks. A concern for optimum timing and pacing should not be restricted to the formal education setting, but needs also to be applied to everyday learning experiences.

Schonfield *et al.* (1972) demonstrated that elderly subjects found difficulty in switching concentration from one item to another. Schonfield (1980) synthesized this observation with the finding that older people are more easily distracted by irrelevancies to (Rabbitt 1965), suggest that the persistence of irrelevant stimuli at the expense of the relevant interferes with learning performance. Being unable to 'switch' from irrelevancies which are the focus of attention to relevant material, is consistent with the theory of stimulus persistence. The provision of 'clutter-free' learning contexts and materials should help aged people focus on those components relevant to the learning activity.

Part learning tasks may be advantageous for older adults insomuch as they lighten the learning load by reducing the volume of material to be acquired at any one time. Dividing learning tasks into sections as a means of reducing the learning load has rarely been researched, however; such a learning strategy possesses face validity and clearing merits investigation.

Older people in general will find meaningful material easier to acquire, and will be helped by instruction in and continuing direction to use cognitive mediators (for example, mental imagery) during learning. Overlearning will invariably generate performance gains, while practice in the use of mnemonic aids will also assist retention following acquisition. Several recent studies have demonstrated that training in targeted mnemonic skills often produces 'domain-specific' improvements in recall. Kliegl and Baltes (1987) showed that both young and old benefit from mnemonic strategies, but suggested that age-related differences could reflect the limit of potential learning capacity in later life. The identification of those mnemonic strategies which are effective, easy to acquire and generalizable remains a focus for current research (Wilson, 1989).

We can conclude this section on learning by stating that if the experience of learning is both relevant and in harmony with the needs of elderly people then education and training can be a rewarding and profitable enterprise. It has even been found that elderly students can be more focused and determined than their youthful counterparts, and are thus able to accomplish significant education goals. As verbal ability holds up well in later life and is the best overall predictor of educational attainment, it should not be surprising that, given supportive learning environments and the motivation to acquire knowledge and skills, elderly people can take full advantage of learning opportunities.

Memory

The ability to remember is a constant human need. It is essential that we are able to retain and retrieve information if we are to make sense of the phenomena we experience and adapt to the demands of life. In many ways it provides the basis for much of what we do. We have already observed the importance of memory in aspects of intellectual performance, problem-solving and information-processing. Memory also enables us to know who we are, what we value and the probability of future successes. Without the ability to remember, our concept of self would be tenuous in the extreme. Yet we tend to take our memory for granted, only being aware of it when we consciously need to recall, or when we are irritated when it fails to work efficiently.

For our purposes the question is, do memory failures become more common with age? This is certainly a stereotypic expectation, and it is true that forgetting is a frequent complaint of elderly people. However, memory never functions perfectly even in younger adults. An inability to remember in old age cannot therefore be regarded as inevitable evidence of the destructive process of ageing. Yet as Cunningham and Brookbank (1988) comment, the commonly held view is that when a young person forgets, it is because they forget; when an old person forgets it is because they are old.

In an entertaining and informative article, Rabbitt (1988) reported that cross-sectional survey data on a population aged between 50 and 96 showed slight and progressive deterioration in memory efficiency as people grow older. Forgetting is a complex phenomenon, however. One point of view is that recall is as efficient in later life as it is in earlier years. Impaired performance in old age is instead the product of deficient learning. In other words, there is no increase in forgetting with age, the difficulty resides in the area of acquisition (including remembering during learning). As we have seen this is a partial explanation, for the experimental evidence clearly indicates that the number of trials required to learn equivalent amounts of material usually increases as people grow older.

Inattention, and peripheral sensory losses can also create or exaggerate a memory deficit. For example, poor hearing can make listening more effortful. As a result, what is said can be misheard and remembering what has been said is harder. Thus one consequence of a slight hearing loss may well be an impaired memory.

The factors involved in the storage and retrieval of information are clearly many and varied, but to what extent is forgetting in later life the conse-quence of actual memory inefficiency? Our understanding of human memory is advanced if we regard it not as a single mechanism but as a sequence of memory stores through which information must be processed. We can then identify whether there is a general decline in memory operations, or whether specific aspects of memory processes are age sensitive while others are impervi-ous to ageing effects.

Sensory Memory

Sensory memory is a very brief short-term memory store which holds data extracted from stimuli detected by the sense organs at a sensory pre-perceptual stage of organization. The information is stored for less than a second in sensory memory and there is one store for each sensory modality. Most information in sensory memory is lost rapidly due to decay, but attentional mechanisms will select some information for processing and possible long-term storage.

There is not much evidence to suggest age changes in the proficiency of the sensory memory system. Only iconic (visual) and echoic (auditory) sensory memory have been investigated with regard to age sensitivity. Visual sensory memory may be measured by the brief tachistoscopic presentation of stimuli, where the subject is asked to recall the stimulus organization. However, Walsh (1982) questions whether this methodology actually measures iconic memory in older people, for the task involves such processing operations as selective attention which may in turn be age-sensitive (see pp. 59). Using a different methodology, Walsh and Thompson (1978) estimated that visual sensory memory in younger people is 15 per cent longer in duration than in older adults. Although very little research has been conducted into echoic sensory memory there appears to be only small or perhaps no reliable age differences.

Overall, while it seems likely that older adults are less efficient at this first level of memory storage the evidence is equivocal and in no way can age differences in memory function be reasonably attributed to deficiencies in the sensory stores.

Semantic Memory

After sensory input, attention and perceptual processes influence the passage of stimuli into a semantic store which contains logical and factual information divorced from personal, temporally dated material. Incoming stimuli are fused with existing knowledge to gain meaning. For example, semantic memory would allow an elderly woman to know what is meant by a purse and where London is, but not where she put her purse or when she moved away from London to live in Coventry.

Howard *et al.* (1980, 1981) reported that semantic memory is not age-sensitive, although older people are very slightly, but consistently slower than younger people to retrieve data from semantic memory. Hultsch and Dixon (1990) reviewed recent studies which have established a number of age-related decrements in various types of semantic memory tasks. Thus the simple conclusion that semantic memory is immune to ageing no longer appears justified. Yet, as with sensory memory, any deterioration in semantic memory function is not of sufficient magnitude to account for either the type or level of forgetting reported in old age. Elderly people are highly unlikely to report they forget the meaning of objects, but they are considerably more likely to report that they cannot remember the outcome of their involvement with objects.

Episodic Memory

As we are yet to establish substantial areas of dysfunction in our hypothesized memory system then it is seemingly inevitable that it is the final stage of memory processing which is age-sensitive, namely episodic memory. Following detection by sensory memory, if information is selected for further processing it will move into episodic memory via the intermediate stage of semantic memory. In episodic memory it can be preserved by repetition or transferred into a permanent store. Once in permanent store information is, in theory, never lost but can be recalled into conscious awareness by processes of retrieval.

Unfortunately there are competing theoretical representations of the encoding and storage aspects of episodic memory which serve to complicate our understanding of remembering and forgetting in old age. However, one of the models of memory function which has generated a significant amount of ageing research and made a notable contribution to our knowledge of later-life performance, is the dual process model. This hypothetical model proposes two episodic memory stores.

Primary memory

The first episodic memory structure is a temporary short-term store or primary memory in which information is maintained by active rehearsal. If information is not transferred to permanent storage the trace is lost. Information in primary memory is vulnerable for capacity is limited and data entering the short-term store can displace existing information. There is little or no information-processing in this system, for it is 'just an input-output operation' (Woods and Britton, 1985).

The ability to retain information in primary memory is traditionally measured by digit span or the immediate recall of, for example, an address. Studies reviewed by Craik (1977) seem to show there is no deterioration in primary memory function in normal ageing until late in life and even then the deficits are negligible. While digit span shows little change in older people, dichotic memory tasks in which different stimuli are presented simultaneously to both ears for recall often reveal age differences. Subjects must report all stimuli presented to one ear first, so information presented to the second ear must be stored for a short period of time. Dichotic listening tasks show deficit in the recall of stimuli from the ear reported second. While dichotic memory decrements are apparent, it is queried whether other factors are implicated aside from recall deficits. For example, Clark and Knowles (1973) conclude that the main problem for elderly people is the *perception* of the stimuli rather than the process of retention and retrieval. However, Parkinson *et al.* (1980) showed that matching old and young people on digit span almost completely eliminated age differences in dichotic memory performance. This indicates that dichotic memory does reflect primary memory and so memory dysfunction is the probable explanation for the impaired task outcomes.

Studies employing different experimental tasks have also reported primary memory deficits. McGhie *et al.* (1965) observed that short-term memory performance declines more rapidly when material is presented in the visual modality than when it is presented in the auditory modality. It is possible, however, that output from primary memory has deteriorated not because the short-term store is impaired, but because information fails to reach adequately the primary memory because of inattention, perceptual decrements or deficits in sensory memory (Neisser, 1967).

Scanning memory span does become slower with age which may have implications for transferring material to the permanent store. This is the most notable age difference in primary memory although age-sensitivity is still slight. Overall, it appears that experimental manipulations of forgetting from primary memory reveal only modest age decrements in functioning. Once again, those losses which have been identified are not of significant magnitude to account for the differences in memory performance with age.

A critical memory system can be distinguished from, although related to, primary store. This is working memory, a concept which includes a central executive capable of attention, selection and manipulation, an articulatory loop and a short-term visual store. It is regarded as a limited capacity system for the temporary storage of information which may not only be domain specific, but task specific. Experimental tasks which involve working memory demand simultaneous storage of recently presented data and the processing of additional material. Although we must accept that there are methodological difficulties in the measurement of working memory, substantial age differences are observed on tasks purporting to assess working memory in favour of younger people (e.g. Light and Anderson, 1985; Wingfield *et al.*, 1988). Craik *et al.* (1989) consider the age decrement lies primarily in the manipulation of information in working memory rather than in storage. Wright (1981) suggests that automatic processing declines with age, so older people have to devote more capacity to storing information, leaving less available to operate other processes within working memory efficiently. Working memory may also be inefficient in later life because age-related decrements in cognitive processes allow irrelevant material to enter the system and inhibit retrieval. The unclear relationship between working memory and age differences in general cognitive performance is discussed in detail by Salthouse (1988) and Salthouse *et al.* (1988).

Secondary memory

Empirical results identify secondary memory as the principal locus of age-related decline (e.g. Craik, 1977). The implications of this observation may be profound, for secondary memory is the major memory function involved in everyday life. The fundamental difference between primary memory and secondary memory is in the level of processing: 'In secondary memory some deeper processing or encoding of the information is thought to have occurred' (Woods and Britton, 1985). With deeper processing the durability of memory is greater so recall is facilitated (Craik, 1977). Deep processing occurs when the meaning of an item or word is examined in relation to the contents of semantic memory (i.e. semantic encoding). Shallow encoding, which is a descriptive operation, does not facilitate retention and recall.

It appears that younger adults are superior at deeper levels of processing, not because elderly people are unable to encode material semantically, but because they fail to carry it out spontaneously in an efficient manner. Woods and Britton (1985) review studies which show that elderly people encode material more generally and neglect to encode the specific meaningful aspects of the item or its context. This may be because deep processing is an effortful operation which is affected by age, whereas encoding an item's global semantic features is a relatively automatic processing activity which is relatively age-insensitive.

We need to introduce a degree of caution into the discussion, however. First, the experimental data are conflicting because different methods used to operationalize depth of processing do not always yield the same results. Second, there are substantial individual differences in performance. Zacks (1982) observed that older subjects who performed as well as young subjects used active encoding strategies, whereas those who were relatively impaired passively registered each item as it was presented.

Experimental studies of secondary memory have investigated various modalities of sensory input and different retrieval mechanisms (for example, recognition, free recall, cued recall). While the general statement, secondary memory loss occurs in old age is accurate, detailed investigation reveals a varied and subtle picture of altered functioning.

Assessing memory performance by recognition rather than recall often reveals negligible age-related decrements. Perhaps this is because recognition is a less effortful operation solely involving a judgment regarding familiarity. It reduces the amount of retrieval that needs to be carried out and possesses a larger automatic processing component than would be the case in the deliberate purposeful process of recall. There is variability in recognition memory in old age, however, and when 'guessing' is controlled for Harkins *et al.* (1979) found recognition to be poorer in older people.

In theory, information which enters secondary memory is never lost and thus is potentially accessible for recall. This potential recall does not mean it is readily retrievable, however. Our recall operations are never perfect, but with advancing age significant changes occur in the ability to retrieve learned information from secondary memory. Experimental studies of free (i.e. unaided) recall, wherein subjects are asked to remember as many items as possible without assistance, indicate that retrieval is highly age-sensitive. The biological basis for this age difference appears to be related to central nervous system inefficiency, probably as a result of cell death in those areas of the brain associated with memory, such as the hippocampus. However, elderly people benefit from cues which facilitate retrieval. Rabbitt (1988) describes a real-life prospective memory task which suggests that information is more easily available if retrieval cues are external (for example, notes and diaries) or associated with routine events rather than being accessed by internal cues. This study also noted that older people who are aware of their memory lapses are more likely to compensate for them by adopting efficient cueing strategies in daily life. The results of cued recall tasks clearly illustrate that information must have been originally stored in secondary memory. Memory decrements in later life must therefore lie at the point of retrieval and cannot reflect impaired storage capacity, although the possibility of inefficient encoding processes will also lead to impoverished retrieval operations. Finally, recall suffers not only because it is an effortful process in later life, but because retrieval is also slower, so older people can no longer access information to keep pace with external demands.

Hultsch and Dixon (1990) review efforts which have been made at establishing age differences in memory for meaningful stimuli, activities and events. In the midst of 'conceptual and methodological problems associated with meaningfulness', they report cross-sectional data which show age differences in favour of younger people in the recall of spoken language and written passages. Several individual and contextual factors appear either to exaggerate or attenuate age differences, however. For example, it is essential when asking young and old subjects to recall written passages that the material is equally familiar and experientially meaningful to both groups, otherwise age differences may be the product of age-related bias in the text to be tested. Hultsch and Dixon (1983) found equivalence in retrieval rates for younger and older adults for passages about an entertainment figure equally well-known by adults of all ages and a figure known best by elderly people. Young adults were superior in their recall of written material about a figure more familiar to them.

Kausler and Lichty (1988) label as rehearsal-independent those daily activities which people remember even though at the time of performance there was no intention to retrieve the information. They are recalled both incidentally and automatically. Although it was expected that rehearsal-independent tasks in contrast to rehearsal-dependent experimental activities (for example, the free recall of items) would reveal negligible age-differences, the results of studies are both inconsistent and inconclusive. Kausler and Lichty (1988) demonstrated that memory for performed activity is a rehearsal-independent dimension of episodic memory, yet they established that on both recognition and recall tasks that younger people were more able than older adults. It is possible that if age-sensitivity does prevail in this area of memory performance it is again indicative of the effortful process of retrieval.

Remote memory
It has been suggested that remote or long-term memory may be a separate dimension within secondary memory which may play a significant role in later life satisfaction and adaptation (see Chapter 3 for a discussion on reminiscence). Botwinick and Storandt (1980) investigated the capacity to recall events going back sixty years and found only slight evidence of memory deficit for major happenings in childhood. It does not appear to be the case, however, that older people are superior in their remote memory when compared with younger adults (Warrington and Sanders, 1971).

Unfortunately, the investigation of remote memory is plagued by methodological weaknesses. For example, is the memory from the past truly remote, or is it the subject of regular retrieval and rehearsal? While a person may retrieve information from their personal memorial store with apparent ease, how can others be assured of the accuracy of the memory? These and other methodological pitfalls may account for the paucity of research into the existence and accessibility of remote memory.

Metamemory

Metamemory refers to a person's awareness and knowledge of their memory functioning. While Hultsch *et al.* (1988) established few age differences in the area of general knowledge of memory, self-evaluation of performance reveals substantial age-sensitivity. Murphy *et al.* (1981) demonstrated that elderly people are less able to judge when they have effectively learned and thus able to recall test items. Sunderland *et al.* (1986) also raised the question whether metamemory is related to actual performance on memory tasks. As this is often not the case it is possible that age-related metamemory deficiencies are highly task-specific and there is no general relationship between performance across activities and deficiencies in self-evaluation. Woods and Britton (1985) suggest that metamemory, including an appreciation of the time needed to acquire information, is not only task and material specific, but is also influenced by subject factors such as motivation. Furthermore, self-reports of memory inefficiency are not only a function of actual forgetting, but are related to lifestyle demands and personal expectations regarding performance. Most people's self-evaluation of memory function is 'strongly affected by their idiosyncratic social environments' (Rabbitt, 1988), which may not be conducive to remembering.

Conclusion

We have not yet achieved a body of theoretical knowledge that enables us to predict when and how age-related changes or differences in memory will appear. Quite clearly there is an interaction of many sources of influence on memory performance in old age. As a result we have an increasingly rich and complex view of the processes and mechanisms involved in remembering and forgetting. There is a growing realization that individual differences may mediate age-sensitive processes in memory functioning. Craik *et al.* (1987) suggest that participation in a range of everyday activities may be related to the maintenance of memory functioning in old age. Older people may display domain- or task-specific expertise effects as a result of years of practice and experience which may be associated with continued high levels of memory performance in these and related areas. To what extent such skills can be generalized to other domains of activity, especially those of everyday life, is open to question.

Substantial variations in memory task performance may be the product of individual differences in abilities relevant to experimental procedures used to measure memory. Verbal speed, an example of a processing resource that may underlie behaviour, may be a predictor of individual variation in memory performance. Hartley (1986) suggests that verbal speed may account for a significant proportion of age-differences in both text and word memory. Aside from information-processing resources, age-differences in memory performance may be mediated by high verbal ability. Meyer and Rice (1989) report that a group of high verbal ability elderly people performed as well as a group of younger people on certain recall measures and Hultsch and Dixon (1990) conclude that 'there is strong evidence that verbal ability is an important predictor of performance....'

Overall, the study of how older people acquire, encode and store information, associate to-be-remembered material with retrieval mechanisms and how individual differences mediate age-related differences requires a shift from artificial laboratory experimentation to real life, ecologically valid tasks. We may then be better able to understand how memory inefficiency exercises an effect on everyday activities such as social behaviour. As Rabbitt (1988) poignantly notes,

> an inability to offer more than the most general outline of your life experiences, to share no more than a scanty summary of a recent common experience, a failure to distinguish between what is generally true and what actually happened on a particular occasion, a loss of working memory capacity which makes it difficult to hold in mind the precise content of more than one or two sentences at a time — all offer very marked obstacles to successful social interaction.

Expending energy in the search for empirical generalizations in traditional experimental situations is unlikely to address effectively such naturally occurring memory phenomena (Coleman, 1986).

A greater emphasis on naturalistic topics and activities may well offer the future prospect of successful remedial intervention, but significantly this will require as a necessary pre-requisite the development of criteria which allow us to differentiate ecologically valid from invalid tasks. At present, we have yet to complete successfully this essential first step on what is likely to be a long march toward answering the questions elderly people have about their memory and enabling many of them to cope effectively with memory inefficiency.

Wisdom, Creative Achievement and Ageing

I conclude this section on the psychological aspects of ageing and old age with an examination of the evidence for personal growth and success in later life. In the previous chapters the focus has been on investigating the prospects of intellectual decay and memory decline with age. The outcome of this review has been the identification of specific, often minor cognitive losses, stability in many areas and wide individual differences. The purpose of this chapter is to uncover the likelihood of not simply holding onto what we already possess in adult life, but whether positive psychological accomplishments can occur in old age.

Wisdom

There may be intellectual products and processes which are only fully developed in old age and which in turn are poorly assessed by standard psychometric testing. An example may be those psychological attributes which are taken as evidence of wisdom.

Simonton (1990) notes that in ancient times and in most traditional societies growing older is equated with the accumulation of wisdom. While this has often been a valued aspect of ageing, less respectful attitudes toward old age in western societies over the past 200 years often associate the characteristics of wisdom as representing archaic behaviour and intellectual obsolescence. Yet how is wisdom defined?

Wisdom is, without doubt, a nebulous concept. It is said to incorporate foresight, a capacity for reflection, the adoption of a broad and meaningful perspective on life, the application of accumulated knowledge and the acquisition of insight. Erikson (1959) saw wisdom as a product of the successful resolution of the life tasks of old age. However, possibly as a result of the difficulty in defining the concept, empirical research data are piecemeal (Simonton, 1990).

One avenue of research has been to evaluate how people perceive wisdom. For example, Sternberg (1985) examined the judgments underlying the concepts of intelligence, creativity and wisdom. Similarly, Clayton and

Birren (1980) investigated the conditions under which a person may be considered wise and whether what is defined as wise differs over age groups. Simonton (1990) concludes that these investigations establish a consensus on what personal attributes constitute wisdom, although certain parameters change with age. For instance, older people are less likely to associate old age with wisdom, unlike younger adults who are inclined to do so.

An uncommon alternative area of research activity is to assess directly those people who are deemed to be wise (e.g. Baltes *et al.*, 1984). These researchers operationally define wisdom in terms of, for example, an accumulation of a rich factual knowledge about life, to establish whether the possession of wisdom is a gift of ageing. The operational definition is taken as the basis for the development of psychometric measures which assess the application of wisdom to everyday life problems. The expectation is that even though the acquisition of wisdom is not guaranteed in later life, people who are considered most wise will be disproportionately represented among older people. Whether this is so is not yet known, but Simonton (1990) considers that 'the approach has immense promise'.

Creative Achievement

Psychometric and Historiometric Data

The stereotypical observation is that wisdom and creativity display opposite longitudinal trends over the life course. While wisdom can be a prominent feature of old age, creativity and achievement are regarded as being the preserve of youth, destined to decline with advancing age. Once again, conceptual obfuscation obstructs the pursuit of empirical confirmation of this view. For the purposes of this chapter, it is thought wise (!) to define creativity as 'the ability to innovate, to change the environment rather than merely adjust to it in a more passive sense' (Simonton, 1990). Clearly, personal effort and ability can lead to successful accomplishments in areas which do not readily lend themselves to creative success. Thus, our interpretation of creative achievement needs to be broad so to capture accomplishments in the domain, for example, of leadership.

There are two distinct approaches to evaluating creative achievement. The first concentrates on the development and application of psychometric measures of the cognitive processes presumed to be implicated in creativity. This methodology measures, in the main, some aspect of 'divergent thinking' rather than the 'convergent thinking' tapped by intelligence tests. The second is a method described by Schaie (1980) as 'archival-archeological reconstruction' which is based on biographical data of actual creative accomplishments. While the methodology is not strictly longitudinal, the development of 'historiometric indicators' enables researchers to plot the age curve of creative output over an individual's lifespan.

Age-related differences on tests which purport to assess creativity by giving people the opportunity to generate novel and imaginative solutions to a given problem show, almost without exception, that older people are less able. Data identify a peak of 'creativity' in the late 30s suggesting a curvilinear age function. Simonton (1990) notes that although there is not a consistent age trend on creativity test performance, in no instance is there evidence to suggest that creativity increases significantly in later life. Thus, psychometric data appear to support the notion that creativity is a privilege of youth.

How valid is this assumption? Although much of the work is cross-sectional with all the attendant confounding of ageing and cohort effects, longitudinal data which have also identified the downturn in creativity with age illustrate that the findings of cross-sectional studies cannot be simply dismissed as artefacts of cohort effects. A concern remains, however, that the psychometric tests employed do not approximate real life creativity. So while age-related differences on creativity tests are prominent, this is not to say that actual creative performance in life adheres to a similar trend. The use of historiometric indicators enables us to address this issue.

The classic research in this area is that of Lehman (1953), who examined both the quality and quantity of significant works in a wide variety of fields. As a general rule, creativity as a function of age tends to rise fairly rapidly to a definite peak somewhere in the 30s or early 40s and thereafter tends to decline gradually. Patterns of achievement differ across disciplines and areas of endeavour, however.

Scientific achievements across a range of disciplines (e.g. astronomy, chemistry, electronics, genetics, mathematics, medicine, physics) consistently reveal peak productivity of significant contributions around ages 30 to 35, with relatively steep descents thereafter. In astronomy contributions peak slightly later in the early 40s while those in psychology peak around the age of 40 and show a moderate decline thereafter (Horner *et al.*, 1986). Yet overall it appears that intellectual productivity in pure and applied science is maximal in the mid 30s. This finding is consistent with the results from psychometric research on creativity. Assuming a normal lifespan, Simonton (1988) states that a creative individual in the last decade of their career will have a productivity rate which is half that recorded at their career peak.

Factors aside from ageing need to be deliberated upon if we are to understand the reasons for this age curve. In some instances, the reduction in creative productivity may not represent an age effect but a change in career direction. Successful research scientists may enter administration or teaching later in their careers. As careers develop, patterns of satisfaction and motivation change, so that the pursuit of knowledge may be replaced by the pursuit of authority and prestige. Miller (1977) also believes that younger scientists have less to unlearn as their training is nearer to current knowledge and thus are more able to keep abreast of and profit from scientific progress. It is too simplistic to assert that the abilities necessary for making significant scientific contributions decline with age. Furthermore, as with all historiometric research, conclusions are drawn on the basis of group averages which obscure individual variation. While average performance may peak in the mid-30s, this does not prevent some people from maintaining a high level of creative activity in later years.

The pattern of average peak productivity in the arts differs from that found in scientific disciplines. The location of the peak for novel writing, history, philosophy and general scholarship is in the 40s and even the 50s with a minimal post-peak decline. To explain this different trend Lehman (1953) suggested that philosophers, for example, need to accumulate experience prior to achieving greatness, and thus peak productivity of significant achievements is delayed. Major contributions in the arts appear to require a period during which ideas and talents are nurtured, and each successive accomplishment is a step toward acknowledged greatness.

Simonton (1990) attempts to integrate the apparent antithetical relationship between creativity and wisdom to explain why the trends of peak productivity are domain specific. 'Chance-configuration' theory holds that over the lifespan there is a gradual change in cognitive style from one that is inefficient and intuitive to a style that is more efficient and analytical. Simonton considers this hypothesized transformation to represent an age-related exchange of creativity for wisdom which may parallel the age distribution of fluid and crystallized intelligence, with the former underpinning creativity and the latter supporting the expression of wisdom. Because certain endeavours such as 'philosophy, history and scholarship' require a fusion of creativity and wisdom, significant contributions in these domains peak later in the lifespan, with a negligible age-decrement in later life. When creativity requires an accumulation of life experience, achievement may manifest itself as leadership, in which instance the career peak may be even later in life. It is even possible that wisdom may determine the source of creativity in those areas where experience is essential for success. Career changes in the life of an innovator may actually represent signs of ever-growing wisdom.

In the domains of music, visual art and literature the achievement curves are highly variable and marked by pronounced individual differences. Not only are there outstanding composers at a remarkably young age (for example, Mozart and Mendelssohn) there are also others producing major compositions in old age (for example, Verdi). While the data on composition tend to reveal peak productivity in the late 30s or early 40s, the overall picture is one of variable peaks and irregular age curves (Cunningham and Brookbank, 1988).

Visual art produces a similar picture to music. While peak productivity of significant paintings is in the 30s or early 40s there are often secondary peaks (notable aged artists include Michelangelo, Titian, Picasso and O'Keefe) and variable age curves. Although, Lehman (1953) noted the age for the peak productivity of literary works is between 35 to 45, once again there is evidence of age variability and marked individual differences. Overall, these creative domains produce historiometric data which are far less orderly than is the case for scientific achievement.

In the area of political and military leadership, older adults are invariably the occupiers of prestigious and influential roles. This phenomenon is also found in the animal kingdom where senior members of the species are often leaders of herds and communities. Why this should be so may well be because leaders are often selected on the basis of both accumulated experience and previous kinds of achievement. Lehman (1953) observed that the peak ages of

United States presidential candidates is between 55 to 60. The same age profile was recorded for British cabinet ministers and 133 presidents of various republics. However, there are considerable age differences with many examples of political leadership being attained by exceptionally aged men (for example, Prime Minister Churchill in Great Britain, Chancellor Adenauer in West Germany, General Secretary Chernenko in the Soviet Union and Ayatollah Khomeini in Iran). Military leadership reveals a differential pattern wherein army commanders (e.g. colonels, generals, fields marshals) have an age curve which peaks between 40 to 45, while naval leaders peak significantly later between 55 to 60. Lehman also observed that the influence of eminent financiers and bankers peaks in the mid-60s. To manage the finances of others requires experience and the ability to adopt a long-term perspective which may well be attributes of ageing.

Overall, leadership is a complex psycho-social phenomenon. Leaving aside the ceremonial function of figureheads who are bereft of authority and power, executive leadership involves personal attributes and characteristics such as a history of accomplishments, patience, tolerance, pragmatism and the creation and use of a network of advisors and supportive subordinates to whom responsibilities can be delegated. Thus it is often through the offices of others that authority is exercised. It is evident that the qualities and attributes which are implicated in leadership are neither the preserve of youth, nor likely to be indicative of such years.

Productivity, Precocity and Longevity

Recently, Simonton (1990) has introduced greater empirical precision to the study of achievement and ageing which serves to increase our understanding of this phenomenon. While controlled experimentation is not possible, statistical manipulation of historiometric data enables us to move away from conclusions derived solely from crude group observations.

For some time it was felt that although the quality of output in many domains declines with age, the quantity of production was less affected by ageing. However, Simonton (1990) reports that the 'quality ratio', in other words the proportion of significant contributions to total output tends to fluctuate randomly over the course of an individual's career. As a consequence it appears that the quality ratio neither decreases or increases with age, nor does it present as a curvilinear trend.

What appears critical in determining the likelihood of producing a significant work is not the age at which it is produced, but the individual's rate of productivity. Simonton (1990) describes this relationship between productivity and creativity as the 'constant-probability-of-success-model of creative output', wherein notable achievement is a probabilistic consequence of productivity. Therefore, on average, those 'creators' who are the most productive will also tend to be the highest creative achievers.

Simonton describes three independent ways of achieving an impressive career total of creative works. First an individual may display outstanding precocity by achieving major creative success at a remarkably early age. Second, a 'creator' may exhibit exceptional productive longevity and thus accumulate an impressive lifetime total. Finally, a person may have an extra-ordinary rate of productivity throughout their career without regard to the onset or longevity of the career. All these factors are positively associated with prodigious lifetime output. Yet, despite the positive relationship of lifetime productivity with precocity, longevity and high rates of contributions, Simonton (1990) concludes that the age at which a person is most productive (according to the constant-probability-of-success model this will be the age period when the most significant contributions are generated) is a function of the domain of creative achievement 'rather than the lifetime productivity or creative eminence of the given individual'.

Achievement in the General Population

A major concern with the historiometric data reviewed in this chapter is whether they have any relevance to the general population. From the tower-ing, rarefied heights of scientific, artistic and political achievement can we deduce how elderly people may experience and display success in everyday life?

Evidence that creative contributions peak in early or middle adulthood and in specific domains decline thereafter is consistent with what we know about age-related alterations and inefficiency in psychometric intelligence, cognitive processes, learning and memory. It is plausible to suggest therefore that the age curves established in historiometric research can be extrapolated to the general population. The wide individual differences in creativity also indi-cate the potential for high achievement by older adults. Furthermore, evidence that creative innovation declines from middle age has to be qualified by the observation that creativity and wisdom may well converge in later life.

Wisdom appears to be a continuing and developing attribute until the very end of life, and so domain-specific achievements which depend on accu-mulated expertise and knowledge can well be a feature of old age. Studies have demonstrated that highly intelligent elderly people can cope well with the demands of life, adjust favourably to reductions in health and adapt to every-day circumstances in a resourceful and satisfactory manner. Schaie (1980) argues that most older people are capable of quite impressive decision-making, while Cornelius and Caspi (1987) suggest that everyday problem-solving ability increases with age. In earlier chapters we have noted the evidence for the plas-ticity of intelligence in later life and reviewed studies that demonstrate that older people can learn, benefit from cognitive re-training and achieve educa-tional goals.

It cannot be argued confidently that older adults are, on average, less motivated to achieve. Despite evidence from cross-sectional research that need achievement declines with advancing age for both men and women, there are conflicting data from both cross-sectional and longitudinal studies. Kausler (1990) concludes that the results are ambiguous, and anyhow we should be aware that tests designed to measure need achievement are constructed with

Part Three

Social Adaptation in Old Age

Chapter 9

Personality, Adjustment and Ageing

The central issue in the field of personality and ageing is the extent and nature of personality stability and change during the course of the lifespan. The view that personality endures with age, especially as people enter later life, does not appear to be supported by cultural stereotypes. As Miller (1977) notes, there is a lot of folk wisdom regarding personality change in old age. As with intellect and memory, evaluation of the aged personality is generally negative. There is an expectation that as people grow old they become introverted, withdrawn, cantankerous, set in their ways and more rigid in their values and opinions. As these undesirable features become more apparent, it is thought that positive characteristics such as enthusiasm and ambition wane.

While it is not easy to trace the origins of these myths about the aged personality, it is hoped that gerontological research will expose the falsehoods of stereotypical expectations and reveal whether people do retain their adult personality as they age. Unfortunately, there is not only 'an unusually wide diversity of concept, assumption and theory with regard to the nature of personality' (Cunningham and Brookbank, 1988), there are also major weaknesses in the research methodology traditionally employed and the age-appropriateness of the personality instruments used.

Issues of Concept, Methodology and Measurement

Theories of Personality

The two dominant traditions in the area of personality and ageing are the psychoanalytic and trait models. Whereas the former is characterized by conceptual richness which often defies operationalization and objective measurement, the latter is empirically based and emphasizes the need for measurement and replicability.

In terms of ageing it is not the early psychoanalytic literature on the structure and development of personality which offers the greatest insight into the personality of older adults, but the 'neo-Freudian' developmental stage model of Erikson (1963). As described earlier, Erikson's work provides us with a rich and detailed description of human development which is difficult to measure and replicate. This 'criticism' cannot be levelled against the ego-developmental stage model of Loevinger (1976), which combines both theoretical insight and the development of an assessment instrument which satisfies rigorous psychometric standards. The popularity of stage-dependent personality theory cannot be said to be in the ascendancy, although, without doubt, Erikson deserves recognition for the significant contribution he has made to our understanding of the issues of change that arise in human development, and encouraging scientific interest in old age.

One of the earliest, yet still influential theories of personality is the trait model which defines people according to their self-descriptions via a range of test questions. Traits have their origins in natural language and can be regarded as the reduction and classification of person-descriptive adjectives. Allport (1937) believes they explain the marked differences between individuals in their responses to the same situations, and the notable consistency in behaviour over time and in a variety of different settings. Each person is regarded as a unique pattern of traits, interpersonal differences being established by differences in scores on traits measures.

To identify the proposed trait dimensions of personality, instruments have been constructed which reflect these aspects of personality. Over time, after interviewing many people, test elements are refined, some are discarded, and through the statistical procedure of factor analysis the constructs are reduced to the optimum number of independent personality dimensions required to encompass the personality domain. Popular personality trait instruments for use with older people are the Cattell Sixteen Personality Factor Questionnaire (16PF) the Eysenck Personality Inventory (EPI) and the Minnesota Multiphasic Personality Inventory (MMPI). Kogan (1990) reports that factor analysis seems to be generating some agreement as to the major trait dimensions of personality. There appears to be a five-factor structure which resembles the NEO–AC (i.e. Neuroticism, Extroversion, Openness to experience — Agreeableness, Conscientiousness) trait model of Costa and McCrae (1985).

An alternative trait method is to embark not upon a comprehensive 'mapping' of the entire domain of personality traits, but instead to focus on a single or limited number of personal characteristics. This approach attempts to operationalize a theoretically derived construct such as rigidity, locus of control or cautiousness and then identify age, group and individual differences.

Overall, theories of personality, regardless of perspective, face the problems of generalizing from a restricted sample to the general population as a whole. Thus, as ever, caution needs to be exercised when interpreting data and extrapolating observations.

Methodology

The study of ageing and its relationship with personality clearly suggests the need for longitudinal research studies. While in recent years the field has been characterized by increasing methodological sophistication so that reliance on cross-sectional data which compare diverse age groups on personality variables appears to be diminishing, it is true that most empirically-based judgments on the aged personality have been based on cross-sectional methodology. So, once again investigators are required to disentangle maturational trends from cohort influences.

In a detailed examination of psychometric testing in later life, Lawton *et al.* (1980) note that sensory and motor impairments penalize aged adults. The assessment procedures require energy, concentration and motivation, as well as a level of intellectual competence, all of which may disadvantage elderly people. It also cannot be denied that cohort-specific cultural norms may mean that certain questions are not only age-inappropriate in terms of language and contextual content, but may also be considered taboo by older adults. There is also the possibility that personality instruments are not measuring the same things at different ages (Miller, 1977). Elderly adults were found by Gilmore (1972) not only to misunderstand questions, but the meanings they attributed to test items differed from those ascribed by younger people.

Woods and Britton (1985) question how relevant personality question-naires are to older people, especially those in extreme old age. Lawton *et al.* (1980) report that when studies have revealed the numbers of older subjects who were untestable, they can constitute over one-third of the sample. It is not simply a case that there are many refusals and incomplete protocols submitted, however. Older people are more likely to be non-committal in their responses, and more inclined to present socially desirable responses in order to deceive or impress either themselves or others. The use of denial by older people as an adaptive mechanism in later life can result in a significant degree of response error (Lawton *et al.*, 1980). Overall, data on personality in old age can be difficult to interpret.

While existing personality inventories may not readily transfer across age-groups, however, Lawton *et al.* (1980) consider that most of the problems identified will not be experienced by the majority of older adults. Furthermore, while there are deficiencies in the use of psychometric tests, many of these are a consequence of the general weaknesses of personality assessment, such as 'the very distressing lack of convincing data on reliability, validity and subgroup norms', rather than being specific to the issues of personality and ageing.

Personality and Ageing

As the trait model is 'the most common conceptual approach in the study of adult and ageing personality' (Costa and McCrae, 1976), it is to this model that I turn in order to determine the case for and against personality change with age. Preference for the trait model stems also from its scientific superiority over developmental-stage models.

The first task is to look at the evidence for personality change or stability across the lifespan from the perspective of interindividual stability over time. Do people retain their approximate rank order on traits within their cohorts across the adult lifespan? From multi-trait studies the answer appears to be an unequivocal yes (Costa and McCrae, 1988).

Conley (1984), using self-report data based on twenty- and forty-five-year intervals, found neuroticism and extraversion measures were significantly stable over time. This demonstration of interindividual stability was later confirmed by peer acquaintance and spouse rating data. Haan *et al.* (1986) established intraindividual consistency in the relative salience of particular personality characteristics over seven age periods from early childhood to late adulthood. While the median correlation across the entire lifespan was a modest (although statistically significant) .25, the median correlations across all of the personality dimensions between adjacent age periods ranged from .40 to .60. The transition between later adolescence and early adulthood yielded the lowest median correlation which suggests that personality development at this time of major life transition is marked by inconstancy and restructuring.

There is mounting evidence that personality stability in the final half of the lifespan is stronger than that found across the first half (Kogan, 1990). Studies by Finn (1986) and Haan *et al.* (1986) identified increased stability on selected measures with age. Haan *et al.* (1986) observed greatest personality instability between the ages of approximately 17 to 35 years.

There has been only very limited longitudinal data collected on the stability of single constructs over time (Kogan, 1990). Studies which have been reported are concerned with the 'locus of control' construct derived from the social learning theory of Rotter (1966). 'Locus of control' refers to the attributions people make with regard to who or what is responsible for their destiny. A person may hold a consistent generalized expectation that they control events (i.e. 'internal control'), whereas those who believe they are dependent on the decisions and actions of others or determined by fate or chance are subject to 'external control'. It is felt that the concept of locus of control may be a significant factor in trying to gain an understanding of the psychology of later life. Kuypers (1971) found that elderly people with a greater sense of internal control were more active, integrated and adaptable. Similar findings were reported by Wolk and Kurtz (1975). Reid *et al.* (1977) found that internal control beliefs, especially among men, were associated with positive self-concept. These observations give credence to the supposition that an individual's sense of control is a core component of the adjustment and self-contentment of elderly people.

The results of studies designed to establish interindividual stability on this seemingly important variable for later life adjustment are consistent. While the data are short-term, rarely exceeding six years, they suggest that attribution of locus of control possesses satisfactory stability over time which approximates that found in multitrait research (Kogan, 1990).

Overall, it appears that personality stability is evidenced by long-term interindividual research for intervals as long as fifty years, although the longer the time, and thus, the longer the age interval between assessments, the greater the instability in rank ordering that is introduced. In early adult life personality growth is more likely to be characterized by instability, while the maturity of later years is indexed by trait consistency. Kogan (1990) is impressed by how similar research outcomes are across studies which have employed both different research designs and personality measures.

While there appears to be general agreement with regard to inter-individual stability over time, controversy surrounds the issue 'of mean-level stability or change across the life span' (Kogan, 1990). There is a substantial body of opinion that argues that there is no universal trend toward change in personality traits over the life course. It is argued that the major source of any change observed is derived from individual differences which are independent of age. Thomae (1980) states that variation on personality traits is related more to sex, education and socio-economic status than to age itself.

Miller (1977) summarizes the findings of cross-sectional research as indicating that age differences are not marked. Some consistent differences are observed, but overall 'personality profiles tend to be very much the same'. While Douglas and Arenberg (1978) found substantial cohort differences on certain personality traits (e.g. thoughtfulness, friendliness, restraint) for a male sample aged between 17 to 98, longitudinal data identified only a few age changes. A longitudinal study by Costa and McCrae (1978) over a ten year period recorded general stability of personality. A cross-sequential study by Siegler *et al.* (1979) addressed similar issues, and also established the relative stability of personality traits with age. Changes which do occur suggest an increase in introversion and social withdrawal, although individual variability is prominent and becomes increasingly so with advancing age.

In contrast to this body of opinion, Haan *et al.* (1986) report significant change in personality traits with age. However, Kogan (1990) maintains that 'given the unique and relatively unfamiliar nature of the analytic procedures employed ... resolution of the apparent disparity simply is not possible'. Critical features of the research methodology which seem to have a major impact on outcome and interpretation are not only the methods of statistical analysis employed, but also the personality traits investigated and the age-spread of the people to be interviewed. It is possible that as the prospect of personality instability declines with chronological age, if samples are recruited and observed during early- and middle-adulthood, changes in personality profiles are more likely to be recorded.

Overall, multitrait studies appear to lead us to the tentative conclusion that age as a maturational variable does not appear to have anything more than a weak relationship with most personality traits. As dramatic change in the ageing personality is not a reasonable expectation, Woods and Britton (1985) believe that if gross changes do occur they are likely to be a consequence of significant psychopathology. There appears to be a case, however, to argue that possibly we are asking if not the wrong question, one that is too general and ambitious. Rather than simply questioning whether personality changes during adulthood, more appropriately we should investigate at what age are changes in personality traits more or less likely to occur, and which traits are more likely to remain stable or change. Kogan (1990) notes that if researchers move away from the five-factor model of personality structure, there is evidence of long-term age-related change. The single construct approach enables us to evaluate the nature and significance of change on specific personal characteristics.

There is a general belief that older people lose a sense of personal control over their lives as they are forced to confront a range of negative life events over which they are able to exercise very little, if any influence. They should, therefore, manifest on locus of control instruments a decline in internal control beliefs with age and a concomitant increase in external control expectancies. A reduction in the sense of control elderly people wish to have in their everyday lives would be expected to lead to raised levels of dysfunctional behaviour and emotional disorder in old age. However, cross-sectional studies have not revealed significant age-differences in the general perception of locus of control in later life, although in the specific domains of health and intelligence it has been found that old people do perceive significantly higher levels of external control (Lachman, 1986). Longitudinal and cross-sequential data are conflicting, for while longitudinal studies by Lachman (1983) and Siegler and Gatz (1985) of people aged between 46 to 89 years reported an age-related decline in internal control, this was not observed in a cross-sequential study of a sample aged from 35 to 69 (Lachman, 1985). Kogan (1990) observed the possibility that the different outcomes may be a function of the different assessment measures used in the studies.

As has already been noted there is a body of opinion that argues that later life is characterized by increased cautiousness (e.g. Botwinick, 1966, 1978). However, when Edwards and Vine (1963) matched old and young subjects on psychometric intelligence, the trend for cautiousness to increase with age disappeared.

The argument that rigidity increases in later life may be related to intellectual decline in old age. An elderly person confronted with a complex, challenging situation may lack the ability to resolve the problem at hand and resort to a rigid, possibly ineffective way of problem-solution. It is likely, however, that there is no single trait of rigidity and so if age-related differences are apparent then intellectual deficits are likely to be only a partial explanation.

It is hypothesized that there should be a continuous change from extraversion to introversion with age. Cummings and Henry (1961) felt that personality changes 'result in decreased involvement with others and increased preoccupation with himself (sic)'. Thomae (1980) regards the case for greater introversion in old age as ambiguous. For example, while Angleitner *et al.* (1971, cited by Thomae, 1980) established no age differences in 'reserved versus outgoingness', Schaie and Parham (1976) found that their oldest cohort was the 'least outgoing'.

The volume of work generated by the single construct approach has not been great, and given that much of it involves cross-sectional data there are evident problems of interpretation. While the methodology employed rules out any definitive statement regarding age-related stability or change, there is little evidence to suggest that trait instability is a prominent feature of ageing.

Before leaving the topic of trait personality theory it is worthwhile to be familiar with those contextual models (e.g. Helson *et al.*, 1984; Caspi, 1987) which represent an elaboration on the traditional trait approach. Trait models examine personality characteristics without giving consideration to the historical or cultural parameters that distinguish one time period from another. Kogan (1990) considers that trait theory focuses on the 'behaviour of variables as opposed to persons'. Thus it is possible to know about the stability or otherwise of achievement in women with age, but to know little about how female achievement manifests itself in different cultural contexts over the lifespan. A contextual perspective would, for example, highlight that those women who entered professional life forty years age were more likely to be 'tough-minded' (e.g. independent, assertive, self-assured, unconventional), than a women who took a similar career decision in 1992. In other words, we can articulate personality traits in terms of their implication for actual life experiences.

The contextual approach strives 'to locate [trait] assessments within the particular sociocultural and historical context in which the respondents are living out their lives' (Kogan, 1990). In this way it is possible to see that personality traits interact with age-graded roles and cultural influences to produce a diversity of life outcomes.

Personality, Behaviour and Adaptation

As the contextual approach suggests, it is one thing to investigate the relationship between ageing and personality, it is another to assume simplistically that trait scores enable us to predict behaviour. In fact the influences on behaviour are varied and many factors have to be taken into account when establishing why people act the way they do. Even though the profile of personality traits remain the same, research has revealed that behaviour in the same person can vary across situations and settings. We are not expected, nor would it be well received, to act at work or college as we do at home. Similarly our behaviour is different when talking to a person in authority than it would be when holding a conversation with a close friend. This is not to suggest an absence of internal consistency, but to propose an interaction between personality and situational specificity.

The weight of evidence clearly indicates that situational factors interact with personality characteristics to produce behaviour. Yet, as Cunningham and Brookbank (1988) note, 'an added degree of complexity occurs in that whether the trait or the situation is the more dominant predictor may vary with the individual's idiosyncratic perception of what is relevant and important for him- or herself in the situation'.

Support for an interactionist model of behavioural determination can be illustrated within the domain of social withdrawal and activity. The theory of social disengagement (Cummings and Henry, 1961) views the stereotypic decline of active interests and the adoption of more solitary and sedentary pursuits in later life as beneficial to both elderly people and society. Social disengagement involves withdrawal from outside activity and the construction of future interpersonal relationships on the basis of greater self preoccupation.

As a consequence, elderly people are presented as inflexible and unsociable. This is not a negative development, however. As disengagement is consistent with the greater introversion of the aged personality, successful 'disengagers' may in fact be better adjusted and have higher life satisfaction (Cummings and Henry, 1961).

Although older people may initiate disengagement, a process of mutual withdrawal transpires as society reduces the number of social roles available to older adults. In this way, society ceases to be dependent on the contribution of aged people and is able to place distance between its institutions and the unwelcome, but inevitable outcome of later life, namely physical decline and eventual death.

This model of later life adaptation is overly simplistic, however, too sweeping in its assertion and unsupported by empirical evidence. First, data on introversion in old age are unclear. Second, research studies have not always confirmed a significant decline in activity among able elderly people (e.g. Palmore, 1970; Stone and Norris, 1966). Thomae (1976) also observed a degree of consistency between two ageing cohorts, one of which was aged from 60 to 65 and another aged between 70 and 75 years.

A further assault on disengagement theory comes from the majority of studies which have consistently demonstrated that active older people are happier. Many investigators have found life satisfaction to be correlated with social activity and integration. Thomae (1980) boldly states, 'only if the elderly can remain active in everyday life will satisfaction be attained'. These findings are consistent with activity theory which points to continued social involvement as an indicator of successful adjustment in later life. This theory sees increased withdrawal and heightened introversion as leading to poor adjustment and relates successful adjustment to the maintenance of activities which characterize mid-life satisfaction and the development of new areas of interest.

However, as Woods and Britton (1985) maintain, it is futile to show that either disengagement or activity theory holds for all elderly people. Life satisfaction in old age is not inevitably associated with the maintenance of involvement in social activities. Similarly, while most elderly people can be crudely assigned to categories of 'active and happy' and 'inactive and unhappy' in accordance with activity theory, the predictions of disengagement theory have been supported by the identification of 'unhappy and active' and 'happy and inactive' groups (Woods and Britton, 1985). As Neugarten *et al.* (1964) observe, people will 'find their maximal adjustment in old age in different ways'. Global interpretations of adaptation need to give way to models which focus on individual differences and diverse reactions in old age.

It is possible that some people have disengaged throughout life and so further disengagement in later years is an unremarkable continuation of the adult process of adjustment. Alternatively, enforced withdrawal after a mid-life of social activity and outdoor pursuits is likely to be experienced as a source of dissatisfaction in later life. Thus, under ideal conditions it is probable that enduring personality traits will determine an elderly person's pattern of adaptation so to achieve maximal life satisfaction. This may result in them being labelled as 'successful disengagers' or categorized as 'happy and active'.

Unfortunately, the majority of elderly people do not enjoy complete good fortune. Low levels of activity are often the product of impoverished social environments. Gordon *et al.* (1973) identified numerous factors such as age, sex, education and wealth as being correlated with quantitative and qualitative aspects of leisure activity. The processes of ageing invariably involve the limiting of choice and the restriction of opportunity to be included in social life (see Chapter 4). As a result, activity declines not because this is consistent with the aged personality, but as a result of an interaction with environmental characteristics.

The levels of social action and occupation are also going to be affected by a person's health status. It is difficult to imagine how an elderly person can successfully maintain an active existence if they are handicapped by arthritis or suffer from chronic respiratory difficulties. The finding that longevity and activity are associated is likely to be mediated by good health.

Overall, it is clear that an interactive model of behavioural determination requires an heuristic equation that incorporates not only personality and situational factors, but cultural, socio-economic and health variables as well. Only with the construction of such an equation can we hope to uncover the nature of adaptive behaviour and life satisfaction in old age. Given that activity is often associated with life satisfaction, and the former is subject to a variety of influences, then it is logical to argue that a complex network of variables are related to life satisfaction scores in old age (Adams, 1971). Investigators have associated life satisfaction with health (Bild and Havighurst, 1976), wealth (Edwards and Klemmak, 1973; Bild and Havighurst, 1976; Chatfield, 1977), socio-economic status, availability of transport, the presence of close, personal relationships (Moriwaki, 1973), internal locus of control (Palmore and Luikart, 1972) and, as previously discussed, lifespan satisfaction. Morale, as another albeit related measure of successful ageing, has been found to be correlated with health (e.g. Kutner *et al.*, 1956; Granick, 1973) and personality variables (Granick, 1973), while socio-economic status is not only directly related to morale, but also exercises a moderating influence on the psychological sequelae of such late life hardships as poor health (Birren and Renner, 1977b, cited by Thomae, 1980).

Behaviour is clearly the outcome of a person's unique reactions to aspects of their external and internal environment. Newcomer and Bexton (1978) have explored the relationship between internal factors, such as personality and intellectual capacity, and the physical and social environment to produce a model of adjustment which can be summarized in the following equation:

$$B = P + I + N + S + PE$$

where: B = Behaviour
P = Personal Competence
I = Interpersonal Environment
N = Normative Environment
S = Supra-personal Environmental Features
PE = Physical Environment

Personal competence refers to the quality of resources (both traits and intellect) an individual brings to a situation. Some people, as a consequence of their unique personal history or experience may possess high levels of competence which enable them to cope with the negative aspects of later life, such as bereavement and retirement. The confidence and wisdom some people accumulate over time can be a potent counterforce to such events. 'In the main older people confront these challenges with a quiet tenacity and inspiring courage' (Cunningham and Brookbank, 1988). Others may develop only a low level of general competence which undermines their ability to cope with and adjust to the losses of old age. While life problems are more common in old age, there is little evidence for age differences in coping skills (Lazarus and Delongis, 1983).

With the passage of time, especially after the age of 75, good health cannot be taken for granted. Being able to adjust to change depends on the availability of resources in the domains of both psychology and physical health. Poor health or sensory deficits can limit a person's adaptive capacity when faced with the 'vicissitudes of old age' (Woods and Britton, 1985) and render coping skills inadequate to prevent entry into a state of disorganization and stress. Thus, personal competence is constrained not only by intellectual and personality deficits, but also by ill health and handicap.

The interpersonal environment refers to the significant others in our social world, who we will see in the next chapter, may be neither supportive nor a source of pleasure in later life. At the very least, major changes in the structure of the family and friendship network will have to be negotiated. The supra-personal environment is indexed by the modal characteristics (for example, the predominating sex, marital status, age and functional ability) of all the people in geographical proximity to an elderly person. Inextricably related to the social environment is the prevailing culture of norms and values which regulates and sanctions behaviour. The question we need to ask is whether elderly people are enabled to live their lives in a socially valued environment? It is not beyond the realms of possibility that culture-inappropriate environments which marginalize older adults and minimize their potential actively discourage independence, activity and adaptive behaviour.

The physical environment embraces the architecture and interior design of the buildings people occupy, the living arrangements in which they reside and the neighbourhoods in which they live. The physical characteristics of the environment and their influence on behaviour can be explored at the level of the immediate built environment or in terms of the 'macro' neighbourhood environment. The onset of dependent behaviour may be a function of the unfamiliar kitchen equipment and power controls an elderly person must understand following a move to a new house, rather than a reflection of a profound impoverishment of personal competence. Similarly, a withdrawn and isolated aged woman may be reacting to the perception of crime and violence on the street rather than remaining true to a life-long personality trait. A detailed analysis of the physical environment will provide powerful evidence as to its role in shaping behaviour.

Woods and Britton (1985) discuss the literature on 'environmental press', which defines environmental demands as negative (i.e. threatening and unhelpful), neutral, or positive (i.e. supportive and enabling). However, it is not the case that a person needs to be satisfied or in harmony with the totality of their interpersonal, cultural and physical (micro- and macro-) environments. Some aspects may be more meaningful or prominent in an individual's life space, and it is only in these areas that congruence needs to be achieved. It is also possible that a person may compensate for dissatisfaction and hardship in one area by establishing a good relationship in another. This compensatory behaviour is inextricably related to personal competence. If a person brings to a situation a high level of competence then positive adjustment may occur even in the face of marked negative press. Conversely, low levels of personal resources may produce maladaptive behaviour regardless of the nature of the environmental press.

This section has identified some of the limitations of the trait model when efforts are made to understand the determinants of behaviour. An interactional approach is needed which takes into account in any given individual-situation interaction, personal history, personality, cognitive functions, health, sensory abilities and micro- and macro-environmental circumstances. The relative balance between the constituent elements of personal competence and aspects of the environment in determining behaviour will vary from situation to situation. However, Woods and Britton (1985) acknowledge that while the importance of the environment cannot be denied, the 'individual differences in cognition and personality were strong determinants to the adjustment of the individual whatever the environment'.

The Structure of Personality in Old Age

While behaviour is the product of an interplay between personal competence and environmental circumstances, the possibility has been investigated that successful adjustment is dependent on the personality characteristics of individuals. Although this is an interesting proposal, a major difficulty is identifying personality types which are independent of the process they are supposed to predict. Many of the typologies which have been produced take as their parameters behavioural descriptions which represent either evidence for or against positive adaptation.

Reichard *et al.* (1962) identified five personality patterns in elderly men using the adjustment process as the criterion for classification. Three of the typologies were considered to be favourably adjusted to the demands of later life. The 'mature' personality was integrated, stable and able to adjust to change. There are obvious similarities between this pattern of traits and the ego-integrated person who has successfully negotiated Erikson's final life-task. The 'rocking chair' man lies back, lets the world go by and contentedly withdraws from social activity. Within the framework of social disengagement theory such people are clearly successful 'disengagers'. The final successful group was labelled 'armoured' individuals. These people keep very much to themselves, and through the adoption of positive defences against the changes of old age maintain a satisfactory lifestyle.

Those elderly people who were least able to adjust were categorized as either 'angry' or 'self-haters'. The former group were hostile, intolerant and at odds with others to the extent that people withdrew from social contact. Those who hated themselves were condemned not only to an equally lonely existence, but were tormented by self-deprecatory beliefs.

Reichard *et al.* (1962) concluded that these personality patterns in old age did not represent evidence of personality change, but were evidence of a continuation of adjustment behaviour going back to childhood. The 'mature' had happy childhoods and had not experienced emotional stress on the path to adulthood. The researchers reported that the 'rocking-chair' person had passive, easy-going fathers and dominant mothers. There were indications that not only had the 'angry' men not adjusted to ageing, but overall they had not led satisfying lives. In a similar vein, Havighurst (1975, cited by Thomae, 1980) assumes that his eight personality types of old age are established by middle age.

The greatest problem with the research programme of Reichard *et al.* (1962) is the small number of people in each of the typologies. The largest group (i.e. 'angry' men) consisted of only sixteen people, while the smallest group (i.e. 'self-haters') was made up of only four men. Related to this problem is the finding that of the eighty-seven men in the sample, 47 per cent could not be classified! While these factors place both a restriction on our ability to generalize these observations to the general population and raises a doubt as to the utility of the typologies of personality, there is a reasonable consistency between the categories of Reichard *et al.* and other approaches to a classification of personality patterns in later life (Woods and Britton, 1985).

Neugarten *et al.* (1968b) identified four personality types in old age, namely those people who were 'integrated', 'passive dependent', 'defended' and 'disintegrated'. Britton and Savage (1966) identified three major personality factors. One reflected general adjustment, another withdrawal and neuroticism, and the third an aggressive–defensive profile. Using cluster analysis, Gaber (1983) produced four patterns of personality traits from a group of elderly people with a mean age of 80. The 'normal' or 'silent-majority' who constituted over 50 per cent of the sample were satisfactorily adjusted to old age. While trait 'weaknesses' were observed, such as a resistance to change, intolerance and suspicion, it is possible these are more appropriately defined as evidence of adaptive behaviour within the elderly person's life space. This group displayed evidence of positive social adjustment. The 'introverted' group comprised 20 per cent of the sample and were found to be shy, withdrawn and predominantly self-sufficient. A 'mature' group of 16 per cent of the sample achieved near 'supernormal' adjustment. Members of this group were highly independent, emotionally stable, resilient and shrewd. The unfortunate remainder (10 per cent of the sample) were poorly adjusted and emotionally disturbed. This 'perturbed' group were suspicious, angry people who reported above average personal difficulties and were poorly integrated.

While the typologies of personality are crude it appears that the majority of elderly people are well-adjusted and socially competent, with a small minority displaying outstanding adaptive resources. Woods and Britton (1985) comment on the probable linkage between the preservation of both cognitive and personality factors. Those people who remain intellectually intact are more likely to be well preserved in personality and able to achieve life satisfaction in old age. Birren (1964) suggests there are two types of personality trait, one which is stable over the lifespan, and the other which develops and adapts with ageing. The key to successful ageing is achieving a balance between these two components of personality, which Woods and Britton (1985) see as being similar to the model of crystallized and fluid intelligence (e.g. Cattell, 1963).

Those elderly people who are poorly adjusted present as either cantankerous and hostile or as withdrawn and self-damning. As Woods and Britton (1985) observe, both these groups present as socially noxious and are thus likely to be shunned by family, neighbours and past friends. These people are the casualties of ageing and invariably form the basis for the stereotypes promulgated by the unaware and the prejudiced. Yet they are without doubt an unfortunate *minority*. The *smallest* group identified by Reichard *et al.* (1962) were 'self-haters', even though a commonly held view is that a general deterioration in self-concept develops with age as advancing incompetence generates negative self-perceptions.

Research does not support major age-effects on self-concept which can be defined as the total collection of attitudes and judgments which a person holds with respect to herself/himself. Mechanisms of denial, distortion and exclusion mean that later life experiences are incorporated into self-concept either as veridical representations of reality or as approximations to the truth. Thomae *et al.* (1977, cited by Thomae, 1980) conducted a study of behaviour and attitudes of elderly pedestrians which illustrated the complex dynamics by which experiences are admitted to or excluded from self-concept. Brubaker and Powers (1976) observed that if a person's sense of self has been positive then only those favourable elements of the stereotype of old age will be accepted, and thus a positive self-concept will be maintained when defining themselves as old. In contrast, if the self-concept has been negatively appraised during adult life, unfavourable features of ageing will be accepted, thereby perpetuating negative self-perception. Thus, psychological defences such as denial are used to reduce threats to self-concept and achieve consistency in self-definition. This is not to suggest that the self-concept is not continually subject to *minor* adjustments in order that new experiences and perceptions can be accommodated. It is only when forced with a major threat to the organization of the self-concept that psychological defence mechanisms are activated to restore a state of 'threat-free' equilibrium.

The study of self-concept in later life has also revealed marked individual differences that 'raise doubt regarding any theory of a universal development of the self-concept from middle to old age' (Thomae, 1980). If a generalization is to be made it is that self-concept of most aged adults is not characterized by self-deprecatory attitudes and low self-esteem, but contrary to public opinion is an organized system of positive self-perceptions. Despite the buffeting people are subjected to in later life as they experience a decline in personal competence and an erosion of their support network, self-definition is remarkably resilient to negative re-appraisal.

Chapter 10

Family Ties and Friendships in Later Life

Throughout life the family is the most basic social institution, enshrining ideals of stability, reciprocity and intimacy. Discourse on the family includes such matters as sex, marriage, parenting and kinship. Yet like any other social entity the family is a process and not a 'thing'. It is a dynamic unit which constantly changes 'in part because the members pass through the life-cycle, in part because it is in a society which changes' (Worsley *et al.*, 1970).

The remarkable social, economic and technological changes which have occurred during this century appear to challenge traditional assumptions concerning family life. Has there been a decline of the family as a primary social institution, especially with regard to the needs of older people? What is the family context of aged adults? Is the commonly accepted belief that significant changes in contemporary family life have disadvantaged elderly members an accurate generalization or a myth? Do older people live alone with infrequent contact with their offspring? Are family relationships inequitable, with younger family members giving more than they receive? Is there evidence of serious intergenerational strain, portrayed in terms of the 'generation gap'?

From the perspective of the individual, as people grow older they face many transitions, some of which are predictable from the standpoint of the lifecycle but remain unanticipated by the individual (Bengtson and Treas, 1980). As each family member ages with the passage of time different people will come to occupy the same role, or the same person will take on different roles. Given that surveys have demonstrated that family roles are the most important ones for most people at all ages (Cunningham and Brookbank, 1988), how an ageing person adapts to changes in such valued role behaviour may facilitate or make more difficult later life adjustment and satisfaction. Adjustment may, however, be a complex process, for adaptation to 'normal' family transitions of ageing is often influenced by how other members negotiate changes in the structure and patterns of family relationships.

While to be part of an intimate family network is seen as an essential requirement for happiness and psychological health, so are interactional ties with friends and neighbours. Non-kin relationships are, for many people, an important source of companionship and support throughout life. To be integrated into a social network not only brings a person a sense of 'belonging' but social relationships are an important source of self identification and esteem. However, established networks are inevitably eroded by death and retirement in later life, so are older people condemned to a life of increasing social isolation within their communities? Can elderly people reconstruct their social networks when faced with the death of friends and colleagues? Friendship develops through the roles a person plays. Does the loss of mid-life roles during the process of 'eldering' (Schroots and Birren, 1990) result in a social age which does not enable older people to establish new friendships to replace those that have been lost?

Overall a profound fear people have is that they will live out their final years lonely and abandoned. As social creatures this is an understandable dread. Yet as we have already seen across a variety of domains, myths and negative stereotypes surrounding the processes of ageing are abundant. So what is the empirical evidence to support the image that elderly people experience pervasive filial and social neglect?

Marriage

The majority of people in the 'young-old' age group (65–74 years) are married and live together apart from other relatives. Health and socio-economic trends in modern times have resulted in marriage partners experiencing years as a self-contained couple. Life expectancy has increased, the years of child-bearing have decreased and elderly people are more likely to live by themselves. As a result, the period of time that older couples are together without children has increased significantly.

Long-term monogamy does not appear to be associated with tedium and disharmony. Quite the reverse, marital satisfaction tends to be higher among the married elderly. Satisfaction is high early in marriage, decreases in middle age and then improves again in later life. Cunningham and Brookbank (1988) note that in most studies marital satisfaction is as high or higher among older couples as it is among newly-married couples. The increase in marital satisfaction may be related to a reduction in conflicts over child-rearing and the cessation of employment following retirement. However, the quality of relationship for elderly married couples is likely to be related not only to a decrease in interpersonal strain, but also reflects an appreciation of the positive emotional and practical supports available in marriage. In old age, the spouse is the person who provides care during illness and is the most significant source of companionship. Furthermore, while the marital relationship is characterized by diminished passion, this does not mean that sexual activity is either absent or not enjoyed (see Chapter 12).

While both spouses are likely to rate the marriage satisfactory, men may be more satisfied than their wives are. However, Cunningham and Brookbank (1988) report that some elderly husbands are unhappy with the respect they receive in the marriage, while many of those who become dependent on their wives because of ill health do not enjoy the dependency relationship. Vinick (1978) observed that elderly women appear less satisfied with communication in the marriage, and are more likely to rate the relationship favourably if they have the support of friends, good housing and an adequate income. Overall married couples are advantaged in longevity (a necessary prerequisite for long-term monogamy!), health, morale and financial security.

Given the emotional and economic benefits of marriage in later life, what is the prevalence of first or remarriage in old age? Marriages do occur, but less frequently than in other age groups. However, getting married is an emerging phenomenon among older adults. As there are more elderly women, men have wider possibilities of choice of prospective marriage partners than do women. First marriages are not common, constituting only 6 per cent of all marriages in later life. While divorced older adults are more likely to remarry than are the widowed, divorce is a relatively rare experience for today's aged cohort. Only about 10 per cent of people aged over 65 have ever been divorced, and less than 5 per cent are currently divorced (Cunningham and Brookbank, 1988). Yet with the overall divorce rate rising, which has already resulted in divorce becoming more prevalent among the 'young-old', future elderly cohorts will undoubtedly have a different divorce profile. Each successive cohort is differentiated from earlier generations as each takes different paths according to prevailing cultural norms. Divorce is a prominent social dimension upon which future cohorts will be readily differentiated. Of those born between 1945–1949, over one-third will have their first marriage end in divorce, while re-marriages are even more likely to be terminated by divorce.

Since women live longer than men and usually marry men older than themselves, they are often the ones who make decisions regarding remarriage. Although, for many women (we must never forget that one of the distinguishing characteristics of people who survive into old age is their diversity, so reactions to event and patterns of behaviour become increasingly individual) widowhood is a deeply traumatic experience of loss, a reluctance to remarry is often found. This reluctance is in part a response to the belief that remarriage can never restore the level of intimacy and companionship which has been lost. Remarriage may also in some way tarnish the memory of the deceased spouse. Approval of children from previous marriages may also be a complicating and inhibiting factor. A particularly salient concern is that one of the marriage partners, in all probability the husband, will become dependent in advanced old age as a result of chronic illness or debilitating handicap. Caring for a partner who is transformed into a shell of their former self is always a difficult and painful situation to bear. If the dependency relationship is not established on many years of shared joys and mutual support, the disabilities of old age can be met with resentment and a reduced capacity to care. To avoid such circumstances elderly widows may not consider remarriage an attractive later life option.

Widowhood

Most elderly men are married, and most older women are widowed. Even among those who are over 75 years, two-thirds of men are married, while two-thirds of women are widowed. Not surprisingly there is more research into widowhood than there is into the experiences of widowers. Cunningham and Brookbank (1988) describe the difficulties widows confront and the supports available to them. Satisfaction can be obtained from the maintenance of certain role behaviours. The roles of mother and to a large extent house-keeper remain intact to provide reward and occupation. However, the elderly widow is likely to live alone and face financial difficulties. As many household tasks remain sex-linked, especially among the current elderly cohort, widows may be inexperienced in practical and financial matters, and may be unwilling or unable to acquire the necessary skills.

Loneliness is a frequent experience of widows and is possibly related to the isolating effects of relative poverty. Some never come to terms with living alone. The death of a spouse may result in a resigned acceptance of loneliness (Burnside, 1980). Role expectations also place limits on acceptable social behaviour. While an interest in the family and other widows is expected, involvement with men is not, and is likely to be frowned upon if it occurs.

It is questionable to what extent elderly widows benefit from having peers who have experienced bereavement and widowhood. While the shared experience of grief may encourage non-kin companionship it is debatable whether it provides a basis for long-term adaptation to widowhood. Evidence shows that elderly widows are in poorer health and have higher suicide rates than their non-widowed peers. Fiske (1980) found little to substantiate the belief that widowhood is associated with mental illness, however, although she observed some evidence for the development of maladaptive reactions to the loss of a spouse among men.

The role expectations of widowers are also limited, but are somewhat more vague. The stricture to avoid showing interest in women exists, but the condemnation attached to mixing with the opposite sex is probably less severe than that shown to widows. Housekeeping may be a source of practical difficulties. Many widowers wish to preserve the memory of their wife, and some have a tendency to idealize their deceased partner (e.g. Coleman, 1986). It needs to be understood that on the death of his spouse, a man not only ceases to be part of a couple, but as his wife is likely to have been his principal confidante, the emotional cost in terms of loneliness may be greater (Cunningham and Brookbank, 1988). While to be a widower is not a rare experience, it is not a typical life expectation. This can result in elderly widowers feeling ill at ease in company. This can well compound their sense of desolation and alienation. MacMahon and Pugh (1965) found that deaths from suicide clustered in the first four years of widowhood, especially among widowers.

Loneliness

Most older adults who live alone are widows. In the United States almost half of white women over 75 years live alone, while for white males at the same age the proportion is just 21 per cent (Bengtson and Treas, 1980). In England and Wales it is predicted that by 2001, 43 per cent of the 5.8 million house-holds headed by an elderly person will be single person female households (Oldman, 1990). Although loneliness is a distressing aspect of widowhood, it cannot be automatically assumed that living alone in old age is an upsetting experience.

For some elderly people, living alone is not equated with loss. These people have been 'loners' throughout their adult life, maintaining non-intimate, primarily instrumental social relationships. Long-term adjustment to solitary living will mean that 'habitual isolates' (Fiske, 1980) will not experience isolation in later life as either anything unusual or unpleasant.

As previously mentioned, many elderly people prefer to live alone because they value their privacy and independence. Lopata (1973) identified differences in lifestyle, the rowdiness of grandchildren and a wish to be 'in one's own kitchen' as reasons why older people prefer independent living arrangements. It is typically those elderly people with high dependency needs, limited personal resources and few options who 'choose' to live with relatives.

Generally, older people do not complain that loneliness is a very serious problem. In the United States, Havighurst (1978) reported that less than 20 per cent of people over 70 felt that not having enough friends was a concern for them, while Harris *et al.* (1975) found only 12 per cent of elderly people had serious problems of loneliness. Nearly thirty years ago, in a classic UK study of 'working class' family life Townsend (1963) estimated that 27 per cent of older people felt lonely.

Many older people who are not integrated into either an active family or social life deny they are lonely. In examining the reasons for this a distinction has been drawn between 'isolates' and 'desolates'. The hypothesis proposed by Townsend (1963) is that desolation and not isolation is the cause of loneliness in old age. Bergmann (1978) also drew a distinction between isolation and loneliness. A person may have few social contacts but not complain of loneliness, while somebody who has a wealth of interpersonal relations may feel lonely. Anybody can be 'lonely in a crowd' for it is not the quantity of social contacts which is important, but the quality of the relationship: a close, confiding intimate friendship may well have greater value than any number of casual acquaintances. Liang *et al.* (1980) noted that measures of 'objective' social integration such as the amount of interpersonal contact and participation in organizations were only indirectly related to morale, whereas feelings of loneliness (i.e. 'subjective' social integration) was directly related to morale. Aside from the quality of relationships, a second mediating factor is the social expectations of older people. If an elderly person has higher expectations for the quality of their interpersonal relationships than actually exist, even though contact is frequent and warm, dissatisfaction and unhappiness will result.

Those elderly people who are lonely are at greater risk of depression and anxiety states. Being less 'socially connected' is related to depression for people of all ages and if a person attributes self-blame for their failure to establish close relationships then mental illness is increasingly likely.

Family Life

The general conclusion ... is that if many of the processes and problems of ageing are to be understood, old people must be studied as members of families .... They are not simply individuals, let alone 'cases' occupying beds or chairs. They are members of families and whether or not they are treated as such largely determines their security, their health and their happiness (Townsend, 1963).

Parenting

In later life people shed 'careers' which have provided occupation, self-identification and personal worth for most of their adult years. A major role change is the loss of active parenting when the last child leaves the family home. The resulting 'empty-nest' phenomenon is often considered to be a significant and common source of stress for middle-aged parents.

Increased life expectancy ensures that married adults will average around three decades of living together as a couple without their children in the house. Clearly the departure of children from home requires parents to adjust to both a loss of role and changed relationships. Cunningham and Brookbank (1988) suggest, perhaps surprisingly, that men rather than women may experience a greater sense of loss. As fathers traditionally spend less time at home, they may feel that they never really got to know their children, nor enjoyed the pleasures of seeing them grow up. As a consequence fathers can be affected by regret and guilt when the last child leaves home.

Concern has, however, more often been focused on the effects the 'empty-nest' phenomenon has on women, especially those with a heavy emotional investment in child-rearing. Some may find the change to a childless house a source of depression. Bart (1968) identified the negative impact on psychological well-being as arising from changes in self-worth and a sense of usefulness. Feelings of loss, anomie and despair for the future, may be accompanied by debilitating psychophysiological symptoms of the menopause, leading to heightened negative affect. Furthermore, the quality of the marital relationship may have been neglected during the years of child rearing. When the children depart the couple may find themselves to be relative strangers inhabiting a loveless unsupportive relationship.

Fortunately, although the departure of children from the family home creates a need for adjustment, longitudinal data suggests that most parents do not find the last child leaving to be a stressful, depressing life event (Palmore *et al.*, 1979). First, a change in the living arrangements of a family is simply that, an alteration in the frequency and content of the interaction. Leaving home rarely results in an absolute break in the parent–child relationship. Children often continue to need their parents' emotional support and frequently remain in close functional contact. Time away from each other can also breed greater mutual respect and, when the occasions arise, an appreciation of time spent with each other.

Second, as we have already seen, evidence indicates that marital disenchantment is not widespread in 'mature' marriages. The quality of marriage in later life may be a positive outcome of the 'empty-nest' years. There is a new sense of freedom from the pressures of child-rearing and attending to the demands of adolescent development. Financial and domestic responsibilities appear both tolerable and less intrusive. Lowenthal (1975) observed that most married couples look forward to the time when child-rearing is successfully accomplished and they can address their own personal needs, so the departure of children from the parental home can be a welcome development. A sense of relief is combined with the enjoyment of greater freedom and the development of new life options. While we cannot automatically assume that the leave-taking of children is a positive life change, Palmore *et al.* (1979) propose that the 'empty-nest' syndrome, with its negative connotations, should be renamed the 'child-free home' with an emphasis on the benefits that can accrue.

Grandparenting

The relationship between chronological age and the organic nature of the family cycle is evident to all with the acquisition of the role of grandparent. This is both a new status for ageing parents and essentially an unchosen role. However, is it a vacuous, ambiguous role or one of the most rewarding aspects of successful ageing?

Being a grandparent is a very common situation, with 75 per cent of elderly people having at least one grandchild. Yet research indicates that the image of kindly grandparents providing love, practical support and wise guidance is not always mirrored by reality. Several styles of grandparenting have been identified: the distant; the reserved and formal; the fun-loving; and being a source of information and wisdom. It is likely that younger grandparents are more likely to be fun-loving and providers of useful information. There is a tendency for same-sex intergenerational bonds to be stronger, although as a generalization grandmothers are closest to their grandchildren.

Age of the child seems to be an important factor in determining the quality of the relationship between grandparent and grandchildren. Children under the age of 10 appear to be closest to their grandparents, although teenagers may turn to grandparents for support and wise counsel.

Cunningham and Brookbank (1988) believe there is considerable positive potential in the role of grandparenting, although it 'can be a delicate, challenging position'. In general they believe that the most valued grandparents are those who are aware of the cultural differences between their generation and the generations of their children and grandchildren, wait to be asked for their opinion before offering it and do not impose their own needs on younger members of the family.

In the future, with continuing advances in health care and life expectancy, great-grandparenting is likely to become an increasingly important phenomenon. Already over one-third of older people have at least one great-grandchild. However, great-grandparenting remains a virtually untouched area of research.

Adult Children, Aged Parents

Demographic trends and cultural change

The family has long been regarded as the social institution to meet the physical, emotional, social and financial needs of elderly people. However, any discussion on the ability of families to provide for those in old age must necessarily take note of contemporary demographic trends. As Bengtson and Treas (1980) state, the 'declining numbers of descendants seem to be on a collision course with the surer survival of ageing kin'. This trend of fewer offspring and more elderly poses questions about the continuing effectiveness of family support systems for aged people.

The phenomenal growth in the numbers of older people this century because of improvements in health care and the associated decline in mortality means that today's middle-aged offspring are more likely to have elderly parents than were their counterparts in earlier times. Increasingly, ageing parents are very old. While the majority of 'old-old' people are not ill, not confused and can look after themselves, there is an inevitable relationship between age, declining health and disability. The very old are more likely to suffer from chronic illness, to fall and injure themselves and suffer from degenerative brain disease than the 'young-old'.

As has been previously documented the numbers of elderly people have not only increased, but their proportion relative to other age groups has also grown dramatically. This reflects the long-term decline in the fertility of younger cohorts. Although reduced fertility is in part offset by the surer survival of those who are born, there remains an overall decline in the numbers of children available to support aged parents.

Smaller families means that the burden of care falls onto fewer family members. This may exhaust the capacity of the family to support ageing parents. A further consideration is that with increasing numbers of 'old-old' people, their children themselves are often past retirement age when called upon to help. The potential consequence of these demographic changes is that the dependency requirements of old age will in the future need to be borne by society as a whole. It is certainly true that in most industrial societies during modern times public welfare and social services have taken greater responsibility for many traditional family support functions in caring for older people.

The drive toward the provision of statutory care services has been influenced not only by demographic trends, but also by the changing aspirations of middle-aged sons and daughters which compete with obligations toward ageing family members. Mid-life is often the age-graded time for a renaissance in non-family activity, a benefit of the 'child-free home'. This postparental era threatens family responsibilities for the everyday care of aged relatives as middle-aged adults rediscover romance within the marriage, take holidays and exploit further education opportunities. Of special relevance are changes in the social and economic roles of middle-aged women. Women have traditionally borne the brunt of supporting aged relatives but with greater employment opportunities for women their continued willingness to meet the needs of ageing relatives is questionable.

These and other developments in society (such as greater geographical mobility which means that children live further from their parents, and housing policies which have led to the destruction of long-established communities) operate against family support. However, before we look in detail at the state of intergenerational relations in contemporary society, how did older family members fare in the past? Are beliefs about the degeneration of family ties based on an idealized conception of traditional family life?

Family life: An historical note
Only a tenth of households in Great Britain today conform to the popular image of the nuclear family (a married couple with two children). The commonest forms of family arrangements are parents and children living together, or the 'rump' of this arrangement following marital breakdown, the departure of adult children or the death of a spouse. The extended family of grandparents, parents and children sharing a home is an uncommon occurrence representing less than 10 per cent of family households in the United Stetes (Cunningham and Brookbank, 1988). The extended family was never as pervasive as is often assumed, however.

Laslett (1976) challenges the historical romanticism which extols the virtues of a past when family elders were revered and were part of a close-knit family network living in 'the warm embrace of multigenerational households' (Bengtson and Treas, 1980). Unfortunately, the past was characterized by the neglect of older family members and the relative absence of extended family households. When they did exist they were invariably based on economic necessity rather than filial sentiment. The perceived breakdown in contemporary family life may reflect the relative affluence of contemporary society which dispenses with the economic need for multigenerational households. If a person could not be a net financial contributor to the household they might be welcomed if they could be of service to the family. Anderson (1977) noted that in the nineteenth century an elderly woman was more welcome than an old man as a member of a household because of their usefulness in child-rearing and housekeeping.

In our society, historical custom has long dictated that young married couples set up independent households rather than move into the parental home. Similarly, aged parents have traditionally preferred to maintain their separate living arrangements rather than be absorbed into the homes of adult children. This is not to propose that in the past multigenerational households did not exist. It is simply that this living arrangement was neither as common (for example, these were relatively fewer older adults to live in multigenerational households) or preferred as is customarily thought. As a consequence family relationships in earlier times fall short of the ideal against which we often evaluate contemporary family behaviour.

Contemporary family life — 'Objective solidarity'
The demographic trends which have led many commentators to question the ability and willingness of families to care for aged parents has resulted in unprecedented opportunities for intergenerational activity and companionship. It is more likely today than ever before that people will be able to share their later life with a surviving spouse and their children. With the advent of smaller families, parents and their offspring can often 'share overlapping years of vigorous adulthood' (Bengtson and Treas, 1980). This makes possible opportunities for reciprocal support unknown to families of earlier generations.

Yet are these opportunities for intergenerational relations taken? Is the structure of contemporary family life not fragmented and dispersed?

An image of the family as a willing and responsible source of support and companionship is replacing the earlier stereotype that the modern nuclear family in industrial societies is unavailable and disinterested in the welfare of older people. Despite momentous demographic and cultural changes this century 'family support remains generally strong' (Woods and Britton, 1985). A contemporary variation of the extended family is for grandparents, parents and children to live apart, but often within easy travelling distance of each other.

Some investigators (e.g. Wroe, 1973) focus on the negative effect geographical mobility has exercised on the ability of families to provide company and care for older people. While geographical distance has been inserted between various generations of a family, survey data indicate that the majority of family members living in the same community interact frequently and those who are separated by long distance have regular contact by letter or telephone. It is suggested that the availability of telephone communication and rapid travel systems means that even active helping networks are not confined to local communities (Warren, 1981).

Shanas *et al.* (1968) report United States survey data that demonstrate that only 10 per cent of aged parents had not seen their adult children within the past thirty days. In Denmark and Great Britain the corresponding figure was 6 per cent. Townsend (1963) established that elderly people 'rarely lived alone in a literal sense'. In a close-knit urban community he found that of those interviewed, 75 per cent saw their children once a week, and as many as a third saw them every day.

Frequency of contact has been observed to be a function of sex, marital status and social class. Sussman (1965) observed that married daughters tend to have closer ties to their parents than do married sons. Lopata (1973) also noted that sons were less frequent supporters of their widowed mothers. Rosow (1969) found that the most powerful predictor affecting whether an aged parent received help or not from their children is the sex of the nearest child. In relation to marital status, unmarried children are more likely to maintain closer ties with their ageing parents. Hill *et al.* (1970) suggests that social class is another differentiating characteristic in so much as it was found that working-class men had greater contact with older family members than did white-collar males.

The reality of ageing and family relationships is varied and ambiguous. While attempts to dismiss the contemporary family system as a major source of support for aged members have clearly been premature, we must be careful not to replace a myth with an overgeneralization. Not all sons and daughters in the 'modified extended family' are paragons of filial loyalty. Yet in general we can confidently state that it is not the case that older people live alone isolated from their families. Instead many of them have frequent contact with their adult children.

A pertinent question to address, however, is not simply what is the frequency of interaction between family members, but what is the nature of the intergenerational contact? Bengtson (1975) identified three dimensions of inter-action; informal activity (for example, conversation and recreational pursuits), family 'ceremonial' activity (for example, birthdays, weddings and funerals), and the exchange of assistance (in other words, helping and being helped). Middle-aged adults and elderly people reported relatively high levels of infor-mal and ceremonial activities. While perception of these aspects of 'objective solidarity' were equivalent for both generations, when estimating the amount of assistance given by middle-aged children, offspring reported a higher level than did parents. Does this reflect a mendacious quality on the part of younger family members or an unfortunate inability to translate good filial intention into practice?

While there might be a slight tendency for families in the United King-dom to rely more on statutory support services and less on family care than in the United States, mutual assistance in times of need is the rule rather than the exception. Sussman (1965), drawing on research data from several studies, identified a general tendency for family members to turn to relatives rather than statutory agencies at times of need. Daughters are often seen as providers of 'warmth' and comfort and sons as being more 'task-orientated' (Lopata, 1973). It is invariably widows and widowers who are more dependent on family support than aged married couples. Taking responsibility for the depend-encies of old age can be a demanding commitment. Newman (1976) found that 20 per cent of adult children caring for aged parents in their homes de-voted time equivalent to that of a full-time job.

A characteristic of the assistance offered between generations is the reciprocal exchange of daily support. The assumption that older adults are de-pendent recipients of intergenerational assistance is not supported by the data. Townsend (1963) was impressed by how often help was reciprocated and considered the helping role of the grandparent to be the most significant finding of his study. Interestingly, Bengtson (1975) noted that aged parents reported giving less help to their children than their children reported receiv-ing. Overall, it appears that older people play down the significance of practi-cal exchanges between generations, and instead place value on the emotional closeness and warmth of family life.

In an illuminating study by Brody *et al.* (1983), the investigators examined the attitudes of three generations of women aged between 17 to 90 years to the care of elderly people. A majority of each generation agreed that adult children should be obliged to help their parents with activities of daily living. However, even though the women interviewed shared similar values about family responsibilities, suggesting that the idea that younger people today do not care as much about ageing parents as they did in the past is unjustified, all three generations believed that this was indeed the trend.

Contemporary family life — 'Affectual solidarity'
It appears that despite demographic changes and the availability of income support and public services the caring role of younger family members has not been eroded. Older people, however, probably place at least as great value on the subjective quality of inter-generational interactions. 'Affectual solidarity'

may be defined as 'mutual positive sentiment among group members and their expressions of love, respect, appreciation and recognition' (Bengtson and Black, 1973). Research has identified a high degree of contact and shared activity between middle-aged children and their aged parents, but to what degree is there tolerance, understanding and affection between family members?

The popular stereotype is that intergenerational relations are characterized by a 'generation gap' which results in conflict and alienation. Successive generations seek to assert their independence by distancing themselves from the existing values, patterns of behaviour and institutions of previous generations, especially those of their parents. Bengtson (1971) considers that this impinges on older adults in two ways. A 'cohort gap' encompasses the perceived differences between the attitudes and behaviour of the elderly person and their peer group and those of younger cohorts. As the older person may have derived status and rewards from existing social institutions, they are the principal stakeholder in the *status quo* and are thus less willing to appreciate the merits of change.

The 'lineage gap' highlights differences between generations within the family. These differences are possibly more personally relevant since they are often related to the expectations parents have for their children. Intergenerational conflict within the family is likely to be the most powerful means by which the currents of change in society as a whole impact on ageing parents.

Bengtson (1971) found that the 'cohort gap' perceived between generations in society is considerably larger than the 'lineage gap' perceived within a respondent's own family. As Bengtson and Treas (1980) succinctly comment, 'yes, there is a generation gap, but not in my family'. The age of the respondent appears to influence the degree to which a 'gap' is perceived. Adults in mid- and later-life may be concerned with a need to create social heirs. Aware that with their death their way of life and personal values may die with them, ageing parents may wish to perpetuate their ideals and achievements in their children. To this end older generations may minimize intergenerational differences. By contrast, younger family members are motivated to develop personal distinctiveness and an individual identity. To be asked or encouraged to perpetuate existing values is inconsistent with this developmental need and so younger adults will exaggerate intergenerational differences in pursuit of their goal. Clearly, each generation has a different developmental stake in the other which varies according to how the relationship enables an individual to achieve their personal goals.

Bengtson and Treas (1980) conceptualize 'the observation that different generations have contrasting perceptions of their common relationship' as representing an application of the 'principle of least interest' (Waller, 1938). The family member with the least commitment for maintaining the relationship is in the strongest position to bargain for influence, for they will have least to lose if the relationship ends. The one with the greatest commitment must often make concessions to the other to avoid severance of the relationship. The implications for older family members are such that as children mature and are able to exercise independence they find themselves in an increasingly weak position. As a consequence, parents tend to minimize intergenerational differences, while the implications for aged family members are such that they may be reluctant to ask for practical help when in need because such demands could place them at a disadvantage in the exchange relationship. This might, in part, account for the observed reluctance of elderly adults both to ask for assistance and play down the significance of this aspect of 'objective solidarity'.

The 'developmental stake' concept and 'the principle of least interest' distorts the perception of intergenerational relationships. Do these distortions and consequent behavioural outcomes achieve a desired level of liking between generations? Bengtson and Black (1973) reported high levels of sentiment between middle-aged children and their elderly parents. However, the data reveal a slightly higher perception of affective solidarity on the part of the age parent insomuch as they perceive higher levels of affection. Bengtson and Treas (1980) see this perception as underpinning the belief that the elderly person's stake in the intergenerational relationship is based on a need for emotional warmth and respect rather than the instrumental dimension of practical assistance.

In sum it appears that first, similarities in attitudes, values and behaviour are not a necessary pre-condition for strong emotional bonds between family members of different generations. Second, the conflicting demands experienced by middle-aged adults, as they address the competing needs of aged parents, offspring and themselves do not appear to have introduced emotional strain into intergenerational relationships. Finally, the caring role of younger family members appears to be founded on sentimental ties and not filial obligation. The historical forces which have reduced ageing parents' reliance on adult children (for example, state benefits, social services), have eliminated the imposed togetherness of families observed in earlier times and with it many of the likely sources of intergenerational tensions. As a result, intergenerational contact is based more on voluntary intention than compulsory obligation. Nor is a concern for an ageing relative motivated by the prospect of a monetary legacy. In the main, socioeconomic changes have reduced the economic authority aged parents might exercise over their adult children insomuch as financial legacies play only a minor role in the plans and security of their middle-aged offspring. As Bengtson and Treas (1980) conclude, inheritance nowadays is no longer a significant intergenerational economic bond, but is rather a cherished sign of special emotional intimacy.

Contemporary family life — Relationships within generations
As Cunningham and Brookbank (1988) note, siblings can be an important source of companionship in later life for they provide interpersonal continuity at a time when middle-aged children are involved in their own households and marriage partners die. Around 80 per cent of elderly people have at least one surviving sibling. Shanas (1968) found that relationships with brothers and sisters gain in importance when the last child leaves home or following the death of a spouse.

Although evidence suggests that grown siblings stay in contact with each other, remain loyal to each other and provide mutual assistance when the need arises, this tends to follow a period in adolescence and early adulthood when relationships were distant. Sisters tend to enjoy the closest relationships. In mid-life caring for an aged parent can bring siblings closer together as they maintain a corporate effort to provide for dependency needs.

Family in absentia

Not all families remain close, whether that be taken to indicate emotional warmth or geographical proximity. Some families can be a source of guilt, regrets and feuds. Stevenson (1981) observed that family support is not a resource available to all elderly adults for in a survey of over-75s it was found that 45 per cent of those living alone were childless. Furthermore, 18 per cent of the women surveyed had never married.

For the minority of old people who have no family in later life, are the odds against them in terms of successful ageing? Are the effects similar for those people who are not without a family, but experience contact as either unsatisfactory or infrequent?

When an elderly person's family is indifferent toward them this may not be the product of filial dereliction, but may result from an aged personality alienating their kin. The quality of a relationship between an aged parent and adult child is critically dependent on the way the former performs their role. The parent may wish to impose their will and share the wisdom of accumulated experience without appreciating that they may alienate their children. An unhappy or depressed personality may also serve to discourage family ties. Responsibility for poor intergenerational relationships cannot be placed solely on the shoulders of elderly adults, however. While they treasure emotional closeness, independence is also valued. Family contact may introduce or confirm a failure of competence. When younger family members violate an elderly adult's autonomy by taking away their right to make decisions and exercise choice, such unsympathetic action can easily contribute to a decline in kin relationships.

Dissatisfaction with the frequency of family contacts may reflect unrealistic expectations rather than actual isolation. Coleman (1986), in his sensitive case-study of older people, exposed both the sadness and joys family relationships can bring. In some instances an elderly person may feel abandoned even when regularly visited because they greatly miss their children being 'around the house'. Seelbach and Sauer (1977) found that a belief that their children should live nearly, visit frequently and take responsibility for their needs was associated with lower morale. Fortunately for all concerned only a minority of elderly people believe children have an obligation to live nearby and visit often (e.g. Streib and Thompson, 1965). It has been suggested that elderly mothers may have higher filial responsibility expectations. Given that elderly women are more likely to be widowed and live alone this is not a surprising observation. In general, however, older people are not inclined to sacrifice independence and assign responsibility to others.

Aside from those adults in later life who hold excessive expectations for their middle-aged children and thus experience family life as a disappointment, there is little evidence that elderly people without a supportive family network are at a psychological disadvantage. For example, in a study of older widows Arling (1976) reported no association between morale and family contact. It would therefore seem that the intuitive belief that family ties promote happiness and adjustment is a simplistic overgeneralization.

Friendship in Later Life

Friendships are of critical and increasing importance in old age, compensating for spouses who have died and providing opportunities for rewarding activity. Generally they are the second most important source of companionship after the spouse. Troll (1982) notes that the role of friend lasts longer than the role of worker, and usually spouse. In the study by Arling (1976), while morale was unaffected by intergenerational ties, contact with friends and neighbours did serve to reduce loneliness and increase feelings of usefulness. Having a stable group of friends helps to maintain autonomy and self-worth in later life.

Successful adjustment to ageing may be dependent on a social network which provides not only companionship and validation, but is also available to provide assistance with daily living and crisis intervention. Wenger (1989) differentiates the support network which is the focus of informal care provision, from the larger social network of which it forms the core. While the family is an important component of the support network, it is only recently in the United Kingdom that research on the totality of the support system has identified the role of friends and neighbours (e.g. Wenger, 1984).

Older women tend to have closer friends, whereas elderly men typically have more remote friends and acquaintances with shared interests. Women tend to have both larger social networks and are more likely than men to have intimate same-sex friends. Social class has an effect on the structure of social networks (Wenger, 1989). Middle-class networks are more dispersed but less constrained by distance, while working-class elderly people have small social networks, which are more family dominated (Mugford and Kendig, 1986) and tend to involve greater contact with neighbours (Warren, 1981). Many friendships, especially for men, are founded on shared interests at the workplace, and as such may not survive the transition to retirement. In addition the social network available to a man shrinks when his wife dies, while widows are able to maintain a stable network.

Although an elderly person's circle of friends inevitably grows smaller in later life, Powers *et al.* (1975) found most older people report the surprisingly high figure of having at least fifteen friends. While these estimates appear somewhat high, it can be confidently stated that even though a significant minority of elderly people are socially impoverished, most retain meaningful social ties and have a number of close friends. Atchley (1985) demonstrated that both a high density of elderly adults and residing in one place for a long time tend to be associated with the number of friends an aged person reports. Good health is a factor as well, for without personal vitality the strength of friendship networks is suspect, for in reality friends and neighbours simply have 'visiting rights'.

As we have already noted in the discussion of loneliness, the significant dimension of friendship is not the number of friends available, but the quality of interaction. Lowenthal and Haven (1968) identified the psychological benefits of having at least one confidant(e) with whom an elderly person can share troubles, fears, as well as happiness. Intimacy is a significant factor in influencing adjustment to the demands of ageing. While it is possible to establish new friendships throughout life to replace those that are lost (although many older people lack the motivation, activity levels and access to social roles to enable them to find new friendships), the emotional significance of these new contacts may not be great. It is doubtful whether they can achieve the warmth and closeness of a lifelong association. As a consequence the loss of just one long-term friend can be especially devastating.

Conclusion

In summary, it is clear that older people do not, in general, experience filial neglect and profound social isolation. While many role-adjustments are necessary, some of which may involve a profound and distressing sense of loss (for example, widowhood), most elderly adults are able to pursue a contented life of supported independence drawing on the sentiment of family and the companionship of friends as and when they desire. What may be interpreted by younger people as a solitary lonely existence, may, in the life space of an elderly person, be a state of affairs compatible with the need for self-determination and privacy. As before, many of our assumptions, this time concerning ageing, family life and friendship, are shown to be little more than unsupported fictions.

Chapter 11

The Meaning of Work, the Impact of Retirement

In any society the economy is the means by which the basic requirements of life are obtained. In capitalist industrial societies direct participation in economic life also enables a person to satisfy a variety of psychological and social needs, as well as providing material benefits (e.g. Stokes, 1983, 1990a). As a consequence, the stability of an adult's emotional and social world is largely dependent on being able to secure employment.

When a person is deprived of a job, they lose access to both the 'manifest' and 'latent' rewards of economic activity. Employment is an exchange relationship that occurs when an individual performs activities within an organizational structure and receives payment determined by market forces (i.e. 'manifest functions'). A person may have negative feelings about their terms of employment and workplace conditions. However, the exchange relationship as well as the activity of work conducted within the employment arrangement possesses psychologically significant 'latent functions'. These include social status, the fulfilment of a moral obligation, the acquisition of personal identity and self-worth, the imposition of a purposeful time structure, the achievement of goals and aspirations, the establishment of social relationships and the provision of active interest. For these reasons being without a job can be psychologically destructive, while being in employment can be psychologically supportive even when conditions are unsatisfactory. Thus a job is meaningful beyond earning a living. Being without employment deprives a person of this meaning even if their standard of living does not suffer.

Unemployment research has identified the importance a job has for personal well-being. Empirical data have established a greater prevalence of poor psychological and physical health, as well as deficient interpersonal behaviour, among long-term unemployed adults and their families. Among the reported ill effects of unemployment are depression, anxiety, loss of identity, feelings of degradation, boredom, loss of drive, a sense of inadequacy and loneliness. There is often a breakdown of an ordered existence and the adoption of a daily routine that is undisciplined and empty. Harrison (1976) concluded that prolonged unemployment is, for most people, a profoundly corrosive experience, undermining emotional stability and atrophying work capacities.

Unemployment and Retirement: Similarities and Differences

There is a certain face validity in assuming that unemployment and retirement are similar experiences, insomuch as they are both examples of a major transition from employment to joblessness. Both involve a loss of status, income and purpose. Does the impact of retirement on psychological and physical well-being therefore approximate that of work deprivation resulting from unemployment?

There are undoubtedly certain dissimilarities that may influence the outcome of these two forms of work-severance. Retirement does not incur the social stigma that is associated with unemployment, nor is it as unexpected. As retirement is a predictable life transition, it is possible for prospective retirees to obtain relevant and necessary information, thereby increasing their preparedness. Evidence suggests most people do little specific planning for retirement, however, and are thus largely unprepared for the financial implications and enforced change in life activities. A reluctance to prepare for 'life after work' reflects 'the common tendency to shut the later years off from the rest of the life cycle' (Hendricks and Hendricks, 1977). Preretirement conselling is a relatively new phenomenon which is not widespread. Limited United States data indicate, however, that it has no significant impact on adjustment or attitudes to retirement (Glamser, 1981).

Unlike redundancy and unemployment, retirement may be perceived as a timely conclusion to a person's occupational career. When reaching retirement age workers may evaluate their employment history and consider that they have achieved their personal goals and satisfied their need to work, thereby rendering further employment-related activity unnecessary.

On the debit side, retirement, unlike unemployment, is immediately experienced as a permanent state with little chance of resolution in terms of re-entering the workforce. For some older people, especially those who have strong attachments for their jobs and express a high level of job satisfaction, this may be an unwelcome and unwanted development in the life course.

Retirement — Theoretical Assumptions

Retirement is a socio-economic phenomenon of modern industrial times. For most of history advancing age had little to do with a person's opportunity to work. Cunningham and Brookbank (1988) established that in the United States in 1880, 70 per cent of people over the age of 65 were working. In 1979 the figure was only 14 per cent, and the trend suggests a continued decrease in the number of older workers.

In the past, when industries were labour intensive, and workers were in short supply, older adults were both expected and obliged to work. There was no financial support for those who were either unable or chose not to work in old age. Technological change, competition between increasingly efficient producer nations and cyclical economic recessions means that in advanced industrial societies the demand for labour has changed from that of shortage, to a situation of perennial high unemployment. By the mechanism of compulsory retirement, older adults are removed from the workforce so as to free job opportunities for younger people.

A non-work policy for older people required the adoption of the principle that in later life a person has earned the right, through years of employment, to share in their nation's prosperity without having to work. In other words, there was a need for the development of state-supported retirement pensions which enabled the basic requirements of life to be satisfied and hopefully a quality of life to be maintained. Unfortunately, many elderly people still have in adequate incomes. Palmore (1972) reported that in the United States 30 per cent of all retired couples, and 64 per cent of retired single people, have incomes below the official poverty line. Thus mandatory retirement at age 65 has created a population of older people who wish to continue working, either because of job satisfaction or because of the need for disposable income, yet are unable to do so.

A second function of retirement benefits is to provide support for those people who are too old or too frail to continue working. It is this function which is promoted by the media and accepted by society as the *raison d'être* of the pension system, rather than the objective of setting a limit on the number of people holding or seeking jobs. As a consequence, retirement is associated with old age, failing physical and intellectual powers and infirmity, with the inference that this commences at 65. This generalization is clearly erroneous and unjust. However, this perception of retirement certainly influences the attitudes of older workers and structures the stereotypes younger people hold about 'old-age pensioners'. There is considerable evidence that most workers consider themselves to be middle aged until they are within a few years of retirement, when they start to define themselves as old (Fiske, 1980).

Stemming from the negative perception of retirement, several investigators have focused on the traumatic potential of this life transition. Back (1977) refers to a profound sense of dislocation produced by the loss of occupational identity and the limitation of role choices on retirement while Kuypers and Bengtson (1973) discuss retirement in terms of a social breakdown syndrome which involves the loss of norms, role and reference groups.

Any crisis of identity is accentuated by the fact that occupational identity is a primary means by which society defines a person and they define themselves. Loss of the work role does not establish what the new identity of the retired person should be and lack of a defined role may lead to feelings of worthlessness and low self-esteem. Sheppard (1976) considers that retired women may face problems even more profound than those experienced by men. Many older women approaching retirement age are concentrated in lower status service positions. As a consequence the financial hardships associated with retirement are often exaggerated, especially when that woman is single, widowed, separated or divorced. Overall, Back (1977) views retirement as involving a surrendering of roles, a relinquishment of established patterns of behaviour and expectations and the acquisition of a culturally devalued status.

An alternative view considers that retirement is not a severe crisis, having little or no negative influence on family life, friendships or social interaction.

'Identity-continuity' is therefore achieved as a person continues to function in a variety of established and meaningful roles. For many older adults this may be an unlikely prospect. While the emotional significance of a person's attachment to the job is critical in determining their reaction to retirement, however, even when other roles are major determinants of self-definition and life-satisfaction, it is likely, if only because of financial considerations, that the end of workforce participation will disrupt the satisfactory performance of other more personally significant roles, and thereby threaten 'identity continuity'.

An intermediate approach to adjustment proposes not an absence of effects, nor does it focus exclusively on the negative impact of retirement. Instead, it considers that role realignment occurs (George, 1980). Despite having to adjust to radical life changes, attitudes and activities can be adopted which are compatible with the status and opportunities available to retired people. Successful adaptation assumes that unlimited leisure-time can provide a sense of usefulness and self-definition. However, can the satisfactions associated with these elective activities compensate for those associated with employment?

Leisure is potentially maximal during retirement; it can provide relaxation, creative activity, exercise, socialization and any other activity that is enjoyable. But can it provide purpose, fulfilment and a sense of value? Can elderly people have a meaningful later life 'career' of leisure? Thompson (1973) believes that retirement can be as rewarding and pleasant as the years of employment as a consequence of leisure roles being an adequate substitute for the work-role. Unfortunately, for people whose work was their life, the prospect of relatively unstructured and unlimited leisure time may be deeply disturbing. In a recent interview, Margaret Thatcher highlighted the despair of workers who are committed to their occupations to the exclusion of all else and who find themselves in retirement confronted with a vacuum that needs to be filled. As she poignantly commented, 'The pattern of my life was fractured. It is like throwing a pane of glass with a complicated map upon it on the floor. And all habits and thoughts and actions that went with it....You threw it on the floor and it shattered' (*Vanity Fair*, 1991). Unless something meaningful enters the 'leisure void', adjustment to retirement can be distressing for this group of retired people.

For others, whose commitment to their employment was marginal, adjustment to increased leisure time may be problematic because of declining health and reduced income. A life comprised of nothing but potential leisure opportunities can only be enjoyed if health, vitality and money are available to people who have retired. A life of enforced idleness and tedium may not only be a source of dissatisfaction, but may be a cause of premature death following retirement (Harrison, 1973).

Attitudes to Retirement

Attitudes to retirement are varied, so attempts to generalize about their nature are likely to be unsuccessful. Furthermore, if it is difficult to establish a consensus of opinion toward the abstract idea of retirement, it is even more problematic to predict a person's reaction to their own retirement.

Barter (1978) established that 82 per cent of people at retirement age would not give up work even if they had the opportunity to do so without loss of pay. In a survey or workers over 50, Sheppard (1976) found that 45 per cent of blue-collar workers would not continue to work if guaranteed an adequate income in retirement. The comparable figure for white-collar workers was only 24 per cent. Ekerdt *et al.* (1980) revealed that older workers typically desire later ages for retirement, some not wishing to retire at all. There appears to be a relationship between advancing age and later retirement preferences, for younger workers are more favourably included toward retirement and the prospect of it occurring at an earlier age. Thus evidence suggests that retirement is perceived as less attractive the more imminent it becomes (Ash, 1966; Atchley, 1980).

Some investigators have considered whether employment attitudes and work involvement are related in a consistent way to retirement attitudes and subsequent adjustment. Goudy *et al.* (1975) found little support for an inverse relationship between work attitudes and retirement. It has been proposed, however, that a positive attitude toward both work and retirement will generate relatively good financial, health and psychological status in retirement, while a negative orientation to both will lead to poor adjustment. A negative view of work because of, for example, monotony and lack of responsibility, allied to a willingness to retire will lead to few adjustment problems. However, high work involvement and a negative perception of retirement will lead to problems of maladjustment in later life.

It seems that those in high status occupations are likely to be characterized by a more positive orientation toward retirement when compared with lower status occupations. Yet in reality people with higher educational and occupational levels tend to retire later, even though they also favour the idea of early retirement.

Back (1977) considered that two types of work experience may facilitate the transition between work and retirement, namely participation in high prestige employment which provides financial security and the knowledge of prior achievements on the one hand, and limited emotional investment in the work role on the other. In contrast, Simpson *et al.* (1966) suggests that high status workers, especially those with high work involvement, will be the least favourably inclined toward retirement. The question seems to be whether prior accomplishments and educational attainment will act as a buffer against any potential negative aspects of retirement, or whether the extent of the losses experienced will frustrate any attempts to adjust to a devalued status. A study by Streib and Schneider (1971) found a curvilinear relationship between occupational status and retirement attitudes. Occupations possessing high and low prestige were least positive in their attitudes toward retirement, while workers in middle level occupations held the most favourable attitudes.

In conclusion, what can be stated with confidence about attitudes to retirement? Cunningham and Brookbank (1988) believe that most workers look forward to retirement, seeing it as a deserved rest from the toil of work.

The minority that fear retirement normally anticipate financial difficulties. Others dread retirement because they have no meaningful involvements outside work with which to occupy their time. Finally, those who work in the professions or who earn high incomes (and expect financial security upon retirement) seem to look forward most to retirement — yet appear to be the most reluctant to seize the opportunity when it actually arrives.

Tedium, Trauma or Tranquillity — The Evidence

Despite suggestions that retirement will initiate or exacerbate health problems and cause severe emotional stress, there is little evidence to associate retirement with long-term problems of health and well-being. While life satisfaction does tend to derease (e.g. Riley and Foner, 1968; Palmore, 1972), any decline in morale is usually temporary (Fiske, 1980). Some people even feel more healthy after retirement, especially if their work was characterized by strain and stressful demands (Woods and Britton, 1985). Martin and Doran (1966) concluded that rather than retirement being detrimental to health, it was associated instead 'with a substantial lowering in the incidence of serious illness'.

It seems that positive adjustment to retirement is the rule, despite major changes in living patterns. Retired people have an increased number of life options, they gain vicarious satisfaction from their children and grandchildren, they benefit from reduced demands and experience the reassuring effect of reminiscing. A number of longitudinal studies indicate continuity of family life, social interaction and community involvement following retirement. Loether (1965, cited by Kasl, 1979) reports that a majority of retired people either miss 'nothing at all' about not working, or only register complaints about missing work colleagues.

Not surprisingly, therefore, there is little evidence to support the idea that retirement has a negative impact on longevity. Haynes *et al.* (1978) monitored the mortality rates of a large cohort of blue-collar workers taking normal (i.e. at 65 years) and early retirement (i.e. 62–64 years). Mortality after early retirement was higher than would be expected in a working group, yet in all probability this simply reflects the tendency of some, although not all, workers in ill health to take early retirement rather than indicating that early retirement causes illness and premature death. This is consistent with the finding that pre-retirement health status was the only significant predictor of survival after early retirement. Normal retirement was not obviously detrimental to survival. While mortality rates were lower than expected in the first two years after retirement, they were greater than expected during the third and fourth years. Other researchers have also found elevations in mortality rates occurring a few years after retirement (e.g. Solem, 1976), and have associated these death excesses to a 'disenchantment phase' (Atchley, 1976) in the retirement process. Again pre-retirement medical history may be a significant risk factor.

When researchers attempt to establish the health consequences of retirement, and offer reasons for possibly elevated mortality and morbidity rates, a significant consideration is with whom to compare the retired population. If it is compared with those elderly adults who are in paid work after retirement age, then the comparator group is very different from the population which has retired and is likely to be in the constituency of those older people described as 'supernormals' (Savage *et al.*, 1973) who are 'free from noticeable physical and mental-health problems, adjustment and social difficulties' (Woods and Britton, 1985).

A potential area of post-retirement tension is the family home. Following retirement many husbands spend their days in the household sphere of the wife for the first time. The retired husband may be seen as an intruder, disrupting the daily routine of his wife. In marriage where roles have been segregated by sex, it is possible that a wife may be irritated by the presence of her husband in the house — he will 'get under her feet'. However, evidence indicates that most retirement couples seem happy with the marital relationship. As detailed in the previous chapter, marital satisfaction may reach its peak during retirement. Indeed the increased marital satisfaction may be related to a blurring of the traditional roles as companionship becomes dominant over the traditional roles of housekeeper or provider.

People who are traumatized by retirement are likely to be those who are committed to their work, or who experience poor health and relative poverty during retirement. In his study of a pattern of working class life that was fast disappearing Townsend (1963) found 'retirement was a particularly tragic event for most men'. This trauma was not simply because they could find little to justify their existence. It was also a result of a sharp fall in income upon giving up work ('a fall of over two-thirds for single people and a half for married people') which meant that established non-work customs could not be maintained. Kasl (1979) noted that among those who were dissatisfied with retirement, reduced income and health problems accounted for most of the reported reasons. Thompson (1973) found that retired people who exhibit lower morale have more negative evaluations of their health, are functionally disabled, are poorer and older.

Overall, the emotional and practical adjustments to retirement are considerable, but the loss of what was previously a central life role is not nearly as devastating as is typically assumed. Although the evidence is at times inconsistent and puzzling, there is no reliable evidence that retirement exercises a significant detrimental effect on physical health and psychological well-being. Attitudes after retirement indicate most people are satisfied with life and cope well with the concomitant social, economic and psychological changes. Those who adjust poorly to retirement are those people who are least prepared for the changes in lifestyle and income, are least flexible in responding to the realities of later life, who focus on unfulfilled life goals, and experience the misfortune of relative impecuniosity and ill health. Evidence which suggests greater life satisfaction among employed older people (who may be a very different and atypical group compared with those who retire), is due largely to differences in health and income, which are undoubtedly major determinants of happiness.

Given the large body of research which documents the importance of work to personal well-being (see Stokes, 1990a), and the regularly reported prevalence of unfavourable preretirement attitudes on the part of older workers, why is it that people largely adjust well to retirement? It is as if retirement is a stage in the life cycle that is relatively independent of previously held values and needs. In all probability, older people accept retirement as a 'normal' part of the life cycle. Dyson (1980) analyzes the adjustment to retirement in terms of social exchange theory. Society exchanges increased leisure time, a retirement pension and release from the obligation to work in return for the availability of additional places in the labour force. Although, as members of society, retired people may accept this as an equitable exchange on an individual level, retirement may be experienced as a psychological cost. Adherence to society's norms and values, however, prevents the expression of discontent.

While passive acceptance of the social prescription to retire may partially explain why older people adapt so well to retirement, such a hypothesis is too simplistic. A model of mechanistic determination denies the capacity of people to perceive, feel and express discontent, and that these psychological phenomena can be the driving force which produce change in society over generations. It is likely that later life postretirement experiences are accepted, not because older adults are prescribed to do so, but because for many people they are compatible with the needs of this stage of the life course. Given good health and adequate income, retirement can be a satisfying release from the burden of employment. The dread of retirement for most people diminishes with the expansion of pension provision and the realistic expectation of reasonably good health during 'young-old' age.

Flexible or Compulsory Retirement

The stereotype of the inefficient, unproductive older worker is certainly, in general, not valid. It is this perception that forms the basis for the age bias in setting the age for retirement, however, even though little basis exists in fact for such generalizations. Ideally employees should be judged individually for their ability to carry out the required tasks that constitute a particular job, for 'chronological age is rarely a reliable index of potential performance' (Havighurst, 1969). Older workers who are compelled to retire when they are gaining many satisfactions from their job and do not wish to relinquish their work role, are the ones who will be disaffected during retirement. With people surviving even longer in the future, and the demographic, biomedical and cultural pressures already resulting in people aged between 65 and 74 being defined as the 'young-old', even more workers may resent the notion that they must retire at an age when they are still fit and look forward to many more years of life.

Palmore (1972) concludes that compulsory retirement is unfair to the capable older worker, psychologically and socially damaging, and economically wasteful. Flexible retirement would avoid people being discarded when they are still capable of working. The methods which organizations use to recruit, dismiss and promote employees under 65, could be used to determine who should be retained and who retired among workers over 65. The measurement of functional ability as a basis for retirement policy is obviously not without drawbacks. Aside from macroeconomic issues such as the effect the retainment of older workers would have on the size of the labour force, and the prospect of able younger workers being denied access to senior positions, flexible retirement reduces predictability for both employers and employees, and removes the psychological protection compulsory retirement offers to the worker who is no longer capable of performing adequately. However, 'saving the face' of such workers has to be set alongside the needs of competent workers who are forced to retire and experience the frustration of their unwanted circumstances.

There is a growing trend for individual flexibility in retirement; suggestions include retirement as a transitional or phased process with workers being allowed to reduce their employment commitments both before and after the accepted age of retirement. Discussion of the relative merits of flexible and compulsory retirement may be a sterile exercise, however, for as there are likely to be too few jobs for at least the foreseeable future, any flexibility that emerges is only likely to enable people to retire earlier, rather than allowing significant numbers of older people to work beyond the existing age of compulsory retirement.

In industrialized youth-centred societies, where life and values are orientated toward the activity of work, debate on the timing and experience of retirement should take place in the wider context of the availability and meaning of employment and leisure. With high levels of joblessness likely to remain a feature of the social and economic landscape (Stokes, 1983, 1990a), are constructive alternatives to employment needed by both younger and older people, so as to ensure that the social fabric is not undermined by the existence of millions of people who are denied access to the material and emotional rewards available to those who do have jobs?

Chapter 12

Sexual Interest and Activity in Later Life

While there are comparatively few studies of sexuality in later life, we do know that there is no age at which sexual activity abruptly ends. For older people, sexual interest and capacity to enjoy sex are not lost. Sexual behaviour may be a less frequent, less vigorous activity but nonetheless it may remain a satisfying experience. Yet this is not the conception we have of sexuality in later life. The generally held belief is that elderly adults are sexually impotent, yet are untroubled by this because of greatly diminished sexual interest. As a consequence, society establishes a climate of social expectation and a range of ill-founded taboos which serve to inhibit older people and, as Hendricks and Hendricks (1977) comment, cause many of them to see themselves as beyond sex. It may be difficult for younger people to accept that a lot of elderly adults may be sexually frustrated because the idea of sexual activity still appeals but opportunities are denied them, but that is the conclusion we can draw from studies which have examined later life sexuality.

Prevalence of Sexual Activity

Corby and Solnick (1980) consider that the physiological responses that appear to decline with age for both men and women do not negate that opinion 'that there is much physiological potential for sexual pleasure remaining for both female and male'. As noted in Chapter 2, it is a misconception to assume that a man's erective capacity is lost as a natural concomitant of biological ageing. Although Bretschneider and McCoy (1988) observed that 61 per cent of men over 80 reported problems of either achieving or maintaining an erection, this is probably due in many instances to an anxiety-provoking 'fear of failure' which arises as a result of the slower erection in old age. While there are some delayed reactions in the male sexual response cycle, this is far removed from the belief that aged men lose their capacity for erection.

The equally inaccurate stereotypic notion that the female menopause leads to a cessation of sexual activity and interest is also unfounded. There is no direct relationship between sexual capacity and menopause, although the menopause may be the excuse some women give for stopping an activity they

Table 12.1: Sexual activity in old age: Longitudinal data (3–4 years)

	Men (%)	Women (%)
No sexual activity at either interview point	27	74
Decreasing sexual activity between interview points	31	10
Equal sexual activity between interview points	22	10
Increasing sexual activity between interview points	20	6

Source: Verwoerdt *et al.*, 1969b

did not enjoy anyway. While the role of the endocrine system in sexual behaviour is not well understood, it is not the case that sex inevitably loses its appeal to women by the end of their procreative years. In fact, women retain the physical capacity to enjoy sex far more satisfactorily than men. Comfort (1980) believes the menopause can mark 'a period of resexualization'.

DeNigola and Peruzza (1974) not only established that 85 per cent of Italian men aged between 62 and 81 years were sexually active, but that both men and women reported sexual satisfaction similar to, or higher than, that reported by younger people. While a woman's capacity for sex may remain intact throughout life, research indicates that fewer women than men remain sexually active. Newman and Nichols (1960) found that 40 per cent of married women over 60 were sexually active compared with 60 per cent of men. Longitudinal data gathered by Verwoerdt *et al.* (1969a,b) also established different levels of sexual activity among elderly men and women. While both sexes displayed a tendency to indulge in sexual intercourse less often over a period of three to four years they revealed a different profile of change (Table 12.1). Over the age of 78 years Verwoerdt *et al.* (1969b) reported that all the women in their study were sexually inactive (i.e. not participating in sexual intercourse) while the comparable figure for men was 50 per cent.

In a study by Bretschneider and McCoy (1988) an attempt was made to study sexuality at even more advanced ages. In a healthy population of people aged between 80 to 102, the most common sexual activity was touching and caressing without sexual intercourse, then masturbation, followed by sexual intercourse. Once again, sex differences were observed with regard to the frequency of sexual activity. Although 63 per cent of men indicated they had intercourse at least sometimes, only 30 per cent of women did so. Similar proportions have been reported in other studies of people over 80 years old. If one includes touching and caressing without sexual intercourse a significant number of men (82 per cent) and women (64 per cent) remain sexually active. Sex differences were also found in the amount of sexual enjoyment experienced. While 76 per cent of men said that sexual intercourse brought them at least mild enjoyment, only 39 per cent of women reported the same level of satisfaction. Men were also more likely to enjoy the activity of touching and caressing.

Bretschneider and McCoy (1988) conclude that for men the frequency of sexual intercourse does not change greatly after 80. It is even possible that there is a moderate increase in the proportion of men in their 80s and 90s who are sexually active but this is probably a function of the greater survival of the more biologically fit. For women the relatively sudden and sizeable increase in the numbers who report having no sexual intercourse occurs in the 50s and 60s and then does not change much after that. Overall, for both men and women, Bretschneider and McCoy (1988) suggest that there is no decade this side of 100 in which sexual activity is totally absent.

Having established that sexual activity continues into extreme old age, the diversity of later life responses needs to be addressed. Group data do not identify 'age-change', but reveal the aggregated experiences 'of a mixture of high- and low-activity individuals, in whom those whose sexual "set" is low for physical or attitudinal reasons drop out early, often with recourse to age as an excuse' (Comfort, 1980).

Factors Affecting Sexual Behaviour

The most significant variables influencing sexual behaviour in later life are probably marital status and the sex of the older person, with being unmarried and being female associated with less sexual activity. In a study of a 70-year-old urban population, Persson (1980) found that the married of both sexes were more often sexually active than unmarried people. Among married men 52 per cent were still active, while 26 per cent of unmarried men were sexually active. The influence of marital status on female sexual behaviour is even more dramatic. Whereas 36 per cent of married women were active, the figure for unmarried women was only 2 per cent. Bretschneider and McCoy (1988) found marital status to be significantly related to the frequency and enjoyment of sexual activities for both men and women.

Although there is conflicting evidence with regard to the effect marital status has on a man's sexual behaviour, there is no doubt that it has a great deal to do with a woman's sexuality. As women tend to outlive their husbands, and therefore constitute the majority of older adults, 'partner availability' is a major influence on female sexual behaviour in later life. As Corby and Solnick (1980) note, with the tendency of men to marry women younger than they, 'available partners for a woman of any age can be described as all single men older than she. For a man, available partners would be all single women younger than he'. With women likely to outlive men of their own age, 'the position of reduced opportunity into which this places women is apparent'. Bretschneider and McCoy (1988) found that while 47 per cent of men in their sample had no regular sex partner, 75 per cent of women found themselves in this position. Corby and Solnick (1980) report survey data which revealed that 48 per cent of women ended sexual intercourse because of the loss of a partner, while only 10 per cent of men gave this as the reason. Overall, the availability of a socially acceptable partner emerges as a most important influence on sexuality in elderly women.

Unfortunately, being married does not in any way ensure that elderly women are able to maintain sexual involvement. For sexual activity to be a dimension of the marital relationship, a woman requires not only an available partner, but a sexually capable partner. Evidence that the husband is usually the determining factor in whether or not a couple will continue to have sexual intercourse comes from Kinsey *et al.* (1953). They noted the decline in the frequency of sexual activity among ageing women was 'controlled by the male's desires, and it is primarily his ageing rather than the female's loss of interest or capacity which is reflected in the decline'. Support for this view comes from several quarters. For example, Christenson and Gagnon (1965) found that older wives with younger husbands are more sexually active than are younger wives with older husbands.

Reports on the relationship between health and sexual behaviour are at times conflicting, but the weight of opinion suggests that health does affect sexual functioning among men. While objective measures of physical health are correlated with the frequency of sexual intercourse, psychological factors are also invariably implicated. Although diseases such as diabetes appear to have a direct effect on sexual functioning, other health problems, for example heart disease, are to varying degrees psychologically mediated. This is evident by the observation that different men with the same disease or disability vary both in their willingness to adjust to their condition and their ability to continue expressing their sexuality. Interestingly, it is not objective indicators of health that appear to determine sexual enjoyment and interest but self-estimates of health.

Among women, health factors appear to be of little significance although Persson (1980) established an association between sexual inactivity and a subjective feeling of not being healthy, but not with any of the specified disorders or symptoms studied. However, for both sexes, sexual activity is associated with better mental health.

In a consideration of marital factors Bretschneider and McCoy (1988) found that elderly men were happier with their partners as both lovers and friends. Given that the sexuality of elderly married women is associated not only with lower age of the husband and their partner's physical health, but also with the rating of the marriage as happy, it is possible that marital conditions also contribute to the diminution of sexual activity. In contrast, Persson (1980) documented that male sexual activity was not related to either age or health of the spouse, nor with the appraisal of marriage with regard to degree of happiness.

Although there appear to be no sex differences in reported past enjoyment of sexual activity, sex differences in present enjoyment represent a much greater decrease from past to present in the enjoyment of partnered sexual activities experienced by ageing women. This is possibly because of hormonal changes which prevent adequate vaginal lubrication and may make intercourse painful (known as dyspareunia). Bretschneider and McCoy (1988) observed that 30 per cent of their female sample suffered from this problem. It is quite probable that reduced sexual enjoyment may be another contributory factor to the significant sex difference in sexual activity found between older men and women.

Woods and Britton (1985) believe that male sexual behaviour in later life is best predicted by past sexual interest, frequency and enjoyment, while for elderly women past sexual enjoyment is most highly correlated with current sexuality. Although Bretschneider and McCoy (1988) did not find that frequency of sexual intercourse in the past to be related to present frequency, they established that past and present importance of sex were highly correlated, and that past importance of sex was significantly associated to present frequency and enjoyment of both sexual intercourse and touching and caressing. Personal characteristics of married men identified by Persson (1980) as being associated with later life sexuality included strength of the sex drive in young adulthood and a positive attitude toward sexual activity among elderly people. In married women, sexual behaviour was associated with having had premarital sexual experience, a positive attitude toward sex in old age and a more positive experience of sexual intercourse. It would appear, as Pfeiffer (1969) stated, 'persons to whom sex was of great importance early in life are more likely to continue to be sexually active late in life.'

The general social expectation that older people will be sexually inactive cannot be discounted as a reason for reduced levels of sexual behaviour in later life. When compared with young and middle-aged people, older adults often consider themselves to be relatively disinterested in sex, less capable of it and less skilful at it. While many elderly people appear to accept their waning sexuality as a product of normal physical ageing, could it not be in part the product of society's attitudes rather than a real consequence of psychobiological ageing? In other words the attitudes older people have about sex for themselves is inextricably related to the folklorist view others have about sex in later life.

Sexual Interest

Another measure of sexuality in later life is not overt sexual activity, but sexual interest. While there is a great deal of variation among older adults in sexual interest, in general women are consistently less interested than men. Even though there is a gradual increase in the proportion of men having no interest in sex, Bretschneider and McCoy (1988) found that even for men in their 90s less than 30 per cent indicated no interest in sex. Pfeiffer and Davis (1972) consider the lower levels of sexual interest in older women is a psychological defence mechanism which 'may well be adaptive to inhibit sexual strivings when little opportunity for sexual fulfilment exists'.

Marital status does not appear to be related to sexual interest for men and has little effect on sexual interest in women. Overall, men appear more positive about sex in later life than women, although advancing age tends to have a conservatizing effect.

Sexual interest is not necessarily reflected in overt sexual action. For example, Pfeiffer *et al.* (1969) found that while sexual interest remained fairly constant in a sample of healthy elderly men over ten years, these same men were actually displaying significant reductions in sexual activity over the same period. Freeman (1961) also found a discrepancy between activity (55 per cent) and interest (75 per cent) among aged men. This gap has led Corby and Solnick (1980) to postulate that male sex interest may not reflect genuine interest as 'there is greater pressure on males than on females to claim sexual interest'. It is not the case that female interest is a veridical representation of their sexual behaviour, however, for expressed interest is also greater than the actual incidence of female sexual behaviour.

Conclusion

While research over the past forty years has given us a greater insight into the sexual behaviour of older people, Bromley (1990) correctly warns that such investigations are difficult and their findings are open to a variety of criticisms related to methodology. In part, research difficulties arise because sexuality is a difficult topic for elderly adults to discuss. It lies within the private domain of life, and as the current cohort of older people were not brought up to be comfortable with their own sexuality, it is likely that many of them may resent or refrain from answering questions. Similarly, others may give socially desirable or culturally appropriate responses which undermine the reliability of outcome data.

We must also be wary of conclusions based on cross-sectional data, for sexual attitudes and morals change across generations thereby rendering such data suspect. It is probable that with presumed changes in sexual morality during recent decades, future generations of elderly people will be less conservative and more sexually active than previous cohorts.

With these reservations in mind we are still able to regard human sexuality as a 'normal' lifelong attribute for both men and women unless compromised by ill health, adverse experience, absence of opportunity or social expectation. However, as Hendricks and Hendricks (1977) touchingly convey, for those older couples who are denied the opportunity to have sexual intercourse, showing tenderness and sensitivity can be valued in such a way that such activity is hardly missed. Intercourse is not the only means of expressing love and affection, and thus it is a mistake to assume that in its absence a couple cannot communicate their sexual feelings. It would not be unusual for intercourse in later life to be experienced as a single element in the communication of emotion, and probably of less importance than other manifestations of the relationship bond.

Chapter 13

Death, Dying and Bereavement

'Whether considering our own potential demise or that of someone close, immortality has long been an impossible dream of human beings' (Cunningham and Brookbank, 1988). For most people this view tends to result in avoidance of the topic of death so it becomes a concealed, unspoken fear in many people's lives. In western society the inevitability of death is neither readily accepted, nor is it considered a matter appropriate for everyday comment. A couple, married for fifty years, may secretly dread the prospect that death will one day part them, yet it is probable that they will neither share these feelings nor prepare for the inevitable event. Denial may promote what is commonly seen as an admirably stoical approach to the prospect of dying, but it is unlikely that such impassive resignation facilitates adjustment when faced with the death of a partner, parent or close friend. Peterson (1980) regards burial and funeral rites as providing further evidence of the denial of death. An elaborate vocabulary (e.g. Chapel of Rest, rest in peace, sleep peacefully, knowing you are in God's care) is employed to convey the feeling that the deceased person is not really dead. In sum, it would appear that we have been prepared for our own deaths and that of others by a subtle denial that this day will ever need to be faced. It is in part the reason why younger members of society construct a social distance between themselves and older adults. To meet with, and know aged people involves explicit recognition that our species has a finite lifespan and a built-in obsolescence.

The prevalence of denial is reflected in the study of ageing and old age. While it would be reasonable to presume that death is a central issue in gerontology, it is in fact a comparatively neglected area of research. Much of what is known about planning for, and reacting to death in later life is based on data from traditional areas of study such as the care of the terminally ill. Peterson (1980) concluded that the study of death and dying 'is severely limited in terms of both methodology and in theory'.

Facing One's Own Death

People tend not to deal with their own mortality. They are willing to prepare for almost everything except their own death. Avoidance is often regarded as the best policy, even if this means for example, risking fatal consequences by not receiving a diagnosis for a persistent health problem. It is as if the diagnosis may be an intolerable, unacceptable confirmation of the nearness of death.

Fear of death often centres around a wish to avoid pain and suffering, the loss of 'self' and a fear of the unknown, along with a sense of sorrow at leaving people one loves. While it is impossible to comprehend oneself as not existing, some people take comfort that this state of 'nothingness' must be like entering a dreamless sleep.

Several investigators have examined how people adjust to the awareness that life will end. Kübler-Ross (1975) observed terminally ill patients and proposed a stage approach to the process of dying. First, there is shock, denial and disbelief, followed by feelings of anger wherein the person becomes hostile and demanding. There then follows a form of denial in the guise of bargaining in which the person may claim they could die in peace if only ... A sign that the acceptance of death has begun is when the individual enters a state of depression. Finally, acceptance is achieved and the person wishes to take care of their affairs, tie up loose ends and be with their loved ones. A concern with what will happen to their property and the need to distribute it to family and friends represents a recognition of approaching death, and a wish to leave the world with some orderly distribution of the products of a life well-lived.

As with all stage theories of adjustment, however, it needs to be accepted that the sequence may be re-ordered and that some people may remain fixed without change at a point in the process until death. Shneidman (1973) is sceptical about a stage approach to dying, believing that there is 'a hive of affect, in which there is a constant coming and going', encompassing feelings such as disbelief, hope, anger, anguish, disinterest, terror and confusion. Some terminally ill people appear at one time to discuss their impending deaths openly and rationally, and at other times to deny the reality of their condition completely. However, as Weisman (1972) states, 'the degrees of denial are never constant'.

Lieberman and Tobin (1983) maintain that older people do not generally have the same reluctance to discuss death and may talk openly about knowing that their life is nearing an end. Without prompting or apparent reason they may start the process of 'tidying up'.

Research reported by Peterson (1980) revealed that the greatest source of comfort older people experience when thinking of death is not religion or love from significant others, but memories of a full life. Over 90 per cent of respondents in this research wanted to die at home and wished for their families to be there at their death. Yet these circumstances are not how death is for most people. The majority of us die 'in an institution of some sort' (Dodd, 1991). It was also recorded that 85 per cent rejected heroic, technological efforts to stave off death, feeling it was better to end life quietly with dignity.

Bereavement

The Process of Mourning

Goode (1964) suggested that the real meaning of death is social, not biological. Among the multiple losses in later life, the loss of a partner, family member or close friend is the most profound crisis experienced by older adults. It devastates the interpersonal environment, and if the relationship was intimate and enduring the impact will be especially great. To describe bereavement as a 'loss' does scant justice to this potentially traumatic experience. It rarely involves a single loss, but rather is the destruction of the totality of what the person represented in the survivor's life space. Because the constituents and qualities of each relationship are unique, the universal experience of death is peculiarly and uniquely painful for each individual.

In modern western society with lower rates of infant mortality and greater longevity, the typical experience until mid-life is not to be acquainted with death (with the probable exception of the death of grandparents). However, it was not many generations ago that the death of parents and one's own siblings in early life brought a close acquaintance with death at a young age. Now death has come to be concentrated in old age.

Death and bereavement in contemporary societies present difficulties which were not experienced in the same way earlier this century. Prior to the First World War there were ritualized patterns of dress and behaviour designed to facilitate and acknowledge the process of mourning. Nowadays these cultural supports are largely ignored. 'Today bereaved people are not expected to show grief, or not for very long, and they are expected to cope without much support' (Dodd, 1991).

When investigating the process of bereavement it is unfortunate, not only for the purposes of this chapter, but as a further indication of the general lack of sensitivity to the issues of later life, that most studies have specifically excluded elderly people. Those which have not will be detailed later, but first we will examine the efforts of investigators (e.g. Parkes, 1972) who have attempted to chart the course of mourning. While they differ in detail there are many common observations.

First, there is a period of shock, which may manifest as hysteria, panic or numbness. This is followed by a time of protest and yearning wherein the person is desperately missed. The survivor may feel vulnerable and unsafe without the reassuring presence of the dead person. Persistent and intrusive thoughts about the lost loved one may urge them to 'search' for the lost person, usually by looking through photographs or visiting places that had a shared meaning. There is a tendency to idealize the dead person, especially if the deceased was a spouse. Grief usually involves episodic experience of psychological pain, rather than sustained feelings of depression. Feelings of guilt and anger may surface. The survivor may condemn themselves for human imperfections. They may feel guilty about the hostile and bitter sentiments held toward the dead person who has left them with the pain of loss. Such bitterness may be misinterpreted by others and be regarded as an unacceptable manifestation of self-pity.

Eventually the grieving person enters a state of disorganization and despair. They may torment themselves by indulging in a painful repetition of the loss experience. During this difficult time auditory and visual misinterpretations may be experienced. Such subjective phenomena are not unusual experiences following the death of someone close. The survivor may 'hear' the turning of the key in the front door lock, or 'see' their partner lying in bed next to them on waking up. A bereaved person may act as if the person is not dead. Recently, an elderly widow was referred to me because of her inability to accept the death of her husband. During each visit she diligently prepared a tray of tea and cakes for the three of us and then politely excused her husband who must have been unexpectedly delayed. Sometimes she even appeared irritated at his lack of consideration.

Finally, the bereaved achieve reorganization and recovery. The majority of bereaved people will re-embark upon a meaningful life after they have mourned their dead in a way appropriate to them. There is a realization that while no-one can replace the person who has died, other sources of love and comfort are available. The time taken to create a new life that excludes the dead person may be lengthy, often much longer than a year. It is misguided automatically to assume, as some investigators do, that a grief reaction which is unresolved after this period is 'abnormal'. Unresolved grieving of over a year is by no means always so, and it is important for the bereaved and those around them to know and accept this. Coleman (1986) observed feelings of loss in an elderly widow forty years the death of her husband!

What more needs to be said about bereavement? Several codicils need to be added. First, bereavement is not a static state of mind and behaviour, but a constantly changing process. Second, the response to the death of another is unpredictable. The intensity and duration of the bereavement process will depend on, for example, how close the bereaved person was to the person who died, their previous experiences of death and the nature of the death (Dodd, 1991). Not only will people display features of bereavement more or less strongly, but not all people will pass through the stages in a given sequence. Finally, 'although grief involves grave departures from the normal attitude to life' (Freud, 1917), to feel anger, sadness and pain is both natural and essential for positive adjustment to occur. Concern arises when the emotions are extreme or long-lasting, although as has been already stated, the process of bereavement is rarely completed in a matter of days or weeks. It is possible, if not probable, that the first anniversary of the person's death will trigger a period of sadness and bitterness.

Abnormal Grief Reaction

For most people the resolution of mourning results in a willingness to get on with living, but some survivors may become fixed in the mourning process and become morbidly preoccupied with the memory of the dead person. Characteristics of maladaptive grief include the absence of grief, enduring physical symptoms, excessive guilt or anger, persistent intense grieving and suicidal thoughts.

Abnormal grief reactions may occur when family and friends pay excessive attention to grieving for too long. Such over-concern prevents the
bereaved person from taking up old activities or starting new ventures and
friendships. A 'conspiracy of silence' wherein family and friends avoid talking
about the loss in order to avoid upsetting the survivor may also result in
pathological grief reaction.

Dodd (1991) identifies the basic environmental supports that encourage
adjustment. In brief, an accepting, supportive climate which allows feelings to
be expressed and enables the survivor to talk about their loss improves the
prospects that after a lapse of time grief will be overcome. Encouraging the
person to find solutions to their practical difficulties will also facilitate adaptive behaviour.

Bereavement in Old Age

Are older adults more fatalistic and resilient when faced with the death of
significant others? Heyman and Gianturco (1973) found that adaptation to
bereavement in older people was remarkably good. Other studies too have
suggested that grief tends to be milder in elderly adults, although somatic
symptoms are more common, as are feelings that life has no purpose. There is
also a greater tendency to idealize the deceased person. A longitudinal study of
widows and widowers by Gallagher *et al.* (1983) found that two months after
bereavement, the survivors' levels of distress were higher than in a comparison
group, although only a small proportion could be said to be manifesting pathological psychological disturbance. No gender differences were reported. While
the evidence suggests that elderly people adjust well to the death of a loved
one (although this may not be so if a child dies before a parent, thus violating
the 'normal' sequence), it is also true that survival may be extremely difficult
for some. This difficulty is most apparent in marriages of many years standing
that are characterized by mutual dependence. Research shows that the
mortality rate of widows and widowers is approximately 40 per cent over
normal expectations in the first six months following death of the partner.

Woods and Britton (1985) review evidence that suggests that in younger
people, while adjustment to the death of a significant other is better when
death is expected, in elderly adults anticipatory grief seems potentially harmful.
This may possibly arise because the strain of caring for a dying partner can
adversely affect the health of the carer, which is reflected in the ensuing process
of bereavement. For some partners caring for a spouse suffering a lingering
death may become their purpose in life and so eventual death may be a traumatic loss leaving them with the despair of endless, pointless time. Woods and
Britton also note that abnormal grief reactions are more likely to follow a
death from chronic illness because the survivor is likely to have held ambiva-
lent feelings toward the dying person. On the one hand they may have wished
for the person to be out of their misery and experienced a sense of relief at the
end. On the other, they never wanted to lose a lifelong partner, and wishing
for that person to die may eventually consume them with guilt. Elderly people

may cope better with unexpected death, however because in later life death is seldom a complete surprise and so a 'sudden' death will be much less unexpected in an older than a younger person.

Conclusion

Confronting the prospect of one's own death and experiencing the deaths of relatives and friends in later life, often in close succession, are major adjustments older people are required to make. The death of a spouse is an especially traumatic event, for it involves the loss of friendship, love, security and sexual satisfaction, the onset of possible financial difficulties, as well as an unwelcome redistribution of household responsibilities. The subsequent process of bereavement is a normal condition, and does not usually lead to chronic emotional or mental health problems. Yet in our youth-centred, growth-orientated culture would movement away from the denial of death toward greater social recognition of the mourning process help bereaved older adults to ameliorate the fears and regrets often felt, if not expressed? We do not know, for the death taboo currently renders dying a forbidden fact of life and an unwelcome (if not a distasteful) topic for investigation.

Part Four

Abnormal Ageing

Chapter 14

Dementia — The Silent Epidemic

Despite the fact that senility is not an inevitable accompaniment of ageing, the prevailing cultural expectation appears to be that it is a normal aspect of growing old. In part this expectation is a consequence of the descriptive language employed. The dictionary definition of 'senile' is 'of or characteristic of old age', while 'senility' is defined as 'mentally or physically weak or infirm because of old age'. From these definitions it can easily be inferred that mental and physical infirmity is a characteristic of old age. Butler (1975) argued strongly against the myth of inevitability of senility, maintaining forcefully that senility, when it occurs, is the result of disease or disorder. In other words senility is abnormal, not normal, and thus the causes are pathological and not the inevitable consequence of biological ageing.

Dementia — Terminology

Whatever term is used to label cognitive impairment in old age (most of which are both inaccurate and pejorative), whether it be senility, senile mental deficiency, mental infirmity or dementia (from the Latin *demens* which means being out of one's mind), intellectual dysfunction is not a disease in its own right. The term dementia essentially represents 'a clinical description without any supposition to an underlying aetiology' (Wade and Hachinski, 1987). If an elderly person displays major signs of intellectual deterioration, behavioural incompetence and social inadequacy the cause needs to be established. For, as has been described in detail throughout this book, such changes are not to be expected in later life.

As long ago as 1838, Esquirol provided a clinical description of dementia which corresponds in many ways with today's concept of the syndrome:

> Senile dementia is established slowly. It commences with enfeeblement of memory, particularly the memory of recent impressions. The sensations are feeble; the attention, at first fatiguing, at length becomes impossible; the will is uncertain and without impulsion; the movements are slow and impractical.

Yet why should such degeneration of personality and performance arise? The discovery of both the cause and neuropathology of syndromes has always lagged behind their clinical delineation, and dementia is no exception.

For most of this century, senile dementia was considered to be an extreme variant of normal age-related changes. Intellectual deterioration was considered to be an almost inevitable consequence of ageing, and as such attracted little interest from either practitioners or researchers. The commonest cause was felt to be cerebral arteriosclerosis — 'hardening of the arteries'. The brain was seen as being starved of its blood supply because of diseased arteries which resulted in a progressive dementia. However, knowledge was disfigured by myth and distorted by disinterest. Only recently have investigators discovered that the role of arteriosclerosis in the cause of dementia had been greatly overestimated (e.g. Tomlinson *et al.*, 1970). Nowadays, dementia is no longer a neglected clinical issue. The Royal College of Physicians (1981) defines the syndrome as:

> the global impairment of higher cortical functions including memory, the capacity to solve the problems of day-to-day living, the performance of learned perceptuo-motor skills, the correct use of social skills and the control of emotional reactions, in the absence of gross clouding of consciousness. The condition is often irreversible and progressive.

Jorm (1987) questions why we persist with the descriptive term of dementia, which is non-specific as to causation, rather than focus on the specific diseases which give rise to it: a valid point. Elderly people are often 'diagnosed' as having dementia, with scant regard as to the nature of the underlying disorder even though it is known that the syndrome is not a specific disease. When used judiciously, however, this general diagnosis can be a useful concept in practice, for the possible causes of dementia are often hard to tell apart, especially in the early stages. It therefore can be seen as a 'compromise diagnosis', which acknowledges a set of characteristic signs and symptoms, and excludes a range of potential causes of intellectual impairment such as Down's Syndrome, traumatic head injury and stroke.

Among the presumptive causes which produce the syndrome of dementia in old age, the three most common disorders are Alzheimer's disease, multi-infarct dementia and a mixed dementia resulting from a combination of the first two. Although there are differences between the disorders at the level of clinical presentation and progression which allow a probable diagnosis, the only completely reliable way to diagnose them is by examination of the brain. Therefore a definite diagnosis is only possible after death when the brain can be examined by autopsy.

Dementia — Prevalence

The great majority of studies have been conducted in Northern Europe, Japan and North America. Among people aged over 65 living in the community, the prevalence (i.e. the proportion of people afflicted at a given time) of severe dementia has been estimated at between 1.3 and 6.2 per cent (Mortimer, 1983). Recently, Lindesay *et al.* (1989) established a prevalence rate of 1.1 per cent for severe cognitive impairment. The wide range in prevalence rates is likely to be the result of different methods of grading and defining severity, rather than indicating actual population differences. The median (i.e. the mid-point) prevalence rate suggests that around 4.15 per cent of adults in later life suffer from severe general impairment of cognitive function. Kay and Bergmann (1980) estimate that the prevalence of moderate or severe dementia (both categories rendering a person incapable of caring for themselves) is generally between 5 and 8 per cent.

One of the most obvious findings from surveys of moderate or severe dementia is that prevalence rises steeply with age. Differences between surveys in the age-prevalence of dementia should not be of great concern as they are probably once again the result of differences in case definition. Of greater significance is the consistency in the relationship between age and prevalence. Whereas approximately 3 per cent of people in their early 70s who live at home suffer from moderate or severe dementia, over 20 per cent of people in their 80s are similarly afflicted. The increase in prevalence with age may not continue into the 90s and beyond, where prevalence is thought to decline again. To date, studies have included too few people over 90 for definitive conclusions to have been reached. Overall, while estimates of prevalence of profound cognitive impairment may vary between studies, there is good agreement as to the rate at which it increases with age. The relationship is exponential rather than linear; Jorm *et al.* (1987) estimates a doubling time of 5.1 years.

As the chance of developing dementia rises steeply in advanced old age, the prevalence of dementia in society as a whole depends on the proportion of the population that survives to be very old. The marked increase in number of people surviving into old age (documented in Chapter 1) will produce what Henderson (1983) has called 'the coming epidemic of dementia'. Henderson and Jorm (1986), using United Nations population data on population projections, show that over the years 1980–2000 there will be an anticipated increase in the number of dementing people of 13 per cent in the United Kingdom, 41 per cent in the United States and 52 per cent in Australia. The epidemic of dementia will reach a peak when the babies of the 'boom' years between 1945 to 1965 become elderly from 2010 onwards. In global terms it is projected that the over-65 population will grow from 260 million people in 1980 to a population of 650 million by 2020. A conservative estimate of the world-wide prevalence of severe dementia thirty years from now may well, as a consequence, be in the region of 27 million cases.

Aside from demographic changes, elderly people with dementia are living longer, and as such this has led to an increase in the numbers alive at any particular time. In the past, many people suffering from dementia in old age died from opportunistic diseases such as pneumonia. However advances in medical treatment mean that infectious diseases kill far fewer people than was the case earlier in the century. As a consequence, people suffering from chronic incurable illnesses such as dementia now live longer. Gruenberg (1977) has referred to this trend as 'the failures of success'. Jorm (1987) adds, 'the "success" of our ability to keep demented people alive longer may lead to the "failure" of an increase in the prevalence of dementia and contribute even further to the epidemic of dementia associated with an aged population'.

Older women with dementia significantly outnumber men with this condition. In large part this is due to the greater life expectancy of women, coupled with the greater prevalence of dementia in the ninth decade of life. This has profound implications for the quality of living arrangement available to dementing elderly women. Only about 20 per cent of older adults with dementia live in hospital or other institutions. The vast majority of dementing people live in the community supported by the family network. However, Kay *et al.* (1964a) observed in a sample of people in Newcastle-upon-Tyne, England, that while none of the men with dementia lived alone, 53 per cent of women did so. This is not a curious feature of the dementing population, but is consistent with general demographic patterns. Elderly men usually live with a spouse, whereas it is common for women in later life to live by themselves. The significance of living arrangements has been documented by Bergmann *et al.* (1978) who found that while 18.5 per cent of dementing elderly people living by themselves survived for one year in the community, 40 per cent of those living with carers did so.

As most prevalence studies have been carried out in advanced industrial societies, little is known regarding the geographic variation in the prevalence of dementia. Data are urgently needed on the prevalence and incidence of dementia in Third World nations. Currently information suggests it is an extremely rare syndrome. However, it needs to be acknowledged that longevity is less common in developing countries, and those people who do survive into advanced old age may constitute a 'survival elite'.

The Causes of Dementia

Alzheimer's Disease (AD)

Alzheimer's disease or senile dementia?
Alzheimer's disease is a neurological disease of the cerebral cortex that is acquired, progressive, irreversible and pursues an insidious unremitting course over a number of years. It was first described by Alois Alzheimer when he presented the case of a 51-year-old woman suffering from generalized dementia. It was regarded as a rare disorder afflicting people in middle age. As a consequence, until recent times, it was described as a pre-senile dementia. A distinction was made between AD and senile dementia, the latter having an onset at or after 65 years. While the characteristic pre-senile picture of intellectual and behavioural deterioration represented an abnormal and tragic deviation from normal ageing in mid-life, senile dementia was considered to be a distinct and separate entity characterized by a sense of inevitability.

Several autopsy studies during the 1960s and 1970s, however, showed that the majority of elderly people with 'senile dementia' had the characteristic neuropathological features of AD. In addition, the clinical picture of senile dementia is, in the main, clinically indistinguishable from AD. In essence, pre-senile dementia and senile dementia differ primarily through an arbitrary age cut-off point. As with other diseases, younger people may be more rapidly and severely affected, but there is little evidence to support the continued use of this age distinction. With the current tendency to refer to all cases as AD regardless of age at onset, AD has been transformed from a rare dementia affecting middle-aged people, to the most common dementing illness.

A continuum of pathological development
Although AD is conceptualized as being a specific disease quite different from 'normal' ageing, the differences between the two are largely a matter of degree. Senile plaques and neurofibrillary tangles (cellular abnormalities characteristic of AD) occur in the brains of most elderly people, and not just in those with dementia. The majority of people in their late 50s and early 60s have some plaques and tangles and, by the time people reach their 90s, few are totally free of them. Less dramatic results were reported by Miller *et al.* (1984), who observed that while 3 per cent of people dying between 55–64 had plaques and tangles, the corresponding figure for those aged 85 or over was 45 per cent.

The critical feature in determining whether an elderly person will experience 'normal' senescence or profound cognitive impairment and behavioural dependency in later life (i.e. dementia) is the severity of the pathological changes found in the ageing brain. Up to a certain point, pathological alterations may be without major psychological consequences. Dementia appears only when the plaques and tangles reach a critical level. Thus changes in brain function found in 'normal' ageing and senile dementia of the Alzheimer type 'can be seen as a continuum which may reflect a single underlying process' (Brayne and Calloway, 1988).

However, the cut-off point between what is considered 'normal' or 'abnormal' is arbitrary. When there is gross impairment of intelligence, memory and adaptive behaviour a diagnosis of dementia of the Alzheimer type is relatively straightforward. However, when cognitive impairment is mild, there is 'a no-man's land where it is unclear at what point normal variation ends and abnormalities begin' (U'Ren, 1987). As Huppert and Tym (1986) observe, the large range of competence within the population of elderly people makes the 'determination of a threshold level of morbidity very difficult'.

In all cases of dementia, impairments of functioning are relatively slight at first, eventually progressing to the point where all cognitive processes and self-care abilities are lost. The question is at what point is the behaviour regarded as demented rather than normal? Many elderly people have neither demonstrable nor subjective memory impairment. Others suffer varying degrees of inefficiency. Kral (1962) identified a population of elderly people whose memory performance fell outside the expected functional range for their age, yet their difficulties were not consistent with the malignant memory impairment characteristic of dementia. People affected by 'benign senescent forgetfulness' (BSF) are unable to remember some of the details of an experience, but have a good memory for the experience itself. The person remains as capable of functioning in domestic and social settings as formerly, but awareness of their forgetfulness may lead to concern, embarrassment and stress, and an accompanying decline in performance.

Kral (1978) also proposed the term BSF to designate a syndrome which for the majority of people with the symptoms will not result in any further decline in cognitive functioning. While the distinction between BSF and progressive dementia has been criticized (Miller, 1977), results from a number of studies seem to support the view that a number of memory impaired people show no evidence of further deterioration at follow-up. Kral (1978) observed a group of elderly adults with a mean age of 80.5 year over a four-year period, and found that only one person suffering with BSF become more severely cognitively impaired.

The model of AD pathology now proposed therefore moves away from a conceptualization of the brain as either diseased or not, to a position of having to establish how severe and widespread are the pathological alterations. As a consequence, in old age, development may be placed on a continuum from normal ageing to dementia of the Alzheimer type, with BSF at an intermediate point on the continuum. However, while we can establish profiles of cognitive function and the ability to perform activities of daily living which have been correlated with the presence of plaques and tangles, as well as reduced acetylcholine levels (a neurotransmitter involved in the process of memory), it is not possible to establish definite biological markers until after death.

Risk factors

With age people move along the continuum. However, some people progress so slowly that even if they reached extreme old age they would not dement. The explanation for this may be that an older person's position on the continuum depends on their exposure to a number of risk factors. Unfortunately, epidemiological studies have identified very few of these risk factors so far and, aside from age (which is the most important risk factor for AD), none have been adequately established.

Family history. Despite methodological difficulties, reliable data suggest that first degree relatives (e.g. siblings, children) of AD victims do have a greater risk of developing the disease. Forty years ago, Kallman (1951) found that if one of a pair of non-identical twins develops dementia in later life, the risk of the other twin getting it is 8 per cent; whereas if the twins are identical, which means they are genetically the same, the risk increases to 43 per cent. Larsson *et al*, (1963) established the risk for senile dementia among first-degree relatives at 4.3 times greater than for the general population. Probably the most rigorous genetic study of AD is that of Heston (1981). He found that the risk to relatives varies greatly depending on the age which AD began. Genetic factors appear to decrease in significance with later age of onset in the index case.

Head trauma. Both early-onset and late-onset cases of AD are more likely to have experienced a serious head injury at some point in their lives. A single severe blow resulting in loss of consciousness can predispose someone to AD in later life. In most cases, this accident occurs several decades before the onset of dementia. Mortimer *et al.* (1985) found the average time elapsing between the head injury and the signs of dementia was thirty-five years. However, it needs to be borne in mind that information about head trauma often comes from relatives. They may more thoroughly review the life history of their loved one and exaggerate the significance of events as a means of coming to terms with the illness.

Environmental toxins. AD could be due to some toxic agent that affects the brain, which reacts by producing plaques and tangles. The most discussed possibility is aluminium. AD sufferers have been shown to have high levels of aluminium in their brains. Although aluminium is a common substance, in geographical areas where the aluminium content in the water supply is high, it is suggested there is a higher prevalence of AD. The case remains unproven, however, although the evidence continues to accumulate.

A dementia of unknown cause. The causes of AD remain unknown. No adequate theory of causation exists, just an awareness of confirmed risk factors. It is possible that there are several causes which act through a common mechanism to produce AD. Another possible explanation is that two or more of the potential causes must be present together to cause dementia. For example, a certain genetic profile may make people more vulnerable to toxic exposures. Neither factor in itself is sufficient to cause AD, but in combination they would do so.

Unfortunately, for the time being AD remains a devastating disease of unknown origin.

Clinical picture
The course of cognitive, behavioural and emotional change varies from person to person. However, while there is no common pathway, a stage model which describes broad characteristics is generally accepted. A typical AD dementia has an insidious onset with progression, which may not be easy to differentiate from normal or benign age-related changes.

The 'forgetfulness phase' (minimal dementia). Evidence of cognitive impairment is a necessary condition for the diagnosis of AD, and in the great majority of cases it is present at the earliest stage. At this point the most prominent feature is an impairment of memory for recent events and a tendency to forget where objects have been placed. Disorientation in time frequently occurs. Names of places and people which were once familiar may also be poorly recalled. Overall, the memory disorder is usually apparent as a mild forgetfulness.

Fatigue and poor concentration may be observed. The learning of new information is deficient. Abstract thinking shows signs of patchy impairment. The structure of conversational speech (e.g. phrase length, grammar) is relatively normal in the early stages of AD, but the speech content tends to be abnormal. There is an over-reliance on stock phrases and mild word-finding difficulties (known as anomia).

Aside from cognitive impairment, there are changes in mood, personality and adaptive behaviour. Huppert and Tym (1986) maintain that it is unlikely that all such changes are secondary to the cognitive deficit, but instead can be seen as direct manifestations of the underlying deterioration of the brain. The new or unexpected is feared or disliked. Sufferers lack curiosity and appear egocentric as they seek sanctuary in established routines. At this early stage activities of daily living in familiar surroundings are usually unimpaired, but when in new situations a shifting pattern of incompetence is revealed. Impairments become apparent more quickly if the person leads an active, varied life than if they have a routine lifestyle.

There may be emotional changes such as anxiety and irritability. While depression is often fleeting and variable, Alexopolous *et al.* (1988) recently estimated that up to 50 per cent of people with dementia may also suffer from depression. Reifler *et al.* (1982) noted that with progressively severe cognitive impairment the prevalence of depression decreases. Whereas 33 per cent of mildly impaired people were depressed, 23 per cent of those who were moderately impaired had depressive symptoms and only 12 per cent of those who were severely deteriorated were clinically depressed. However, in some people mood disturbance and anxiety are conspicuously absent. Gilleard (1984) notes that in such cases 'it is their apparent emotional indifference that is the more striking'. In the early stages of AD, most people display some form of insight into their impairments, although awareness is often less apparent in late-onset dementia. However, insight may be distorted by memory dysfunction, cultural expectation and psychological defence mechanisms. Reactions to the distressing changes may not simply manifest as appropriate concern, but instead result in the onset of additional psychopathology which may obscure the advancing cognitive decline. Denial may be used as a defence against the emotional trauma of losing one's intellectual capacity. The dementing person may also appear 'paranoid' as they attempt to avoid the frightening implications of a deteriorating memory: 'Making accusations against others to explain why items cannot be found or why an arrangement was forgotten can provide external sources of blame for internally caused errors' (Stokes, 1990b).

The 'confusional phase' (mild-moderate dementia). This stage is characterized by progressively failing memory, increasingly poor attention-span and a generalized decline in intellectual performance. Learning becomes increasingly impaired and retrieval of very familiar information from secondary memory store is affected. Disorientation in place can result in the person getting lost in unfamiliar surroundings. Forgetting internally produced plans and objectives is, in many ways, responsible for the discontinuity and lack of purpose that characterizes the dementia. Behaviour is seen to be increasingly random and disorganized.

All aspects of language become more impaired, especially knowledge of meaning, although structural features show slowest deterioration. Berrios (1987) notes that the interacting effects of memory loss, cognitive degeneration and perceptual dysfunction lead to a peculiar disintegration of spoken, written and read language in dementia. Defects in comprehension become evident.

Judgment and the capacity for abstract thought are significantly deteriorated. Parietal lobe (the two hemispheres of the cerebral cortex are divided into four areas, each known as a lobe) deficits such as apraxia and agnosia evolve. Apraxia is the impairment of the ability to carry out purposeful movements even though motor skills and comprehension of the action to be carried out are intact. Agnosia is a disorder of recognition which results in an inability to identify an object by sight alone. As Holden (1990) writes, it 'is not only an inability to name or demonstrate the use of an object without touching it, but also a lack of recognition of the object's meaning or character'. A person may be unable to recognize familiar faces (prosopagnosia). It appears that when prominent parietal lobe deficits are associated with AD it constitutes a more malignant variant usually resulting in early death.

Complex tasks are slovenly and inaccurately performed. Mistakes are not acknowledged or corrected. Skills necessary for social independence are the first to be markedly eroded, although during this stage basic self-care skills are also compromised. Behaviour is considered to be increasingly 'risky'. There is a withdrawal from demanding situations. Mood is characterized by emotional flattening. Indifference towards family news, apathy and a loss of interest in events in general is to be expected.

Rationalizations and confabulation (giving an imaginary account of activities and actions) are used to conceal failures of memory. The environment may be seen as threatening as demands exceed limited competence. Heightened confusion may result in disruptive behaviour such as wandering and aggression. While there is little empirical investigation of socially challenging behaviour, clinical impressions indicate that in part such disruptive actions are the consequence of an inability to articulate significant emotional needs.

The dementia phase (moderate-severe dementia). This can be defined as beginning at the point at which remaining intellectual and self-care abilities would no longer sustain survival if the person were left on their own. Profound difficulties in fundamental activities of daily living are the hallmarks of this phase. There is gross destruction of all intellectual capacities. Memory worsens to such an extent that personal history is eroded. As this stage progresses recognition of oneself and close relatives is lost. All aspects of language are severely impoverished and ultimately lost. Sufferers lose the urge or ability to practise intimate self-care skills and so need assistance in dressing, toileting and eating.

The dementing person is unaware of their experiences and surroundings. The personality is now submerged by the disease. There is a progressive physical wasting as the person declines to a state of passive, incoherent dependency. General motor abilities overtly decline. Ultimately, physical feebleness will mean they require help with walking. Life may continue for one or more years in an almost vegetative state. At this point the person is unable to control their bodily functions and is either chairbound or bedfast. Attention is not focused on stimuli, and the person appears to stare blankly and is invariably unresponsive.

Comment

Without longitudinal data, the temporal gradient in AD cannot be truly identified. However, clinical data based on cross-sectional methodology give general support to this stage approach. Progress through each of these stages is gradual. A person may spend several months, if not years, in each phase. Stokes and Holden (1990) note that while remorseless deterioration is inevitable, a surprising number of 'islands' of relatively intact ability may be found until late in the process. What functions are preserved and for how long will depend on the personal characteristics and history of the dementing person, as well as the encouragement received from supporters.

Multi-Infarct Dementia (MID)

With a few exceptions (e.g. Kay *et al.*, 1964a), the consensus is that late-onset AD is a considerably more common disorder than MID. It is estimated that as many as 60 per cent of older people with dementia suffer from AD (Tomlinson *et al.*, 1970), approximately 20 per cent have MID, and around 20 per cent have a mixed diagnosis of AD and MID (Sinex and Merril, 1982). In Japan, however, the most common cause of dementia is MID. Kay and Bergmann (1980) suggest that men are more prone to MID in 'young-old' age (65–74 years), whereas women mainly suffer from AD in 'old-old' age (75 or over). Most of these estimates are obtained from neurohistological data obtained at autopsy. There is no reliable distinction between AD and MID yet possible in field settings, and until reliable and valid criteria are established for the diagnosis of presumed cause, prevalence rates derived from epidemiological studies must be treated with caution.

Cerebral pathology

Despite possibly accounting for, or being implicated in 40 per cent of later-life dementia, MID has not been subject to anywhere near the same volume of research as AD. MID is a vascular dementia, and thus the old concept of cerebral arteriosclerosis was not completely wrong. Although restriction of the blood supply to the brain does not cause dementia, narrowing of the arteries has been found to make people more prone to stroke. In a stroke, or infarct, there is a blockage of an artery supplying blood to a region of the brain. After several strokes, sufficient brain tissue may be destroyed to result in dementia. Hackinski *et al.* (1974) labelled this form of dementia, multi-infarct dementia. At post-mortem the brain may present with a 'moth-eaten' appearance as the surface is marked by many infarcts.

Strokes do not always lead to dementia. Most often they produce quite specific deficits, the nature of which depends on the region of the brain affected. A person may even suffer several strokes without showing signs of dementia, despite evidence of marked physical disability. In contrast, a person can suffer from severe MID with only minor physical handicap. Pitt (1982) offers the explanation that in MID the cerebral infarcts mainly affect the smaller vessels nearer the brain's surface, and thus mainly spare the tracts lying deeper in the brain which govern movement.

Risk factors

Ageing. As with AD, the prevalence of MID rises sharply with age. There may also be a fall-off in the prevalence among people who survive past 90.

Family history. Parents and siblings of people with MID have a greater risk of developing the dementia themselves, although there is no data on whether the children of parents with MID are at greater risk.

High blood pressure. As has already been noted, not all stroke victims develop dementia. A comparison between stroke victims with and without dementia revealed that high blood pressure was the main difference between them. Ladurner *et al.* (1982) found that while 68 per cent of stroke patients with dementia had high blood pressure, only 23 per cent without dementia had raised blood pressure.

Stroke is much more common in Japan. This frequency is possibly related to high salt levels in the Japanese diet. Salt raises blood pressure, and as high blood pressure predisposes to stroke, this could be why MID is the most common cause of dementia in that country.

Life habits. Smoking and alcohol use are possibly related to MID. As a consequence it is possible that lifestyle changes may lead to a decline in its incidence. In fact there is good evidence from several countries that the incidence of stroke is declining (there was a decline of 37 per cent between 1968 and 1978 in the United States), and so it is almost certain the MID is on the decline as well.

Clinical picture
MID is a fluctuating and remitting dementia characterized by an abrupt onset. It is generally observed in the seventh and eighth decades of life, although it may occur as early as the mid-40s.

The course is typically that of a series of small strokes or 'strokelets' which vary in frequency, intensity and location from individual to individual. They cause episodes of confusion and loss of specific cognitive function, sometimes associated with minor neurological signs (e.g. slurring of speech, weakness down one side of the body). After the infarct there is usually limited clinical improvement until the next episode, which sometimes takes place in a matter of weeks or months, and sometimes not for more than a year.

Although the vascular disease is extensive, the cortex is less uniformly affected than in AD. As a consequence the clinical picture is patchy, inconsistent and at times intriguing. Certain intellectual functions are significantly deteriorated, while others are unimpaired. Emotions are often labile and weeping may be induced easily. Not all emotionalism is shallow, however. There is a relative preservation of personality and insight, and as a consequence profound depression is more frequently encountered.

Eventually, after a succession of infarcts there is less and less recovery, until by a process of 'step wise' deterioration, dementia as widespread as AD develops. However, many victims die before they reach the stage of advanced dementia, most often from a major stroke.

Psychological Models of Dementia

Although many investigators consider that dementia 'is a unique clinical syndrome with a characteristic onset and progression' (Reisberg *et al.*, 1982), this commonly accepted model, which assumes a simple linear causal relationship between neuropathology and dementia fails to acknowledge that in dementia the origins of behaviour remain complex. Although the underlying pathology eventually determines 'a homogenous pathway of ultimate decline' (Gilleard, 1984), in the early stages of dementia psychogenic and environmental factors will influence the rate and pattern of decline. As a consequence, an interactionist model is required in order to explain the heterogeneity of behaviour in dementia. Environmental and psychological factors do not cause dementia, but they offer an explanation for the individual behavioural consequences of the presumptive disease. As such they challenge the determinism and pessimism that pervade the accepted 'medical-disease' model.

While it is often assumed that brain pathology is a sufficient explanation of the behaviour observed in dementia, Kitwood (1989) reports that the correlations between the degree of dementia and the extent of neuropathological change established at post mortem leaves 'some 80 per cent of the variance unexplored in moderate or severe dementia'. Without doubt, the dementing illness is inextricably woven into the pattern of an individual's life history, personality, physical health, social relationships and environmental circumstances. Sensory deprivation arising from visual and auditory handicaps and unstimulating environments may interact with and exacerbate memory dysfunction to produce heightened confusion. A failure to support and encourage adaptive behaviours in the dementing person's environment will lead to progressive dependency. The means by which a sufferer from dementia seeks to cope with 'a kind of psychological pain whose persistence and intensity we can scarcely envisage' (Kitwood, 1989) may influence cognitive performance. Too often the experience of dementia is regarded as a passive process and as such the importance of the reaction of the dementing person to the disorder is underestimated.

In an attempt to synthesize the biological, psychological and environmental levels into a single framework, Stokes and Allen (1990) propose a model of the 'multiple pathway to behaviour'. The model illustrates how each of the 'pathways' needs to be considered when seeking an explanation as to why a dementing person displays a particular behaviour or loss of function. Similarly, Kitwood (1990) has developed these basic equations:

$$SD = NI + MSP$$

(Senile Dementia is compounded from the effects of Neurological Impairment and of Malignant Social Psychology).

$$(NI)a \leftarrow MSP$$

(Neurological Impairment in an elderly person attracts to itself a Malignant Social Psychology).

Kitwood (1990) sees malignant social psychology as being the process by which the sufferer from dementia is depersonalized, disempowered, labelled and stigmatized. As a result, behaviour deteriorates and expectations of progressive decline set up a self-fulfilling prophecy. The tragedy is that 'the malignant social psychology is so much a part of the taken-for-granted world of later life that it generally passes unnoticed' (Kitwood, 1990). Identifying the interactionist nature of the dementia process introduces a more effective understanding of dementing behaviour, which 'is much closer to real life than those rather abstract schemes which aim to classify the various 'stages of dementia', as if the dementing process were a simple consequence of an advancing pathology in the brain tissue' (Kitwood, 1990).

The psychological models of the dementing process described in this section not only have greater explanatory power than do the simple disease model, they also enable us to see how psychological intervention may help sufferers from dementia regain 'lost' behaviours or functions.

Psychological Intervention in Dementia

In the absence of a cure for the presumptive diseases, it is encouraging to see the rapid growth of interest in developing psychological strategies for working with dementing people. The principles of rehabilitation and relearning, namely 'helping someone reach his or her highest attainable level of skill and function' (Reifler and Teri, 1986) are relevant and essential to the special needs of people with dementia. While the concept of rehabilitation for people with dementia is comparatively new, thirty years ago the first steps were being taken in the United States with the development of Reality Orientation (Taulbee and Folsom, 1966). This is a therapeutic method which increases motivation and reduces dependency through the use of cued recall. It uses the repeated presentation of verbal information and environmental cues such as memory boards, colour coding and directional signs to correct confused behaviour and to enhance the elderly person's ability to live as independently as possible within their environment.

In the last ten years there has been a huge growth of interest in psychological approaches to 'therapy' and management. The development of Reminiscence Therapy, which is in part based on the life review concept of Butler (1963), has become increasingly popular, as has the development of individual care planning to help dementing people regain skills in specific areas such as self-care and toileting, as well as providing strategies to manage problem behaviour such as aggression and wandering.

As a person's behaviour is the product of an interaction between individual attributes and environmental influences, an essential aspect of the psychological approach to rehabilitation is effecting change in the quality of social interactions and the design of the built environment. A dominant concept in achieving enabling environments that are not devaluing or demeaning, but instead promote dignity, individuality and self-determination is *normalization*. The principle of normalization is the use of means which are valued in our society to achieve and support age-appropriate and valued lifestyles and living arrangements for disabled people.

Increasingly, interest is also being shown in the internal, emotional world of the dementia sufferer with the development by Goudie and Stokes (1989) of Resolution Therapy, a method of counselling people suffering from organic dementia. The underlying premise is that the cerebral pathology acts as a barrier between the dementia sufferer and their social environment, and thus the disorientated messages received and the confused behaviour observed by others are possibly forlorn attempts to express emotional needs, such as a need for security, tenderness or respect. When these actions are misinterpreted and emotional needs are not met, the outcome may be behaviour that is labelled as disruptive and difficult.

To summarize, the psychological analysis and management of dementia has considerable potential. Many of the methods of intervention remain unproven, and thus there is a definite need for evaluation of therapeutic interventions. Yet with the continuing creative application of psychological theory and practice to the needs of older dementing people, it is to be hoped that clinical psychologists will continue to build on the current utility of their interventions.

Chapter 15

Emotional Disorder and
Physical Disability in Later Life

This volume has challenged the prejudice which typically surrounds old age. However, it would be a pointless exercise to replace distortion and myth with unrealistic expectation. Thus, a section on abnormal ageing must cover not only dementia, but to ensure a balanced perspective must also examine other disorders and disabilities of later life which are of either psychological origin or have major psychological sequelae and result in a minority of older people becoming the casualties of ageing.

Epidemiology

Mental Illness

'The older we get the more liable we are to mental disorder' (Pitt, 1982), yet the mental health problems of elderly people have only been seriously considered comparatively recently. In many ways this was because the obvious evidence of the physical effects of ageing led to the acceptance of an inevitable parallel decline in psychological well-being. Since the pioneering work by Roth (1955) in hospital settings and Kay *et al.* (1964a) in the community of Newcastle-upon-Tyne, England, an appreciation of the epidemiology of mental disorders among aged adults has grown. Kay *et al.* established that around 15 per cent of older people in their sample had a functional mental illness (i.e. neurotic, paranoid and depressive disorders) or personality disorder of at least moderate severity.

The chance of admission to psychiatric hospital increases sharply in later life, especially for women. Pitt (1982) reports that the first admission rate to mental hospitals in those over 75 is more than double that in midlife, while one in four adults admitted to hospital are 65 or over. Yet only the minority of elderly people with mental disorders are cared for or receive treatment in psychiatric hospitals. Ouslander and Beck (1982) note that 20 per cent of older adults living at home receive some psychotropic medication, of whom only 1 per cent are under the care of a psychiatrist. In a pioneering community survey, Williamson *et al.* (1964), in a random sample of people 65 or over living at home, found 27 per cent were suffering from a functional psychiatric disorder, most of which were not known to their general practitioners.

Obviously, not all these people are suffering from mental health problems of ageing as a consequence of maladjustment in later life. Many are, in fact, ageing problems reflecting unresolved difficulties and a continuation of earlier issues. In such cases recovery and restoration of mental health is improbable.

Although some of the mental health difficulties encountered in old age are similar to problems of adjustment experienced by younger people, the circumstances of older adults can make some distinguishable in significant ways. As LaRue *et al.* (1985) describe, younger people rarely present 'with emotional or cognitive problems who are also affected by multiple chronic physical illnesses, taking several types of medication, and adjusting to a series of potentially traumatic life changes', as can be the situation for some elderly people. Furthermore, sensory handicaps are common in later life. The majority of people registered as blind, partially sighted or hard of hearing are elderly. Not only does the presence of serious sensory deficits often make diagnosis of certain conditions, such as dementia, difficult, some psychological problems in later life, for example, mild paranoia, can develop from age-related losses.

Physical Ill-Health and Disability

The major physical illnesses encountered in old age are heart disease, cancer, stroke, bronchitis and diabetes. Not only do elderly people more frequently suffer from a variety of illnesses when compared with younger people, the diseases and disorders are often experienced simultaneously rather than sequentially. Sloane (1980) reported that 86 per cent of people aged 65 or over have one or more chronic health problem. In the survey by Williamson *et al.* (1964), they considered their 'most striking observation was the frequency of multiple disabilities'. Only 4 per cent of their sample were disability free. On the other hand, 9.5 per cent were either bedridden, immobile or capable of only limited indoor mobility. Most of the disabilities unknown to GPs were slight or moderately severe, suggesting that most older people do not report their complaints to their GPs until the condition is well-advanced. The conclusion must be that a family practitioner service based on the self-reporting of illness is likely to be seriously deficient in meeting the health needs of older adults.

Woods and Britton (1985) report that half the hospital in-patient population in the United Kingdom is aged 65 or over. Sanford (1975) notes that 12 per cent of geriatric admissions are for patients whose relatives or friends can no longer cope with them at home.

The volume of medication prescribed to elderly people is high. Approximately 25 per cent of all prescriptions are made out to older adults. In addition, rates of self-medication are also high. Not surprisingly, 20 per cent of deaths by accidental poisoning from medication occur in elderly people.

While the devastating nature of irreversible dementia focuses attention on this condition, there are clearly other problems of health in later life which have profound psychological effects. As McCally *et al.* (1984) state, there now exists 'an unprecedented new population of persons suffering from multiple chronic illnesses, functional disabilities and dependence'. Unfortunately, we are often unaware of the psychological sequelae of many of the disabling physical ailments commonly found in later life.

Problems of Psychological Health

Depression

Prevalence

Depression is the most common emotional disorder affecting elderly people, yet too often it is regarded as an inevitable feature of old age rather than a potentially treatable condition. As we have already seen (p. 22) depression in old age is a vague and difficult concept to grasp, with no consensus regarding typology or aetiology, and so efforts to establish prevalence rates are somewhat unreliable. Investigators adopt different criteria for case definition, some including transient changes in mood, others focusing on the syndrome of major depression.

Stenback (1980) considers that epidemiological data 'point to a prevalence of 20–25 per cent of depressive states in the old population'. In a survey by Murphy (1982), about 30 per cent of elderly people were found to be moderately or severely depressed. Estimates of the rates of severe levels of depression only are typically in the range between 2 and 5 per cent (e.g. Blazer, 1980). Most studies find higher rates of depression in women (e.g. Copeland *et al.*, 1987).

States of depression are clearly common in later life, but they are not more common in older people. It is possible, however, especially in instances of mild depression, that the condition is underdiagnosed. Balier (1968, cited by Stenback, 1980) comments that depression in later life is often unnoticed behind a barrier of social isolation, inactivity, fatigue and health complaints which are either wrongly attributed to 'normal' ageing or are put down to physical illness.

Origins of depression

Life experiences. Murphy (1982) compared elderly depressed adults with 'normal' people of the same age and found the former were more likely to have experienced major stressful life events, such as the death of or serious illness in someone close. They were more likely to have housing problems and relationship difficulties. Those who were most vulnerable were those who lacked a close, confiding relationship to act as a buffer at times of adversity.

Brown and Harris (1978) established that what may precede the onset of depression is an accumulation of mostly minor adverse life experiences. Stenback (1980) considers that depression is not necessarily the outcome of distressing loss, but the consequence of a loss of futurism. A limited forward time perspective may mean the person considers it is not worthwhile to attempt to find replacements for losses experienced.

Negative emotion is a natural response to loss, dissatisfaction and disappointment. It is only characteristic of a pathological emotional disorder when it is out of proportion, in terms of severity or duration, or both, and impairs personal and social functioning. An extreme emotional reaction to adverse personal or social circumstances, as distinct from low morale or life dissatisfaction, is often defined as a 'reactive depression'. In a study of one hundred patients with depression, Post (1962) found a precipitating factor in 65 per cent of cases. A significant question is, why is it that most people can cope with the vagaries of life, while 'the prospective depression patient [is] unable to rise after the smarting blow'? (Stenback, 1980).

Cultural factors. The prevailing negative attitudes, prejudice and stereotypes about old age in western industrial societies lower self-esteem, invoke a sense of uselessness and produce a state of depressed mood.

Physical illness. Poor physical health is also related to depression. Kay *et al.* (1964b) found moderate or severe physical disability in 41 per cent of their elderly sample with functional mental illness, compared with 16 per cent among their 'normal' group. The impact of poor health on mood may be mediated by the inability to perform personally significant activities.

Cerebral changes in depression. Although social circumstances appear to be significant risk factors, a biological basis of depression cannot be denied. Some older people experience no adverse circumstances prior to their depression, which may indicate a biological predisposition to depressive illness. This is often referred to as an 'endogenous' depression.

The question of how organic brain changes are related to the emergence of depression in later life is old and as yet unresolved. As early as the fifth century BC, Hippocrates considered that depression was due to a biological factor, namely black bile. Contemporary work suggests that when depression occurs for the first time in later life, it is more likely to be associated with degenerative brain changes than if depression occurs earlier in life. Reding *et al.* (1985) found that 57 per cent of depressed elderly people developed dementia within three years of the depression being diagnosed. Whether the depression represents a reaction to the insidious onset of the dementia, or is related to the same biological changes as the presumptive dementing illness is unclear.

Heredity. Heredity is a factor, for there is a family history of major depression in 44 per cent of those developing the disorder after 65 (Pitt, 1982). However it appears that heredity is of less significance in late-onset depression than in episodes of depressive disorder in early adult life.

Comment. The aetiology of depression is likely to be multi-factorial. Cunningham and Brookbank (1988) suggest that 'a person could be vulnerable to depression in an organic sense, but that a strongly negative life event may be necessary to trigger a latent depressive response'. What is certain is that the causes of depression can only be understood in terms of an interplay between a number of elements — life experience, social support, physical health, biochemistry, cerebral changes, genetics and psychological factors.

Psychological models of depression
Various psychological theories have been developed to explain the onset and maintenance of depression.

Learned helplessness. Seligman (1975) proposes that depression arises as a result of believing that life events are beyond control. Faced with the role transitions and losses in later life, older adults may feel impotent to influence events and a pervasive sense of helplessness may result. Given that many of the losses associated with ageing are independent of the aged person's actions (e.g. loss of occupation, income, status, health, spouse, family, friends and possibly home) it is easy to see how the belief in the uncontrollability of life may arise. The subsequent decline in mood, characterized by hopelessness and helplessness, may lead the elderly person to give up activities of which they are quite capable, and which could have contradicted the belief of uncontrollability.

The theory of learned helplessness has been developed to take into account the person's perception of who or what is responsible for the absence of control. It is felt that the locus of attribution for their helplessness influences the severity and duration of the mood disturbance following the distressing life experience(s). If the person blames her/himself, the effects will be worse than if a transitory external influence is held responsible. Mood disturbance is greatest when the desirability of the situation that cannot be controlled is high, when the certainty of uncontrollability is strong and when the uncontrollable event presages a general deterioration in the quality of life (Woods and Britton, 1985). Once depression arises, Goudie (1990b) notes that positive life experiences are perceived as being uncontrollable and happening rarely, rather than within their control and constituting enduring aspects of their life. Depression is thereby maintained.

Several studies have shown a correlation between controllability and depression in later life. Reid *et al.* (1977) demonstrated an inverse relationship between the extent to which people attain the control they desire over their lives and depressed mood. There is possibly a sex difference, insomuch as the association between controllability and mood is stronger in elderly men (Hanes and Wild, 1977).

A synthesis of the learned helplessness model, attributional style and the 'locus of control' construct of Rotter (1966) may provide us with a valuable insight into later life maladjustment. Does a person's belief that they can generally control their environment and future destiny lead them also to selecting an internal cause for their helplessness when 'life goes wrong'? As we saw earlier (p. 88), internal control expectancies may hold up well in elderly people. While these expectations may contribute to positive adjustment in old age, it may not be so when confronted with adverse life circumstances. A generalized expectation that they control events may result in internal attribution for their misfortune. Focusing on perceived inner failings can then lead to a more serious decline in mood.

Loss of social reinforcement.   Lewinsohn (1974) believes that loss of mastery over and pleasure in life's activities, especially those which provide access to social rewards, can be associated with the development and maintenance of depression. A reduction in the availability of social reinforcement in the environment, or reduced activity in later life because of role transitions or failing health, may lead to depressed mood. Not only may participation in potentially reinforcing events be denied because they are deemed age-inappropriate, but involvement in formerly enjoyable social activities may be diminished or lose its impact as a source of reinforcement because of pain, illness or reduction in physical mobility. Even the most simple of activities may be an unwelcome effort, rendering them punitive rather than positively reinforcing behaviours.

Depression may result in social avoidance. Withdrawal from social activity further reduces a person's prospects of being in receipt of positive reinforcement, and mood continues to deteriorate. However, we have already seen that the activity and disengagement theories of adjustment in old age are somewhat simplistic. We cannot naively equate activity with psychological health and social withdrawal with depression. For example, research demonstrates that the relationship between engagement and depression is not significant (Simpson *et al.*, 1981; Davies and Gledhill, 1983). The critical variables are how a person perceives, thinks and feels about activity in old age. As Woods and Britton (1985) note, passive behaviour, such as reminiscing or onlooking, may be preferred by some elderly adults to more active social engagement. Thus, Lewinsohn's behavioural model can only further our understanding of why many people become depressed for the first time in later life if cognitive factors are included in the equation. Only then will an awareness of observable behaviour be complemented by an appreciation of the value placed on engagement.

Life review.   In Chapter 3 the life review theory of Butler (1963) was discussed. While successful review may lead to the achievement of positive adjustment in old age, depression may be the process outcome if historical conflicts cannot be either resolved or accepted. Present circumstances may have little bearing on the prospects for success and current mood.

Cognitive theory.   Beck (1967) maintains that depression is a consequence of a negative cognitive appraisal of self, environment and future. A person has a 'negative cognitive set' which distorts the experience of life. They overgeneralize, so a circumscribed failure becomes an all-embracing principle. Only the negative aspects of an experience are perceived, while a moment of success or enjoyment is degraded or dismissed as chance experience. When cause is being established, misattributions occur. In addition, a person may restructure their belief system so that dysfunctional attitudes toward the past are adopted. Eventually, the negative cognitions are repeated as 'automatic thoughts', thereby helping to maintain the depressed mood.

It is clear that cognitive distortions are present in depression, but do they lead to depressed mood or are they simply associated with the condition? Woods and Britton (1985) believe that a coming together of cognitive theory and the model of learned helplessness provides ' a clear mechanism for understanding how stressful life-events, like a bereavement or physical ill health, can lead to depression in elderly people'. The experience of adverse life circumstances generates a negative view of the world and future and leads to general and stable attributions of helplessness being made.

Depressive pseudodementia

In some instances, depression in later life is accompanied by a number of alterations in memory and intellectual function. The changes can be so profound that the person becomes disorientated, forgetful and unable to care for themselves. The more severe the depression, the greater the cognitive impairment. However, the cognitive deficits are invariably inconsistent, patchy and fluctuate over time.

Unfortunately, depressive pseudodementia is frequently confused with Alzheimer's disease. The tragedy is that with appropriate antidepressant treatment the cognitive impairments associated with severe depression are often reversible, unlike those associated with AD. In an Australian study, Smith and Kiloh (1981) found that 5 per cent of patients admitted to hospital with 'dementia' were suffering from depression.

Prognosis

Pessimism has long been typical of the attitude toward therapeutic approaches for depression in later life. The reasons for this sense of therapeutic nihilism are complex. Woods and Britton (1985) believe some elderly people are simple 'written off'. Cumulative losses, poor physical health, anticipated decline in intellectual functioning as part of the 'normal' ageing process and the 'rigidity' of old age which prevents shifts in attitude and perspective are seen as precluding the likelihood of significant improvement. Post (1962) observed that 46 per cent of his sample of depressed elderly patients showed sustained emotional decline, for 35 per cent life remained tolerable despite subsequent periods of emotional disturbance, and only 19 per cent revealed no detrimental long-term effects. Similar findings were reported in Post's later study (1972). Murphy (1983) found that only one-third of depressed elderly people recovered and did not subsequently relapse. At a 4-year follow-up, Murphy *et al.* (1988) identified increased mortality in elderly depressed patients even after allowing for the severity of coexistent physical illness.

Despite what Woods and Britton (1985) call the 'gerophobia' of therapists, there is increasing evidence that psychological therapies can benefit older people (e.g. Gallagher and Thompson, 1983), if the content areas of therapy are 'modified to take physical and psychological issues relevant to the ageing process into account' (Goudie, 1990c). Not only do Nemiroff and Colarusso (1985) consider that elderly people are good candidates for psychotherapy, Knight (1983) suggests that in some cases older adults may respond better than younger patients.

It is probable that elderly people do not traditionally respond well to therapeutic intervention because they typically present themselves (or are presented) for treatment when their emotional disorder has become chronic, at which time they are offered treatments which are not tailored to their specific needs. For example, while antidepressant medication is useful with many older depressed people, in instances of reactive depression if medication is the only therapeutic response it is rarely of value. Plopper (1990) suggests that effective treatment requires a multifocal approach, including psychological therapy, family and social intervention and, when indicated, pharmacological treatment.

Suicide
Suicides are disproportionately common among older people although Stenback (1980) argues that the general belief that the frequency of suicide rises with age is incorrect. While this increase occurs in many countries, such as England and Wales, especially for men (McClure, 1984), the overall picture suggests there is 'no regular relationship between higher rates and higher age'. Addario (1990) points to a decrease in both suicide attempts and completed suicides in women 65 or over.

While elderly people constitute around 15 per cent of the UK population, approximately 25 per cent of all suicides involve people 65 or over (Lindesay, 1986). It is possible, however, that attempted suicide is less common in this age group. In other words, if an elderly person is intent on committing suicide they are much more likely to carry out the act successfully than a younger person. This 'success' is partly because of physical frailty, partly a result of greater opportunity and possibly most significantly, because depression in later life is either not recognized or responded to by others, being seen instead as a 'normal' concomitant of ageing.

In comparison with younger people who commit suicide, fewer older suicides are of unstable personality (Pitt, 1982). The majority are suffering from depression, most of whom will not be receiving treatment for their emotional disorder (Barraclough, 1971). An elderly man living alone, with a history of social isolation and in poor physical health is a great suicide risk. Chronic alcoholism especially heightens the risk (Addario, 1990). Sainsbury (1955) found moving house for elderly men was a risk factor, suicides often taking place within two years after the move. As noted in Chapter 10, rates of suicide are higher among widowed than among married elderly people.

Sainsbury (1955) estimated that physical illness contributed toward suicide in 35 per cent of elderly cases, compared with 27 per cent of those in middle age and 10 per cent in young people. In an analysis of suicide notes, Kulawick and Decke (1973, cited by Stenback, 1980) found physical illness most frequently mentioned, especially for elderly women. The relationship between ill health and suicide is complex, however, and is often mediated by pain (Cattell, 1988).

Although social isolation and loneliness are frequently cited as precipitants of suicidal behaviour (e.g. Cattell, 1990), Stenback (1980) found that suicidal intent was not associated with the frequency of social contact, but with the intimacy experienced in social relationships ('qualitative isolation').

Anxiety

Prevalence

There have been few estimates of the prevalence of anxiety in old age, and differences in definition have resulted in a wide range of results. In the UK, Lindesay *et al.* (1989) established a prevalence rate for generalized anxiety of 3.7 per cent, with the highest rate among women 75 or over (4.6 per cent). As is often observed, anxiety was significantly correlated with depression.

Phobic anxiety (particularly agoraphobia) is relatively common among elderly people, particularly women, with a recorded prevalence rate of around 10 per cent (Lindesay *et al.*, 1989). However, as with generalized anxiety, the rates reported for phobias are varied, with some studies revealing much lower prevalence. Such variation may again be the result of differences in case definition, for example differences in severity criteria.

Clinical picture

In old age, generalized anxiety (often labelled 'free-floating' anxiety) is often not considered as a cause of dependency in activities of daily living. Anxiety, like unhappiness, is a normal reaction. However, a state of intense and enduring anxiety that acts as a handicap in everyday life whether it be generalized, associated with specific phobias or related to fear of physical disease is evidence of an emotional disorder. In old age, an episode of ill-health or trauma is a common precipitant of neurotic anxiety. If left undiagnosed and untreated, functional decrements may be attributed to intellectual decline (Goudie, 1990c). The symptoms of anxiety — restlessness, perspiring, heart palpitations, poor appetite, feelings of nausea and diarrhoea, sleep disturbance, butterflies in the stomach, muscle tension, hyperventilation and abnormal bodily sensations — often mimic problems of poor physical health, and are as a consequence often misdiagnosed.

Attacks of acute anxiety may be associated with particular events. Phobic anxiety is also often unrecognized, as 'disabling fears in old people may be dismissed by the subject, their family and others as being "reasonable for their age"' (Lindesay *et al.*, 1989). In order to avoid panic, and gain security and reassurance, the phobic situation has to be avoided. This may result in a flight from reason. Avoidance behaviour may be a significant reason why some elderly people become housebound. Exton-Smith *et al.* (1976) found that 20 per cent of housebound elderly adults had no physical reason for their functional impairment, with 'nervousness' and 'loss of confidence' being given as explanations instead. The onset of the problem may be traced to a specific incident, such as a fall when outside the house. However as Lindesay *et al.* (1989) note, while older people are justifiably cautious about dangers in their environment (such as the fear of street crime), there is no reason to expect that 'a chronic state of fear with disabling generalised avoidance is a normal or inevitable consequence of the ageing process'.

Paraphrenia

Paraphrenia is a schizophrenic-like illness occurring first in late life, and affecting perhaps 1 or 2 per cent of people aged 65 or over. Although in terms of prevalence it is less common than either dementia or depression, because of the disruptive nature of the condition almost every sufferer is likely to create considerable problems sooner or later (Post, 1980), and thus bring their maladaptive behaviour to the attention of family, neighbours and health professionals.

Clinical picture

Paranoid phenomena are the prominent features of paraphrenia. The sufferer is tormented by circumscribed delusional ideas of a persecutory nature. The focus of their paranoia is typically a neighbour whose 'voice' they hear giving instructions or providing a commentary on their activity. The delusions are not attributed to the whole neighbourhood or people in general, but solely involve the neighbour, who is believed to be spying upon or robbing the paraphrenic. Erotic delusions are also common. The person may be able to escape from the increasingly intrusive auditory hallucinations if they go out, but sometimes they pursue sufferers wherever they go.

Surprisingly, the experience of sustained delusions and auditory hallucinations does not lead to a major disintegration of personality. In the early stages of the illness the person may be able to live a relatively normal life. Intellectual functioning may be only mildly impaired (Hymas *et al.*, 1989), while confusion is never a consequence of paraphrenia. There is no insight into the illness, however.

As the psychotic phenomena progressively dominate their waking hours, behaviour becomes increasingly bizarre and the sufferer is unable to carry out the activities of daily living effectively. The build-up of extraordinary suspiciousness and persecutory beliefs can result in complaints to the police, abuse of supposed persecutors or entry into a state of siege. If they enter a state of siege, they may refuse to open the front door to visitors, may operate under the cover of darkness to avoid observation and may become wary of eating in case their food has been contaminated. As a consequence, self-neglect is a prominent clinical feature. Sometimes the elderly person is so frightened of their 'persecutor', they move away. Unfortunately, after a period of relief the delusions reappear, this time localized on a new neighbour.

Pitt (1982) describes untreated paraphrenia as running a chronic, unremitting course, which once fully developed is likely to continue unchanged until the person's death. However, because the disorder is so intrusive, it is unlikely to be unnoticed by others and remained untreated. The condition usually improves in response to drug treatment. Post (1966) found that of seventy-one paraphrenic patients, 20 per cent recovered fully, 41 per cent recovered, but without complete insight, 31 per cent made social recoveries only, retaining some of their delusions, and 8 per cent made no improvement at all. Prognosis is closely linked to the maintenance of drug treatment.

Risk factors

Post (1980) considers the causes of paranoid disorders in later life are 'little known'. Kay and Roth (1961) found the typical paraphrenic patient to be female, socially isolated, partially deaf and eccentric, but without a past history of serious psychiatric illness until pathological suspiciousness developed in later life.

Paraphrenic patients often have an atypical interpersonal history. They have a low marriage rate. Sometimes marriage was delayed until an unusually late age. Thus, the life of paraphrenic patients is characterized by a relative fail-ure in intimate relationships, resulting in fragile or absent interpersonal con-tacts in later life.

There is ample evidence of an association between paraphrenia and poor hearing. The illness may be precipitated by sensory deprivation, or as Cooper *et al.* (1976) maintain, deafness may be a causal mechanism arising from the impact hearing impairments have on psychological functioning and social adaptation.

Alcohol-Related Problems

Prevalence and definition

'An alcoholic is a person whose dependence upon alcohol has reached a degree such that it interferes with his (sic) health, interpersonal relationships, social adjustment, and economic functioning' (Simon, 1980). It is not only a physical problem, but it also has a profound detrimental effect on psychological and social performance.

While few studies have been made of alcoholism in old age, James (1983) believes that alcohol may result in more problems in elderly people than has been realized. Similarly, Mishara and Kastenbaum (1980) identify a seemingly growing problem of alcoholism among older adults in the United States. Although the incidence of alcoholism may decline with age, the number of alcoholics in later life is significant. Hopson-Walker (1990) calculates that about 10 per cent of elderly people in the United States have an alcohol-related problem, with men outnumbering women at the rate of twelve to one in alcohol abuse. Overall, the issue of alcohol-related problems in later life represents the survival of early-onset alcoholics (prior to age 40), the preva-lence of late-onset alcoholism (people who began having problems in their 40s and 50s) and the practice of heavy drinking in old age. The group classified by Barnes (1982) as heavier drinkers included 14 per cent of men and 7 per cent of women aged 60 or over.

It appears that there is a significant proportion of women who increase their alcohol consumption in their 70s (Goudie, 1990c), while for a man meta-bolic changes in later life can mean that alcohol may have a more pronounced effect than it used to. A major issue is the extent to which the problem of alcohol misuse in later life is underdiagnosed. Presenting difficulties (e.g. social isolation, falls, physical malaise, intellectual deterioration) are frequently unrecognized as alcohol-related. Performance changes may be attributed to anxiety, depression, physical illness or even the process of 'normal' ageing.

Attempts have been made to associate heavy drinking with later-life adjustments. However, no correlation has been identified in men or women between alcohol use and death of a spouse, retirement, degree of life satisfaction, activity levels and state of health. The age of onset of heavy drinking tends to be later in women, who also tend to be solitary, rather than social drinkers.

Data on the number of elderly alcoholics are few and much remains to be learned about the correlates of alcoholism in old age. Alcoholism, as distinct from heavy drinking, has been associated, however, with a range of adverse life events. The majority of actively drinking elderly alcoholics suffer from late-onset alcoholism, which has been associated with depression, bereavement, loneliness, marital disharmony and physical illness. Although psychological problems are invariably present,the co-existence of alcoholism and emotional disorder cannot prove causation. Overall, elderly alcoholics cannot be considered to constitute a homogeneous group.

Cognitive change
Aside from the transient confusion and disorientation associated with bouts of heavy drinking, the chronic consumption of alcohol over many years can lead to damage of the cerebral cortex and progressive intellectual deterioration. Psychological studies of elderly alcoholics suggests that cognitive impairments are apparent on a wide range of tasks. Overall, general intelligence is impaired compared with both younger alcoholics and their age cohorts. While some of the intellectual deficits are reversible, prolonged alcohol abuse can lead to a progressive dementia similar to Alzheimer's disease. Alcohol-related dementia can be distinguished from another alcohol-induced problem known as Korsakoff's disease which also produces memory loss. However, general intellectual performance is not affected in Korsakoff's disease, nor is there progressive memory decline resulting in the destruction of remote memory and a sense of self as it observed in Alzheimer's disease. The affected person is alert, has no insight into their condition, and their memory loss may be obscured by the person's ability to confabulate. Within the limits of their memory dysfunction, reasoning and judgment are often unimpaired. If Korsakoff's disease is identified and treated early enough some remission is possible.

Physical Disease and Disability

Most of the physical diseases of old age are rarely placed in a framework of psychological theory, and thus insights are few. For example we are poorly equipped to understand the psychological correlates of diabetes or arthritis. However, the psychological sequelae of some illnesses commonly encountered in geriatric medicine are better understood.

Parkinson's Disease (PD)

In 1817 James Parkinson first described the disease which now bears his name. It is the most common degenerative neurological disease that results in progressive impairment of mobility in older people. The prevalence rate is approximately 1.5 per cent (Agid *et al.* 1986), with the disease predominating among men. With age, prevalence increases. Two-thirds of people with PD show the first sign of symptoms between the ages of 50 and 69 (Goudie, 1990c). The cardinal features of PD are impoverished and slow movements, rigidity, tremor, gait disorder, postural instability and, in some people, marked cognitive decline. With treatment survival for between ten and fifteen years after onset is common. It is even possible that life expectancy may not be reduced.

The discovery by Hornykiewicz (1982) of a striking reduction in the neurotransmitter, dopamine, led to the introduction of a drug (levodopa) as a successful treatment for PD. However, recent findings suggest that while levodopa provides symptom relief, it does not stop the progress of the disease.

Depression is often reported in PD and is considered an integral part of the disease. Forty per cent of PD sufferers have been found to have depression. This may be related to problems of adjustment to a debilitating illness, or possibly to a chemical imbalance caused by the disease which increases the person's susceptibility to depression.

The prevalence of intellectual impairment in PD is a longstanding subject of investigation. Originally, cognitive changes were thought to be absent in PD. However, Agid *et al.* (1986) consider that a minimum of 20 per cent of people with PD develop dementia, while Boller (1980) reports that it is an even more frequent (30 to 50 per cent) feature of the disease. Pirozzollo *et al.* (1982) go so far as to assert that sensitive psychological testing reveals that all PD patients show some degree of cognitive deterioration.

Although intellectual performance may be affected by tremor and retardation of movement, the obvious PD motor disorders cannot wholly explain the range of observed cognitive dysfunction. Similarly, the association between depression and intellectual impairment in PD appears weak or non-existent (Oyebode *et al.*, 1986).

To explain the intellectual deterioration that has been observed in PD, reference has been made to the role of alterations in the brain. Controversy remains, however, as to whether the profound cognitive changes seen in PD are typical of Alzheimer's disease or whether they constitute a distinct sub-cortical dementia produced by diseases of the sub-cortex (for example, Parkinson's disease).

Boller (1983) concluded that there is considerable evidence from both neuropathological and clinical studies suggesting that a sizeable number of PD patients demonstrate changes indistinguishable from AD. Very little is known as to why PD and AD (which is a disease of the cerebral cortex) should co-exist, other than to say they may share a common pathogenic mechanism. Boller *et al.* (1980) found that all PD patients with severe dementia had cortical degeneration compatible with a neuropathological diagnosis of AD. If future studies are to confirm the association between the two diseases, they need to establish whether the existence of cerebral cortical degeneration is more extensive in the brains of people with PD than in the brains of age-matched controls, and prevalence is greater than chance alone would predict.

Oyebode *et al.* (1986) argue that the true prevalence of dementia of the Alzheimer type in PD is significantly lower than was originally thought. They demonstrated that in only 7 per cent of cases were the cognitive deficits typical of AD. While the prevalence rate is higher than that expected in the general population, it appears that the significant cognitive impairments that are a frequent concomitant of PD cannot be attributed solely to AD.

Peretz and Cummings (1988) maintain that while AD may account for a portion of dementia associated with PD, especially the most severe intellectual impairments, the characteristic cognitive deficits 'conform to the pattern of subcortical dementia'. Yet this concept is currently of 'uncertain status' (Smith and Mindham, 1987). Knight *et al.* (1988) believe that studies with PD patients show that what has been termed sub-cortical dementia is nothing other than the early stages of AD. However, evidence is accumulating that cortical and sub-cortical dementia are separate 'clinical concepts that correlate with the principal site of dysfunction in the central nervous system' (Peretz and Cummings, 1988).

Stroke

Stoke occurs most commonly in elderly adults. After age 55 incidence doubles with each additional decade. Seventy per cent of victims are 65 or over (Mulley, 1981) which results in an old age prevalence rate of about 0.5 per cent. Although major advances have been made in the prevention of stroke, it remains one of the most common causes of death, disability and dependence for people in later life.

Onset is sudden and unexpected, and the consequences are frequently devastating. A stroke may cause 'one-sided' paralysis or weakness. The psychological effects depend largely on the site and extent of the brain lesion. Disorders of language and speech occur in nearly 50 per cent of victims. Confusion is a common problem in elderly stroke patients. For some stroke victims the location of the stroke may cause a syndrome characterized by impaired initiative, lack of empathy, emotional lability, impulsivity and poor judgment. Others may display perceptual abnormalities, the most common of which are neglect of the affected side and distortion in body image. There may be major changes in physical abilities, self-care skills may be impoverished, the expression of feelings may be curtailed and hobbies and social activities may be less easy to accomplish. Such transformations in physical capacity and lifestyle may cause anger, frustration and resentment. Grief may also be an initial emotional response to a stroke. Goodstein (1983) suggests that a person's reaction depends on how they perceive the specific functional losses and their implications, the response of significant others and their social network, and the effect of the stroke on personal appearance and sexuality.

Depression is a frequent concomitant of stroke. A longitudinal study of stroke patients showed 47 per cent of victims had marked depressive disorder as an early clinical feature, while prevalence had increased to 60 per cent six months after the stroke (Robinson *et al.*, 1984). Such an emotional response may not simply be a reaction to the experience of isolation and disability, for there may be a neurophysiological basis for post-stroke depression. Depression can occur any time up to two years following the brain lesion and without treatment may persist for up to a year.

While many stroke victims have difficulty adjusting to limitations imposed by a stroke, the prognosis for most long-term survivors is good. Unlike dementia, some restoration of function may be possible, although as time passes recovery of lost or damaged abilities is increasingly unlikely. Gresham (1986) reports that 80 per cent of victims will achieve independent mobility, while 65 per cent will regain independence in activities of daily living. Unfortunately, depression may be a barrier to rehabilitation.

Acute Confusional State (Delirium)

Acute confusional state is a common disorder in old age, which is poorly understood and frequently misdiagnosed as dementia. Given the risk to life and the reversibility of many of the conditions which cause delirium, it is essential that acute confusional state is distinguished from dementia.

An acute confusional state is the result of a widespread disturbance of brain metabolism which leads to fever, delirium, disorientation, memory loss, poor concentration, hallucinations, delusions, restlessness, 'clouding of consciousness' and self-neglect. Cognitive processes are slowed and coherent thought is difficult. Insight is diminished.

As can be seen an acute confusional state shares many of the cardinal features of dementia. Delirium is distinguished by the fact that onset is characteristically sudden, arising over a few hours or days, and the profile of cognitive impairment is inconsistent.

The major causes of delirium are the toxic effects of prescribed medication, infections, neoplasms and arteriosclerosis. It may occur at a time of major physical illness or trauma. In many cases there is no single cause, but is usually the consequence of multiple deficits, some of which produce delirium. In a substantial minority of confusional states in older people, no underlying organic factors are identified. Delirium may then be associated with major environmental changes, sensory deprivation and psychological stress.

The outcome of an acute confusional state is either recovery or death. Following successful treatment of the underlying cause delirium usually shows itself to be a reversible condition. However, an acute confusional state can also indicate a risk of imminent death (Rabins and Folstein, 1982). Overall, the mechanisms of causation and the psychological sequelae of delirium are neglected research topics in comparison with the syndrome of dementia, probably because the effects are usually temporary and often overshadowed by physical illness (Pitt, 1987).

Conclusion

The 'problems of ageing' described in this chapter are, in the main, either common in old age (e.g. depression), become more prevalent with advancing age (e.g. stroke) or arise for the first time in later life (e.g. paraphrenia). Others can be seen as neglected consequences of later life maladjustment (e.g. alcohol misuse). They are not normal manifestations of the ageing process. As Woods and Britton (1985) state, the elderly people experiencing these disorders are statistically abnormal.

To a large extent, the scale of handicaps and illnesses in later life remain unknown. Addario (1990) suggests this is because the psychology of those involved — elderly people, their families and health care providers — is flawed. Older adults often associate growing old with discomfort and sadness and cannot distinguish stereotypical expectations from actual illness. Similarly, families often share the same misbeliefs of ageing and therefore mistakenly interpret the signs. Health care professionals, however, are the most culpable. Historically they receive little training in the health problems of older adults, and thus often see symptoms of disease as part of ageing and neglect to treat them. If illnesses are acknowledged, they may be incorrectly perceived as being treatment-resistant or having a poor prognosis thereby rendering treatment a questionable option.

This section was written in the hope that it will contribute to a growing awareness of the need to provide improved health care to older adults who have chronic, disabling disorders. Only when this goal is achieved can we promote a quality of life for all people throughout the whole lifespan, regardless if they age well or not. This argument should resonate throughout centres of learning and practice if for no other reason than *On Being Old* is inevitably about our future selves.

References

ABRAHAMS, J.P. and BIRREN, J.E. (1973) 'Reaction time as a function of age and behavioural predisposition to coronary heart disease', *Journal of Gerontology*, **28**, pp. 471–8.

ABRAMS, M. (1978) *Beyond Three Score and Ten: A First Report on a Survey of the Elderly*, Mitcham, Surrey, Age Concern Publications.

ADAMS, D.L. (1971) 'Correlates of life satisfaction', *Gerontologist*, **II** (4, Part II), pp. 64–8.

ADDARIO, D. (1990) 'Treating mental health conditions in the rehabilitative setting', in KEMP, B., BRUMMEL-SMITH, K. and RAMSDELL, J.W. (Eds) *Geriatric Rehabilitation*, Boston, College-Hill Press.

AGID, Y. RUBERG, M., DUBOIS, B. *et al.* (1986) 'Parkinson's disease and dementia', *Clinical Neuropharmacology*, **9**, 22.

ALEXOPOLOUS, G.S., MEYERS, B.S., YOUNG, R.C., ABRAMS, P.C. and SHAMO-LAN, C.A. (1988) 'Brain changes in geriatric depression', *International Journal of Geriatric Psychiatry*, **3**, pp. 157–61.

ALLPORT, G.W. (1937) *Personality: A Psychological Interpretation*, New York, Harper.

ANDERSON, M. (1977) 'The impact on the family relationship of the elderly of changes since Victorian times in governmental income maintenance provision', in SHANAS, E. and SUSSMAN, M. (Eds) *Family, Bureaucracy and the Elderly*, Durham, NC, Duke University Press.

ANGLEITNER, A., SCHMITZ-SCHERZER, R. and RUDINGER, G. (1971) 'Altersabhangigkeit der Personlichkeit im Sinne von R.B. Cattell', *Actuelle Gerontologie*, **I**, pp. 721–9.

ARENBERG, D. (1974) 'A longitudinal study of problem-solving in adults', *Journal of Gerontology*, **29**, pp. 650–8.

ARENBERG, D. (1982) 'Changes with age in problem solving', in CRAIK, F.I.M. and TREHUB, S. (Eds) *Aging and Cognitive Processes*, New York, Plenum Press.

ARLING, G. (1976) 'The elderly widow and her family, neighbours and friends', *Journal of Marriage and the Family*, **38**, pp. 757–68.

ASH, P. (1966) 'Pre-retirement counselling', *Gerontologist*, **6**, pp. 97–9.

ATCHLEY, R.C. (1976) *The Sociology of Retirement*, New York, Halsted Press.

ATCHLEY, R.C. (1980) *Social Forces in Later Life*, 3rd edn, Belmont, CA, Wadsworth.

ATCHLEY, R.C. (1985) *The Social Forces and Ageing*, Belmont, CA, Wadsworth.

BACK, K.W. (1977) 'The ambiguity of retirement', in BUSSE, E.W. and PFEIFFER, E. (Eds) *Behaviour and Adaptation in Late Life*, Boston, Little, Brown and Co.

BALIER, C. (1968) 'Les états névrotiques chez les personnes agées', *Gazette Medicale de France*, **75**, pp. 3415–20.

BALTES, P.B. and WILLIS, S.L. (1982) 'Plasticity and enhancement of intellectual functioning in old age: Penn State's Adult Development and Enrichment Project (ADEPT)', in CRAIK, F.I.M. and TREHUB, S. (Eds) *Ageing and Cognitive Processes*, New York, Plenum Press.

BALTES, P.B., DITTMANN-KOHLI, F. and DIXON, R.A. (1984) 'New perspectives on the development of intelligence in adulthood: Toward a dual-process conception and a model of selective optimisation and compensation', in BALTES, P.B. and BRIM, JR., O.G. (Eds) *Life-Span Development and Behaviour*, **6**, New York, Academic Press.

BARNES, G.M. (1982) 'Patterns of alcohol use and abuse among older persons in a household population', in WOOD, and ELIAS (Eds) *Alcoholism and Ageing*, Boca Raton, FL, CRC Press.

BARRACLOUGH, B.M. (1971) 'Suicide in the elderly', in KAY, D.W.K. and WALK, A. (Eds) *Recent Developments in Psychogeriatrics, British Journal of Psychiatry*, Special Publication, No. 6.

BART, P. (1968) 'Social structure and vocabularies of discomfort: What happenend to female hysteria?' *Journal of Health and Social Behaviour*, **9**, pp. 188–93.

BARTER, J. (1978) *Computers and Employment*, London, National Opinion Polls Ltd.

BECK, A.T. (1967) *Depression: Clinical, Experimental and Therapeutic Aspects*, Staple Press, London.

BECK, A.T. (1976) *Cognitive Therapy and the Emotional Disorders*, New York, International Universities Press.

BENGTSON, V.L. (1971) 'Inter-age differences in perception and the generation gap', *Gerontologist*, Part II, pp. 85–90.

BENGTSON, V.L. (1975) 'Generation and family effects in value socialization', *American Sociological Review*, **40**, pp. 358–71.

BENGTSON, V.L. and BLACK, K.D. (1973) 'Intergenerational relations and continuities in socialization', in BALTES, P. and SCHAIE, K.W. (Eds) *Life-Span Development Psychology: Personality and Socialization*, New York, Academic Press.

BENGTSON, V.L., KASSCHAU, P.L. and RAGAN, P.K. (1977) 'The impact of social structure on ageing individuals', in BIRREN, J.E. and SCHAIE, K.W. (Eds) *Handbook of the Psychology of Aging*, 1st edn, New York, Van Nostrand Reinhold.

BENGTSON, V.L. and TREAS, J. (1980) 'The changing family context of mental health and ageing', in BIRREN, J.E. and SLOANE, R.B. (Eds) *Handbook of Mental Health and Aging*, Englewood Cliffs, NJ, Prentice-Hall.

BERGMANN, K. (1978) 'Neurosis and personality disorder in old age', in ISAACS, A.D. and POST, F. (Eds) *Studies in Geriatric Psychiatry*, New York, John Wiley and Sons.

BERGMANN, K., FOSTER, E.M., JUSTICE, A.W. and MATHEWS, V. (1978) 'Management of the elderly demented patient in the community', *British Journal of Psychiatry*, **132**, pp. 441–9.

BERRIOS, G.E. (1987) 'The nosology of the dementias: An overview', in PITT, B. (Ed.) *Dementia*, Edinburgh, Churchill Livingstone.

BILD, B.R. and HAVIGHURST, R.J. (1976) 'Senior citizens in great cities. The case of Chicago', *Gerontologist*, **16** (1, Part II), pp. 3–82.

BIRREN, J.E. (1959) 'Principles of research on ageing', in BIRREN, J.E. (Ed.) *Handbook of Aging and the Individual*, Chicago, University of Chicago Press.

BIRREN, J.E. (1964) *The Psychology of Aging*, Englewood Cliffs, NJ, Prentice-Hall.

BIRREN, J.E. (1965) 'Age changes in speed of behaviour: Its central nature and physiological correlates', in WELFORD, A.T. and BIRREN, J.E. (Eds) *Behaviour, Aging and the Nervous System*, Springfield, IL, Thomas.

BIRREN, J.E. (1970) 'Toward an experimental psychology of ageing', *American Psychologist*, **25**, pp. 124–35.

BIRREN, J.E. (1973) 'A summary: Prospects and problems of research on the longitudinal development of man's intellectual capacities throughout life', in JARVIK, L.F., EISDORFER, C. and BLUM, J.E. (Eds) *Intellectual Functioning in Adults*, Springer, New York.

BIRREN, J.E. and RENNER, V.J. (1977a) 'Research on the psychology of ageing: Principles and experimentation', in BIRREN, J.E. and SCHAIE, K.W. (Eds) *Handbook of Aging and the Individual*, New York, Van Nostrand Reinhold.

BIRREN, J.E. and RENNER, V.J. (1977b) 'Health, behaviour and aging', in BIRREN, J.E., MUNNICHS, J.M. and THOMAE, H. (Eds) *Institut de la Vie: Proceedings of the World Conference on Ageing: A Challenge to Science and Policy. Section: Behavioural Sciences*, Oxford, Oxford University Press.

BIRREN, J.E. and RENNER, V.J. (1980) 'Concepts and Issues of Mental Health and Ageing', in BIRREN, J.E. and SLOANE, R.B. (Eds) *Handbook of Mental Health and Aging*, Englewood Cliffs, NJ, Prentice-Hall.

BIRREN, J.E., WOODS, A.M. and WILLIAMS, M.V. (1979) 'Speed of behaviour as an indicator of age changes and the integrity of the nervous system', in HOFFMEISTER, F. and MULLER, C. (Eds) *Brain Function in Old Age*, Berlin, Springer-Verlag.

BLAZER, D. (1980) 'The diagnosis of depression in the elderly', *Journal of the American Geriatrics Society*, **28**, pp. 52–8.

BOLDY, D., ABEL, P. and CARTER, K. (1973) *The Elderly in Grouped Dwellings. A Profile*, The Institute of Biometry and Community Medicine, University of Exeter.

BOLLER, F. (1980) 'Mental status of patients with Parkinson's disease', *Journal of Clinical Neuropsychology*, **2**, 157–72.

BOLLER, F. (1983) 'Alzheimer's disease and Parkinson's disease: Clinical and pathological associations', in REISBERG, B. (Ed.) *Alzheimer's Disease*, Free Press, New York.

BOLLER, F., MIZUTANI, T., ROESSMANN, U. *et al.* (1980) 'Parkinson's disease, dementia and Alzheimer's disease: clinico-pathological corrections', *Annals of Neurology*, **7**, pp. 329–35.

BONDAREFF, W. (1980) 'Neurobiology of Aging', in BIRREN, J.E. and SLOANE, R.B. (Eds) *Handbook of Mental Health and Aging*, Englewood Cliffs, NJ, Prentice-Hall.

BOTWINICK, J. (1966) 'Cautiousness with advanced age', *Journal of Gerontology*, **21**, pp. 347–53.

BOTWINICK, J. (1978) *Ageing and Behaviour*, New York, Springer.

BOTWINICK, J., BRINLEY, J.F. and BIRREN, J.E. (1958) 'The effect of motivation by electric shocks on reaction time in relation to age', *American Journal of Psychology*, **71**, pp. 408–11.

BOTWINICK, J. and KORNETSKY, C. (1960) 'Age differences in the acquisition and extinction of GSR', *Journal of Gerontology*, **15**, pp. 83–4.

BOTWINICK, J. and STORANDT, M. (1980) 'Recall and recognition of old information in relation to age and sex', *Journal of Gerontology*, **33**, pp. 755–62.

BRAUN, H.W. and GEISELHART, R. (1959) 'Age differences in the acquisition and extinction of the conditioned eyelid response', *Journal of Experimental Psychology*, **57**, pp. 386–8.

BRAYNE, C. and CALLOWAY, P. (1988) 'Normal ageing, impaired cognitive function, and senile dementia of the Alzheimer's type: A continuum?' *Lancet*, **4** June, pp. 1265–7.

BRETSCHNEIDER, J.G. and MCCOY, N.L. (1988) 'Sexual interest and behaviour in healthy 80- to 102-year-olds', *Archives of Sexual Behaviour*, **17**, 2, pp. 109–29.

BRITTON, P.G. and SAVAGE, R.D. (1966) 'The MMPI and the aged: Some normative data from a community sample', *British Journal of Psychiatry*, **112**, pp. 941–3.

BRODY, E.M., JOHNSEN, P., FULCOMER, M.C. and LANG, A.M. (1983) 'Women's changing roles and help to elderly parents: Attitudes of three generations of women', *Journal of Gerontology*, **38**, pp. 597–607.

BROMLEY, D.B. (1990) *Behavioural Gerontology*, Chichester, John Wiley.

BROWN, G.W. and HARRIS, T. (1978) *Social Origins of Depression: A Study of Psychiatric Disorders in Women*, Tavistock, London.

BRUBAKER, T.H. and POWERS, E.A. (1976) 'The stereotype of old', *Journal of Gerontology*, **31**, pp. 441–7.

BUCKS, R. (1990) 'Depression: A new name for old', Unpublished MSc Thesis, University of Birmingham.

BURNSIDE, I.M. (1980) 'Symptomatic behaviours in the elderly', in BIRREN, J.E. and SLOANE, R.B. (Eds) *Handbook of Mental Health and Aging*, Englewood Cliffs, NJ, Prentice-Hall.

BUSSE, E.W. (1985) 'Normal ageing: The Duke longitudinal studies', in BERGENER, M., ERMINI, M. and STRAHELIN, H.B. (Eds) *Thresholds in Aging*, New York, Academic Press.

BUSSE, E.W. and BLAZER, D.G. (1980) 'The theories and processes of ageing', in BUSSE, E.W. and BLAZER, D.G. (Eds) *Handbook of Geriatric Psychiatry*, New York, Van Nostrand Reinhold.

BUTLER, R.N. (1963) 'The life review: An interpretation of reminiscence in the aged', *Psychiatry*, **26**, pp. 65–76.

BUTLER, R.N. (1975) *Why Survive? Being Old in America*, New York, Harper and Row.

BUTLER, R.N. and LEWIS, M.I. (1977) *Ageing and Mental Health*, St Louis, C.V. Mosby and Co.

CASPI, A. (1987) 'Personality in life course', *Journal of Personality and Social Psychology*, **53**, pp. 1203–13.

CATTELL, H.R. (1988) 'Elderly suicide in London: An analysis of coroners' inquests', *International Journal of Geriatric Psychiatry*, **3**, pp. 251–61.

CATTELL, H.R. (1990) 'Suicide in the elderly', *Psychiatry in Practice*, **9**, 2, pp. 14–17.

CATTELL, R.B. (1963) 'The theory of fluid and crystalline intelligence', *Journal of Educational Psychology*, **54**, pp. 1–22.

CENTRAL OFFICE OF INFORMATION (1977) *Care of the Elderly in Britain*, London, HMSO.

CERELLA, J. (1990) 'Aging and information-processing rate', in BIRREN, J.E. and SCHAIE, K.W., *Handbook of the Psychology of Aging*, 3rd edn, London, Academic Press.

CHATFIELD, W.F. (1977) 'Economic and sociological factors influencing life satisfaction of the aged', *Journal of Gerontology*, **32**, pp. 593–9.

CHOWN, S.M. (1961) 'Age and the rigidities', *Journal of Gerontology*, **16**, pp. 353–62.

CHRISTENSON, C.V. and GAGNON, J.H. (1965) 'Sexual behaviour in a group of older women', *Journal of Gerontology*, **20**, pp. 351–6.

CLARK, L.E. and KNOWLES, J.B. (1973) 'Age differences in dichotic listening performance', *Journal of Gerontology*, **28**, pp. 173–8.

CLARK, M. and ANDERSON, B.G. (1967) *Culture and Aging: An Anthropological Study of Older Americans*, Springfield, IL, Charles C. Thomas.

CLAYTON, V.P. and BIRREN, J.E. (1980) 'The development of wisdom across the lifespan: A re-examination of an ancient topic', *Life-Span Development and Behaviour*, **3**, pp. 103–35.

COLEMAN, P.G. (1986) *Ageing and Reminiscence Processes*, Chichester, John Wiley and Sons.

COMFORT, A. (1980) 'Sexuality in later life', in BIRREN, J.E. and SLOANE, R.B. (Eds) *Handbook of Mental Health and Aging*, Englewood Cliffs, NJ, Prentice-Hall.

CONLEY, J.J. (1984) 'Longitudinal consistency of adult personality: Self-reported psychological characteristics across 45 years', *Journal of Personality and Social Psychology*, **47**, pp. 1325–33.

COOPER, A.F., GARSIDE, R.F. and KAY, D.W.K. (1976) 'A comparison of deaf and non-deaf patients with paranoid and affective psychoses', *British Journal of Psychiatry*, **129**, pp. 216–26.

COPELAND, J.R.M., GURLAND, B.J., DEWEY, M.E., KELLEHER, M.J., SMITH, A.M.R. and DAVIDSON, I.A. (1987) 'Is there more dementia, depression and neurosis in New York?' *British Journal of Psychiatry*, **151**, pp. 466–74.

CORBY, N. and SOLNICK, R.L. (1980) 'Psychosocial and physiological influences on sexuality in the older adult', in BIRREN, J.E. and SLOANE, R.B. (Eds) *Handbook of Mental Health and Aging*, Englewood Cliffs, NJ, Prentice-Hall.

CORNELIUS, S.W. and CASPI, A. (1987) 'Everyday problem solving in adulthood and old age', *Psychology and Aging*, **2**, pp. 144–53.

CORSELLIS, J.A.N. (1976) 'Some observations of the Purkinje cell population and on brain volume in human aging', in TERRY, R.D. and GERSHON, S. (Eds) *Neurobiology of Aging*, New York, Raven Press.

COSTA, P.T., JR. and McCRAE, R.R. (1976) 'Age differences in personality structure. A cluster analysis approach', *Journal of Gerontology*, **31**, pp. 564–70.

COSTA, P.T., JR. and McCRAE, R.R. (1978) 'Age differences in personality structure revisited', *Ageing and Human Development*, **8**, pp. 131–42.

COSTA P.T., JR. and McCRAE, R.R. (1985) *The NEO Personality Inventory Manual*, Odessa, FL. Psychological Assessment Resources.

COSTA P.T. and McCRAE, J.R. (1988) 'Personality in adulthood: A six year longitudinal study of self-reports and spouse ratings on the NEO Personality Inventory', *Journal of Personality and Social Psychology*, **54**, pp. 853–63.

CRAIK, F.I.M. (1977) 'Age differences in human memory', in BIRREN, J.E. and SCHAIE, K.W. (Eds) *Handbook of the Psychology of Aging*, 1st edn, New York, Van Nostrand Reinhold.

CRAIK, F.I.M., BYRD, M. and SWANSON, J.M. (1987) 'Patterns of memory loss in three elderly samples', *Psychology and Aging*, **2**, pp. 79–86.

CRAIK, F.I.M., MORRIS, R.G. and GICK, M.L. (1989) 'Adult age differences in working memory', in VALLAR, G. and SHALLICE, T. (Eds) *Neuropsychological Impairments of Short-Term Memory*, New York, Cambridge University Press.

CUMMINGS, E. and HENRY, W. (1961) *Growing Old: The Process of Disengagement*, New York, Basic Books.

CUNNINGHAM, W.R. and BROOKBANK, J.W. (1988) *Gerontology: The Psychology, Biology and Sociology of Aging*, New York, Harper and Row.

CUNNINGHAM, W.R., SEPCOSKI, C.M. and OPEL, M.R. (1978) 'Fatigue effects on intelligence test performance in the elderly', *Journal of Gerontology*, **33**, 541–5.

CUTLER, R.G. (1976) 'Evolution of longevity in primates', *Journal of Human Evolution*, **5**, pp. 169–202.

DALE, A., EVANDROU, M. and ARBER, S. (1987) 'The household structure of the elderly in Britain', *Journal of Social Policy*, **7**, 1.

DAVIES, A.D.M. and GLEDHILL, K.J. (1983) 'Engagement and depressive symptoms in a community sample of elderly people', *British Journal of Clinical Psychology*, **22**, pp. 95–106.

DENIGOLA, P. and PERUZZA, M. (1974) 'Sex in the aged', *Journal of the American Geriatrics Society*, **22**, pp. 380–2.

DODD, B. (1991) 'Bereavement', in COCHRANE, R. and CARROLL, D. (Eds) *Psychology and Social Issues*, London, The Falmer Press.

DOUGLAS, K. and ARENBERG, D. (1978) 'Age changes, cohort differences, and cultural change on the Guilford-Zimmerman Temperament Survey', *Journal of Gerontology*, **33**, pp. 737–47.

DYSON, J. (1980) 'Sociopolitical influences on retirement research', *Bulletin of the British Psychological Society*, **33**, pp. 128–30.

EDWARDS, A.E. and VINE, D.B. (1963) 'Personality changes with age: Their dependency on concomitant intellectual decline', *Journal of Gerontology*, **18**, pp. 182–4.

EDWARDS, J.N. and KLEMMAK, D.L. (1973) 'Correlates of life satisfaction: A re-examination', *Journal of Gerontology*, **28**, pp. 497–502.

EISDORFER, C., BUSSE, E.W. and COHEN, L.D. (1959) 'The WAIS performance of an aged sample: The relationship between verbal and performance IQs.', *Journal of Gerontology*, **14**, pp. 197–201.

EKERDT, D.J., BOSSE, R. and MOGEY, J.M. (1980) 'Concurrent change in planned and preferred aged for retirement', *Journal of Gerontology*, **35**, 2, pp. 232–40.

ENDERBY, P. (1990) 'Promoting communication in patients with dementia', in STOKES, G. and GOUDIE, F. (Eds) *Working with Dementia*, Bicester, Oxon., Winslow Press.

ERIKSON, E.H. (1959) 'Identity and the life cycle', *Psychological Issues*, 1, pp. 1–171.

ERIKSON, E.H. (1963) *Childhood and Society*, New York, Norton.

ERIKSON, E.H., ERIKSON, J.M. and KIVNICK, H.Q. (1986) *Vital Involvement in Old Age*, New York, Norton.

ESQUIROL, J.E.D. (1838) *Des Maladies Mentales*, Paris, Baillière.

EVERITT, A.V. and HUANG, C.Y. (1980) 'The hypothalamus, neuroendocrine and autonomic nervous systems in aging', in BIRREN, J.E. and SLOANE, R.B. (Eds) *Handbook of Mental Health and Aging*, Englewood Cliffs, NJ, Prentice-Hall.

EXTON-SMITH, A.N., STANTON, B.R. and WINDSOR, A.C.M. (1976) *Nutrition of Housebound Old People*, London, King Edward's Hospital Fund.

FARKAS, M.S. and HOYER, W.J. (1980) 'Processing consequences of perceptual grouping in selective attention', *Journal of Gerontology*, **35**, pp. 207–16.

FEIL, N. (1985) 'Resolution: The final task', *Journal of Humanistic Psychology*, **85**, 2, pp. 91–105.

FIELD, D., SCHAIE, K.W. and LEINO, E.V. (1988) 'Continuity in intellectual functioning — The role of self-reported health', *Psychology and Aging*, **3**, pp. 385–92.

FINN, S.E. (1986) 'Stability of personality self-ratings over 30 years: Evidence for an age/cohort interaction', *Journal of Personality and Social Psychology*, **50**, 813–18.

FISKE, M. (1980) 'Tasks and crises of the second half of life: The interrelationships of commitment, coping and adaptation', in BIRREN, J.E. and SLOANE, R.B. (Eds) *Handbook of Mental Health and Aging*, Englewood Cliffs, NJ, Prentice-Hall.

FLYNN, J.R. (1984) 'The mean IQ of Americans: Massive gains 1932 to 1978', *Psychological Bulletin*, **95**, pp. 29–51.

FOULDS, G.A. and RAVEN, J.C. (1948) 'Normal changes in the mental abilities of adults as age advances', *Journal of Mental Science*, **94**, pp. 133–42.

FOX, D. (1981) 'Housing and the elderly', in HOBMAN, D. (Ed.) *The Impact of Ageing: Strategies for Care*, London, Croom Helm.

FREEMAN, J.T. (1961) 'Sexual capacities in the aging male', *Geriatrics*, **16**, pp. 37–43.

FREUD, S. (1917) 'Mourning and melancholia', in *Standard Edition of the Works of Sigmund Freud*, **14**, London, Hogarth Press.

FREUD, S. (1973) 'Femininity', in *New Introductory Lectures in Psychoanalysis*, Harmondsworth, Penguin Books.

FURRY, C.A. and BALTES, P.B. (1973) 'The effect of age differences in ability extraneous performance variables on the assessment of intelligence in children, adults and the elderly', *Journal of Gerontology*, **28**, pp. 73–80.

GABER, L. (1983) 'Activity/disengagement revisited: Personality types in the aged', *British Journal of Psychiatry*, **143**, pp. 490–7.

GALLAGHER, D. and THOMPSON, L.W. (1983) 'Effectiveness of psychotherapy for both endogenous and non-endogenous depression in older adult out-patients', *Journal of Gerontology*, **38**, pp. 707–12.

GALLAGHER, D.E., BRECKENRIDGE, J.N., THOMPSON, L.W. and PETERSON, J.A. (1983) 'Effects of bereavement on indicators of mental health in elderly widows and widowers', *Journal of Gerontology*, **38**, pp. 565–71.

GANZLER, H. (1964) 'Motivation as a factor in the psychological deficit of ageing', *Journal of Gerontology*, **19**, pp. 425–9.

GEORGE, L. (1980) *Role Transitions in Later Life*, Monterey, Brooks/Cole.

GILBERT, G.N., DALE, A., ARBER, S., EVANDROU, M. and LACZKO, F. (1989) 'Resources in old age; ageing and the life course', in JEFFREYS, M. (Ed.) *Growing Old in the Twentieth Century*, Routledge, London.

GILLEARD, C.J. (1984) *Living with Dementia*, London, Croom Helm.

GILMORE, A.J.J. (1972) 'Personality in the elderly: Problems in methodology', *Age and Ageing*, **1**, pp. 227–32.

GLAMSER, F. (1981) 'The impact of pre-retirement preparation programs for industrial workers', *Journal of Gerontology*, **36**, pp. 244–50.

GOODE, W.J. (1964) *The Family*, Englewood Cliffs, NJ, Prentice-Hall.

GOODSTEIN, R.K. (1983) 'Overview: Cerebrovascular accident and the hospitalized elderly — A multidimensional clinical problem', *American Journal of Psychiatry*, **140**, p. 141–7.

GORDON, C., GAITZ, C.M. and SCOTT, J. (1973) 'Value priorities and leisure activities among middle-aged and older Americans', *Diseases of the Nervous System*, **34**, pp. 13–26.

GOTTSDANKER, R. (1982) 'Age and simple reaction time', *Journal of Gerontology*, **37**, pp. 342–8.

GOUDIE, F. (1990a) 'Attitudes to aging and dementia', in STOKES, G. and GOUDIE, F. (Eds) *Working with Dementia*, Bicester, Oxon., Winslow Press.

GOUDIE, F. (1990b) 'Depression in dementia', in STOKES, G. and GOUDIE, F. (Eds) *Working with Dementia*, Bicester, Oxon., Winslow Press.

GOUDIE, F. (1990c) 'Problems of ageing', in STOKES G. and GOUDIE, F. (Eds) *Working with Dementia*, Bicester, Oxon., Winslow Press.

GOUDIE, F. and STOKES, G. (1989) 'Dealing with confusion', *Nursing Times*, **85**, 39, 27 September, pp. 35–7.

GOUDIE, F. and STOKES, G. (1990) 'Reminiscence with dementia sufferers', in

STOKES, G. and GOUDIE, F. (Eds) *Working with Dementia*, Bicester, Oxon., Winslow Press.

GOUDY, W.J., POWERS, E.A. and KEITH, P. (1975) The work-satisfaction, retirement-attitude typology: Profile examination, *Unpublished Paper*.

GRANICK, S. (1973) 'Morale measures as related to personality, cognitive and medical functioning of the aged', *Proceedings of the 31st Annual Convention of the American Psychological Association*, **8**, pp. 785–6. Montreal, Canada.

GRESHAM, G.E. (1986) 'Stroke outcome research', *Stroke*, **17**, p. 358.

GRUENBERG, E.M. (1977) 'The failures of success', *Milbank Memorial Fund Quarterly*, **55**, pp. 3–24.

GRUNDY, E. (1989) 'Longitudinal perspectives on the living arrangements of the elderly', in JEFFERYS, M. (Ed.) *Growing Old in the Twentieth Century*, London, Routledge.

HAAN, N., MILLSAP, R. and HARTKA, E. (1986) 'As time goes by: Change and stability in personality over fifty years', *Psychology and Aging*, **1**, pp. 220–32.

HABOT, B. and LIBOW, L.S. (1980) 'The interrelationships of mental and physical status and its assessment in the older adult: Mind-body interaction', in BIRREN, J.E. and SLOANE, R.B. (Eds) *Handbook of Mental Health and Aging*, Englewood Cliffs, NJ, Prentice-Hall.

HACHINSKI, V.C., LASSEN, N.A. and MARSHALL, J. (1974) 'Multi-infarct dementia: A cause of mental deterioration in the elderly', *Lancet*, **ii**, pp. 207–10.

HANES, C.R. and WILD, B.S. (1977) 'Locus of control and depression among non-institutionalised elderly persons', *Psychological Reports*, **41**, pp. 581–2.

HARKINS, S.W., CHAPMAN, C.R. and EISDORFER, C. (1979) 'Memory loss and response bias in senescence', *Journal of Gerontology*, **34**, pp. 66–72.

HARRIS, L. and ASSOCIATES (1975) *The Myth and Reality of Aging in America*, Washington, DC, The National Council on the Aging, Inc.

HARRISON, P. (1973) 'Living with old age', *New Society*, November, pp. 265–8.

HARRISON, R. (1976) 'The demoralizing experience of prolonged unemployment', *Department of Employment Gazette*, **LXXXIV**, 4.

HARTLEY, J.T. (1986) 'Reader and text variables as determinants of discourse memory in adulthood', *Psychology and Aging*, **1**, pp. 150–8.

HAVIGHURST, R.J. (1959) 'Social and psychological needs of the aging', in GORLOW, L. and KATKOVSKY, W. (Eds) *Readings in the Psychology of Adjustment*, New York, McGraw-Hill.

HAVIGHURST, R.J. (1969) 'Research and development goals in social gerontology', *Gerontologist*, **9**, Part II.

HAVIGHURST, R.J. (1975) 'Life styles transitions related to personality after age fifty', Paper presented at the International Society for Study of Behavioural Development Symposium. The Problem of Transitions in the Human Life Cycle, Kibbutz Kiravim, Israel.

HAVIGHURST, R.J. (1978) 'Ageing in western society', in HOBMAN, D. (Ed.) *The Social Challenge of Ageing*, London, Croom Helm.

HAYFLICK, L. (1982) 'The strategy of senescence', *Journal of Gerontology*, **14**, pp. 37–45.

HAYNES, S.G., McMICHAEL, A.J. and TYROLER, H.A. (1978) 'Survival after early and normal retirement', *Journal of Gerontology*, **33**, 2, pp. 269–78.

HELSON, R., MITCHELL, V. and MOANE, G. (1984) 'Personality and patterns of adherence and non-adherence to the social clock', *Journal of Personality and Social Psychology*, **53**, pp. 176–86.

HENDERSON, A.S. (1983) 'The coming epidemic of dementia', *Australian and New Zealand Journal of Psychiatry*, **17**, pp. 117–27.

HENDERSON, A.S. and JORM, A.F. (1986) *The Problem of Dementia in Australia*, Canberra, Australian Government Publishing Service.

HENDRICKS, J. and HENDRICKS, C.D. (1977) *Aging in Mass Society*, Cambridge, MA, Winthrop.

HERTZOG, C., SCHAIE, K.W. and GRIBBIN, K. (1978) 'Cardiovascular disease and changes in intellectual functioning from middle to old age', *Journal of Gerontology*, **33**, pp. 872–83.

HESTON, L.L. (1981) 'Genetic studies of dementia: With emphasis on Parkinson's disease and Alzheimer's neuropathology', in MORTIMER, J.A. and SCHUMAN, L.M. (Eds) *The Epidemiology of Dementia*, New York, Oxford University Press.

HEYMAN, D.K. and GIANTURCO, D.T. (1973) 'Long-term adaptation by the elderly to bereavement', *Journal of Gerontology*, **28**, pp. 359–62.

HILL, R., FOOTE, N., ALDOUS, J., CARLSON, R. and MACDONALD, R. (1970) *Family Development in Three Generations*, Cambridge, Schenkman.

HOLDEN, U.P. (1990) 'Dementia: Some common misunderstandings', in STOKES, G. and GOUDIE, F. (Eds) *Working with Dementia*, Bicester, Oxon., Winslow Press.

HOLLAND, C.A. and RABBITT, P. (1991) 'Ageing memory: Use versus impairment', *British Journal of Psychology*, **82**, 1, pp. 29–38.

HOPSON-WALKER, S.D. (1990) 'Substance abuse in older persons with disability: assessment and treatment', in KEMP, B., BRUMMEL-SMITH, K. and RAMSDELL, J.W. (Eds) *Geriatric Rehabilitation*, Boston, College-Hill Press.

HORN, J.L. (1970) 'Organization of data on life-span development of human abilities', in GOULET, L.R. and BALTES, P.B. (Eds) *Life-Span Development Psychology*, New York, Academic Press.

HORN, J.L. (1985) 'Intellectual ability concepts', in STERNBERG, R.L. (Ed.) *Advances in the Psychology of Human Intelligence*, **3**, Hillsdale, NJ, Erlbaum.

HORN, J.L. and DONALDSON, G. (1976) 'On the myth of intellectual decline in adulthood', *American Psychologist*, **31**, pp. 701–9.

HORNER, K.L., RUSHTON, J.P. and VERNON, P.A. (1986) 'Relation between aging and research productivity', *Psychology and Aging*, **1**, pp. 319–24.

HORNYKIEWICZ, O. (1982) 'Brain neurotransmitter changes in Parkinson's Disease', in MARSDEN, C.D. and FAHN, S. (Eds) *Movement Disorders*, London, Butterworth.

HOWARD, D.V., LASAGA, M.I. and MCANDREWS, M.P. (1980) 'Semantic activation during memory encoding across the adult life span', *Journal of Gerontology*, **35**, pp. 884–90.

HOWARD, D.V., MCANDREWS, M.P. and LASAGA, M.I. (1981) 'Semantic priming of lexical decisions in young and old adults', *Journal of Gerontology*, **36**, pp. 707–14.

HOWE, M.J.A. (1990) 'Does intelligence exist?' *The Psychologist*, **3**, 11, pp. 490–3.

HULTSCH, D.F. and DIXON, R.A. (1983) 'The role of pre-experimental knowledge in test processing in adulthood', *Experimental Aging Research*, **9**, pp. 7–22.

HULTSCH, D.F. and DIXON, R.A. (1990) 'Learning and memory in aging', in BIRREN, J.E. and SCHAIE, K.W. (Eds) *Handbook of the Psychology of Aging*, 3rd edn, London, Academic Press.

HULTSCH, D.F., HERTZOG, C., DIXON, R.A. and DAVIDSON, H.A. (1988) 'Memory self-knowledge and self-efficacy in the aged', in HOWE, M.L. and BRAINERD, C.J. (Eds) *Cognitive Development in Adulthood: Progress in Cognitive Development Research*, New York, Springer-Verlag.

HUNT, A. (1979) 'Some aspects of the health of elderly people in England', *Health Trends*, **11**, pp. 21–3.

HUPPERT, F.A. and TYM, E. (1986) 'Clinical and neuropsychological assessment of dementia', *British Medical Bulletin*, **42**, 1, pp. 11–18.

HUSSAIN, R.A. (1981) *Geriatric Psychology: A Behavioral Perspective*, New York, Van Nostrand Reinhold.

HUYCK, M.H. (1990) 'Gender differences in aging', in BIRREN, J.E. and SCHAIE, K.W. (Eds) *Handbook of the Psychology of Aging*, 3rd edn, London, Academic Press.

HYMAS, N., NAGUIB, M. and LEVY, R. (1989) 'Late paraphrenia: A follow-up study', *International Journal of Geriatric Psychiatry*, **4**, pp. 23–9.

JAMES, O.F.W. (1983) 'Alcoholism in the elderly', in KRASNER, N., MADIN, S. and WALKER, R. (Eds) *Alcohol-related Problems — Room for Manoeuvre*, Chichester, John Wiley.

JARVIK, L.F. (1973) 'Discussion: Patterns of intellectual functioning in the later years', in JARVIK, L.F., EISDORFER, C. and BLUM, J.E. (Eds) *Intellectual Functioning in Adults*, New York, Springer.

JEFFRIES, V. and RANSFORD, H.E. (1979) *Multiple Hierarchy Stratification: Class, Ethnicity, Sex, Age*, Boston, Allyn and Bacon.

JOHNSON, M.L. (1975) 'Old age and the gift relationship', *New Society*, 13 March.

JOHNSON, M.L. (1978) 'That was your life: A biographical approach to later life', in CARVER, V. and LIDDIARD, P. (Eds) *An Ageing Population*, Sevenoaks, Kent, Hodder and Stoughton.

JORM, A.F. (1987) *Understanding Senile Dementia*, London, Croom Helm.

JORM, A.F., KORTEN, A.E. and HENDERSON, A.S. (1987) 'The prevalence of dementia: A quantitative integration of the literature', *Acta Psychiatrica Scandanavica*, **76**, pp. 465–79.

KALLMAN, F.J. (1951) 'Comparative adaptational social and psychometric data on life histories of senescent twin pairs', *American Journal of Human Genetics*, **3**, p. 65.

KALLMAN, F.J. and SANDER, G. (1949) 'Twin studies on senescence', *American Journal of Psychiatry*, **106**, 29.

KASL, S.V. (1979) 'Changes in mental health status associated with job loss and retirement', in BARRETT, J.E., *Stress and Mental Disorder*, New York, Raven Press.

KAUSLER, D.H. (1982) *Experimental Psychology and Human Aging*, New York, John Wiley and Sons.

KAUSLER, D.H. (1990) 'Motivation, human aging and cognitive performance', in BIRREN, J.E. and SCHAIE, K.W. (Eds) *Handbook of the Psychology of Aging*, 3rd edn, London, Academic Press.

KAUSLER, D.H. and LICHTY, W. (1988) 'Memory for activities: Rehearsal independence and aging', in HOWE, M.L. and BRAINERD, C.J. (Eds) *Cognitive Development in Adulthood: Progress in Cognitive Development Research*, New York, Springer-Verlag.

KAY, D.W.K., BEAMISH, P. and ROTH, M. (1964a) 'Old age mental disorders in Newcastle-upon-Tyne, I. A study of prevalence', *British Journal of Psychiatry*, **110**, pp. 146–58.

KAY, D.W.K., BEAMISH, P. and ROTH, M. (1964b) 'Old age mental disorders in Newcastle-upon-Tyne, II. A study of possible social and medical causes', *British Journal of Psychiatry*, **110**, pp. 668–82.

KAY, D.W.K. and BERGMANN, K. (1980) 'Epidemiology of mental disorders among the aged in the community', in BIRREN, J.E. and SLOANE, R.B. (Eds) *Handbook of Mental Health and Aging*, Englewood Cliffs, NJ, Prentice-Hall.

KAY, D.W.K. and ROTH, M. (1961) 'Environmental and hereditary factors in the schizophrenias of old age ("late paraphrenia") and their bearing on the general problem of causation in schizophrenia', *Journal of Mental Science*, **107**, pp. 649–86.

KENDRICK, D.C. (1982) 'Why assess the aged? A clinical psychologist's view', *British Journal of Clinical Psychology*, **21**, pp. 47–54.

KIMBLE G.A. and PENNYBACKER, H.S. (1963) 'Eyelid conditioning in young and aged subjects', *Journal of Genetic Psychology*, **103**, pp. 283–9.

KINSEY, A.C., POMEROY, W.B., MARTIN, C.E. and GEBHARD, P.H. (1953) *Sexual Behaviour in the Human Female*, Philadelphia, W.B. Saunders.

KITWOOD, T. (1989) 'Brain, mind and dementia: With particular reference to Alzheimer's disease', *Ageing and Society*, **9**, pp. 1–15.

KITWOOD, T. (1990) 'The dialectics of dementia: With particular reference to Alzheimer's disease', *Ageing and Society*, **10**, pp. 177–96.

KLEEMEIER, R.W. (1962) 'Intellectual changes in the senium', *Proceedings of the Social Statistics Association*, American Statistical Association, pp. 290–5.

KLIEGL, R. and BALTES, P.B. (1987) 'Theory-guided analysis of mechanisms of of development and aging through testing-the-limits and research on expertise', in SCHOOLER, C. and SCHAIE, K.W. (Eds) *Cognitive Functioning and Social Structure Over the Life Course*, Norwood, NJ, Ablex.

KLINE, D.W. and SCHIEBER, F. (1985) 'Vision and aging', in BIRREN, J.E. and SCHAIE, K.W. (Eds) *Handbook of the Psychology of Aging*, New York, Van Nostrand Reinhold.

KNIGHT, B.G. (1983) 'Assessing a mobile outreach team', in SMYER, M.A. and GATZ, M. (Eds) *Mental Health and Aging: Programs and Evaluation*, Beverley Hills, Sage.

KNIGHT, R.G., GODFREY, H.P.D. and SHELTON, E.J. (1988) 'The psychological deficits associated with Parkinson's disease', *Clinical Psychology Review*, **8**, pp. 391–410.

KOGAN, N. (1990) 'Personality and aging', in BIRREN, J.E. and SCHAIE, K.W.

(Eds) *Handbook of the Psychology of Aging*, 3rd edn, London, Academic Press.

KRAL, V.A. (1962) 'Senescent forgetfulness: Benign and malignant', *Canadian Medical Association Journal*, **86**, pp. 257–60.

KRAL, V.A. (1978) 'Benign senescent forgetfulness', *Aging*, **7**, pp. 47–51.

KÜBLER-ROSS, E. (1975) *Questions and Answers on Death and Dying*, New York, Macmillan.

KULAWIK, H. and DECKE, D. (1973) 'Letzte Aufzeichnungen — eine Analyse von 223 nach vollendeten Suiziden hinterlassenen Briefen und Mitteilungen', *Psychiat. Chin.*, **6**, pp. 193–210.

KUTNER, B., FANSHEL, D., TOGO, A.M. and LANGER, T.A. (1956) *Five Hundred Over Sixty*, New York, Russell Sage Foundation.

KUYPERS, J.A. (1971) 'Internal-external locus of control and ego functioning correlates in the elderly', *Gerontologist*, **12**, pp. 168–73.

KUYPERS, J.A. and BENGTSON, V.L. (1973) 'Social breakdown and competence: A model of normal aging', *Human Development*, **16**, pp. 181–201.

LABOUVIE-VIEF, G., HOYER, W., BALTES, M.M. and BALTES, P.B. (1974) 'Operant analysis of intellectual behaviour in old age', *Human Development*, **17**, pp. 259–72.

LACHMAN, M.E. (1983) 'Perceptions of intellectual ageing: Antecedent or consequence of intellectual functioning?' *Development Psychology*, **19**, pp. 482–98.

LACHMAN, M.E. (1985) 'Personal efficacy in middle and old age: Differential and normative patterns of change', in ELDER, JR., G.H. (Ed.) *Life-Course Dynamics: Trajectories and Transitions*, Ithaca, NY, Cornell University Press.

LACHMAN, M.E. (1986) 'Locus of control in aging research: A case for multidimensional and domain-specific assessment', *Psychology and Aging*, **1**, pp. 34–40.

LADURNER, G., ILIFF, L.D. and LECHNER, H. (1982) 'Clinical factors associated with dementia in ischaemic stroke', *Journal of Neurology, Neurosurgery and Psychiatry*, **45**, pp. 97–101.

LARSSON, T., SJOGREN, T. and JACOBSON, G. (1963) 'Senile dementia: A clinical sociomedical and genetic study', *Acta Psychiatrica Scandinavia* (Suppl. 167) **39**, pp. 1–259.

LARUE, A., DESSONVILLE, C. and JARVIK, L.F. (1985) 'Aging and mental disorders', in BIRREN, J.E. and SCHAIE, K.W. (Eds) *Handbook of the Psychology of Aging*, Van Nostrand, New York.

LASLETT, P. (1976) 'Societal development and aging', in BINSTOKC, R.H. and SHANAS, E. (Eds) *Handbook of Aging and the Social Sciences*, New York, Van Nostrand Reinhold.

LAWTON, M.P., WHELIHAN, W.M., BELSKY, J.K. (1980) 'Personality tests and their uses with older adults', in BIRREN, J.E. and SLOANE, R.B. (Eds) *Handbook of Mental Health and Aging*, Englewood Cliffs, NJ, Prentice-Hall.

LAZARUS, R.S. and DELONGIS, A. (1983) 'Psychological stress and coping in ageing', *American Psychologist*, **38**, pp. 245–54.

LEAF, A. (1973) 'Every day is a gift when you are over 100', *National Geographic*, **143**, pp. 93–118.

LEBOWITZ, B.D. (1980) 'Old age and family functioning', *Journal of Gerontological Social Work*, **1**, 2, pp. 111–18.

LEECH, S. and WITTE, K.L. (1971) 'Paired-associate learning in elderly adults as related to pacing and incentive conditions', *Developmental Psychology*, **5**, p. 180.

LEHMAN, H.C. (1953) *Age and Achievement*, Princeton, NJ, Princeton University Press.

LEWINSOHN, P.M. (1974) 'A behavioural approach to depression', in FRIEDMAN, R. and KATZ, M. (Eds) *The Psychology of Depression*, New York, John Wiley.

LEWIS, C.N. (1971) 'Reminiscing and self-concept in old age', *Journal of Gerontology*, **26**, pp. 240–3.

LIANG, J., DVORKIN, L., KAHANA, E. and MAZIAN, F. (1980) 'Social integration and morale: A re-examination', *Journal of Gerontology*, **35**, pp. 746–57.

LIEBERMAN, M.A. and TOBIN, S.S. (1983) *The Experience of Old Age, Stress, Coping and Survival*, New York, Basic Books.

LIGHT, L.L. and ANDERSEN, P.A. (1985) 'Working memory capacity, age and memory for discourse', *Journal of Gerontology*, **40**, pp. 737–47.

LINDESAY, J. (1986) 'Suicide and attempted suicide in old age', in MURPHY, E. (Ed.) *Affective Disorders in the Elderly*, Edinburgh, Churchill Livingstone.

LINDESAY, J., BRIGGS, K. and MURPHY, E. (1989) 'The Guy's/Age Concern Survey. Prevalence rates of cognitive impairment, depression and anxiety in an urban elderly community', *British Journal of Psychiatry*, **155**, pp. 317–29.

LOETHER, H.J. (1965) 'The meaning of work and adjustment to retirement', in SHOSTAK, A.B. and GOMBERG, W. (Eds) *Blue Collar World*, Englewood Cliffs, NJ, Prentice-Hall.

LOEVINGER, J. (1976) *Ego Development: Conception and Theory*, San Francisco, Jossey-Bass.

LOPATA, H. (1973) *Widowhood in an American City*, Cambridge, Cambridge University Press.

LOWENTHAL, M.F. (1975) *Four Stages of Life*, San Francisco, Jossey-Bass.

LOWENTHAL, M.F. and HAVEN, C. (1968) 'Interaction and adaptation: Intimacy as a critical variable', *American Sociological Review*, **38**, pp. 20–31.

MACMAHON, B. and PUGH, T.F. (1965) 'Suicide in the widowed', *American Journal of Epidemiology*, **81**, pp. 23–31.

MADDOX, G.L. (1970) 'Themes and issues in sociological theories of human aging', *Human Development*, **13**, 1, pp. 17–27.

MARSH, G. (1980) 'Perceptual changes with ageing', in BUSSE, E.W. and BLAZER D.G. (Eds) *Handbook of Geriatric Psychiatry*, New York, Van Nostrand Reinhold.

MARTIN, J. and DORAN, A. (1966) 'Evidence concerning the relationship between health and retirement', *Sociological Review*, **14**, pp. 329–43.

MATARAZZO, J.D. (1972) *Wechsler's Measurement and Appraisal of Adult Intelligence*, 5th edn, Baltimore, Williams and Wilkins.

MAZESS, R. and FORMAN, S. (1979) 'Longevity and age by exaggeration in Vilcabamba, Ecuador', *Journal of Gerontology*, **34**, pp. 94–8.

McCALLY, M., GREENLICK, M. and BECK, J.C. (1984) 'Research in geriatrics: Needs and priorities', in CASSEL, C. and WALSH, J.R. (Eds) *Geriatric Medicine*, **2**, New York, Springer.

McCLURE, G.M.G. (1984) 'Trends in suicide rate for England and Wales, 1975–1980', *British Journal of Psychiatry*, **144**, pp. 119–24.

McCULLOCH, A.W. (1985) 'Adjustment to Old Age in a Changing Society', PhD Thesis, University of Southampton.

McGHIE, A., CHAPMAN, J. and LAWSON, J.S. (1965) 'Changes in immediate memory with age', *British Journal of Psychology*, **56**, pp. 69–75.

McGRATH, J.E. and KELLY, J.R. (1986) *Time and Human Interaction: Toward a Social Psychology of Time*, New York, Guilford.

McMAHON, A.W. and RHUDICK, P.J. (1964) 'Reminiscing: Adaptational significance in the aged', *Archives of General Psychiatry*, **10**, pp. 292–8.

MEYER, B.J.F. and RICE, G.E. (1989) 'Prose processing in adulthood: The text, the learner and the task', in POON, L.W., RUBIN, D.C. and WILSON, B.A. (Eds) *Everyday Cognition in Adulthood and Old Age*, New York, Cambridge University Press.

MILLER, D.F., HICKS, S.P., D'AMATO, C.J. and LANDIS, J.R. (1984) 'A descriptive study of neuritic plaques and neurofibrillary tangles in an autopsy population', *American Journal of Epidemiology*, **120**, pp. 331–41.

MILLER, E. (1977) *Abnormal Ageing*, London, John Wiley and Sons.

MISHARA, B.L. and KASTENBAUM, R. (1980) *Alcohol and Old Age*, New York, Grune and Stratton.

MOLINARI, V. and REICHLIN, R.E. (1985) 'Life review reminiscence in the elderly: A review of the literature', *International Journal of Aging and Human Development*, **20**, pp. 81–92.

MONGE, R. and HULTSCH, D. (1971) 'Paired-associate learning as a function of adult age and the length of the anticipation and inspection intervals', *Journal of Gerontology*, **26**, pp. 157–62.

MOORE, W.E. (1963) *Man, Time and Society*, New York, John Wiley and Sons.

MORIWAKI, S.Y. (1973) 'Self-disclosure, significant others and psychological well-being in old age', *Journal of Health*, **14**, pp. 226–32.

MORONEY, R.M. (1976) *The Family and the State: Considerations for Social Policy*, Harlow, Longman.

MORTIMER, J.A. (1983) 'Alzheimer's disease and senile dementia: Prevalence and incidence', in REISBERG, B. (Ed.) *Alzheimer's Disease*, New York, The Free Press.

MORTIMER, J.A., FRENCH, L.R., HUTTON, J.T. and SCHUMAN, L.M. (1985) 'Head injury as a risk factor for Alzheimer's disease', *Neurology*, **35**, pp. 264–7.

MUGFORD, S. and KENDIG, H. (1986) 'Social relations: Networks and ties', in KENDIG, H. (Ed.) *Ageing and Families: A Social Networks Perspective*, Sydney, Allen and Unwin.

MULLEY, G.P. (1981) 'Stroke rehabilitation: What are we all doing?' in ARIE, T. (Ed.) *Health Care of the Elderly*, Croom Helm, London.

MURPHY, E. (1982) 'Social origins of depression in old age', *British Journal of Psychiatry*, **141**, pp. 135–42.

MURPHY, E. (1983) 'The prognosis of depression in old age', *British Journal of Psychiatry*, **142**, pp. 111–19.

MURPHY, E., SMITH, R., LINDESAY, J. and SLATTERY, J. (1988) 'Increased mortality rate in late life: Depression', *British Journal of Psychiatry*, **152**, pp. 347–53.

MURPHY, E.A. (1978) 'Genetics of longevity in man', in SCHNEIDER, E.L. (Ed.) *The Genetics of Aging*, New York, Plenum Press.

MURPHY, M.D., SANDERS, R.E., GABRIESHESKI, A.S. and SCHMITT, F.A. (1981) 'Metamemory in the aged', *Journal of Gerontology*, **36**, pp. 185–93.

MURRELL, K.F.H. and FORSAITH, B. (1960) 'Age and the timing of movement', *Occupational Psychology*, **34**, pp. 275–9.

NEISSER, U. (1967) *Cognitive Psychology*, New York, Appleton-Century-Crofts.

NEMIROFF, R.A. and COLARUSSO, C.A. (1985) *The Race Against Time: Psychotherapy and Psychoanalysis in the Second Half of Life*, Plenum Press, New York.

NETTLEBECK, T. (1990) 'Intelligence does exist', *The Psychologist*, **3**, 11, pp. 494–7.

NEUGARTEN, B.L. and DATAN, N. (1973) 'Sociological perspectives on the life cycle', in BALTES, P.B. and SCHAIE, K.W. (Eds) *Lifespan Developmental Psychology: Personality and Socialization*, New York, Academic Press.

NEUGARTEN, B.L. and HAGESTAD, G.O. (1976) 'Age and the life course', in BINSTOCK, R.H. and SHANAS, E.L. (Eds) *Handbook of Aging and the Social Sciences*, New York, Van Nostrand Reinhold.

NEUGARTEN, B.L., HAVIGHURST, R.J. and TOBIN, S.S. (1961) 'The measurement of life satisfaction', *Journal of Gerontology*, **16**, pp. 134–43.

NEUGARTEN, B.L., CROTTY, W.F. and TOBIN, S.S. (1964) *Personality in Middle and Late Life*, New York, Atherton Press.

NEUGARTEN, B.L., MOORE, J.W. and LOWE, J.C. (1968a) 'Age norms, age constraints and adult socialization', in NEUGARTEN, B.L. (Ed.) *Middle Age and Aging: A Reader in Social Psychology*, Chicago, University of Chicago Press.

NEUGARTEN, B.L., HAVIGHURST, R.J. and TOBIN, S.S. (1968b) 'Personality and patterns of aging', in NEUGARTEN, B.L. (Ed.) *Middle Age and Aging: A Reader in Social Psychology*, Chicago, University of Chicago Press.

NEWCOMER, R.J. and BEXTON, E.F. (1978) 'Ageing and the environment', in HOBMAN, D. (Ed.) *The Social Challenge of Ageing*, London, Croom Helm.

NEWMAN, G. and NICHOLS, C.R. (1960) 'Sexual activities and attitudes in older persons', *Journal of the American Medical Association*, **173**, pp. 33–5.

NEWMAN, S. (1976) 'Housing Adjustments of Older People: A Report from the Second Phase', Ann Arbor, Institute for Social Research, University of Michigan.

OFFICE OF POPULATION, CENSUSES AND SURVEYS (1989) *Mortality Statistics, 1987, England and Wales*, London, HMSO.

OLDMAN, C. (1990) *Moving in Old Age*, London, HMSO.

OUSLANDER, J.G. and BECK, J.C. (1982) 'Defining the health problems of the elderly', *Annual Review of Public Health*, **3**, p. 55.

OYEBODE, J.R., BARKER, W.A., BLESSED, G., DICK, D.J. and BRITTON, P.G. (1986) 'Cognitive functioning in Parkinson's disease', *British Journal of Psychiatry*, **149**, pp. 720–5.

PALMORE, E. (1969) 'Physical, mental and social factors in predicting longevity', *The Gerontologist*, **9**, pp. 103–8.

PALMORE, E. (1970) 'The effects of aging on activities and attitudes', in PALMORE, E. (Ed.) *Normal Aging*, **I**, Durham, NC, Duke University Press.

PALMORE, E. (1972) 'Compulsory versus flexible retirement: Issues and facts', *The Gerontologist*, **12**, 4, pp. 343–8.

PALMORE, E., CLEVELAND, W.P., NOWLIN, J.B., RAMM, D. and SIEGLER, I.C. (1979) 'Stress and adaptation in later life', *Journal of Gerontology*, **34**, pp. 841–51.

PALMORE, E. and LUIKART, C. (1972) 'Health and social factors related to life satisfaction', *Journal of Health and Social Behaviour*, **13**, pp. 68–80.

PALMORE, E. and MANTON, K. (1973) 'Ageism compared to racism and sexism', *Journal of Gerontology*, **28**, pp. 363–9.

PARKES, C.M. (1972) *Bereavement: Studies of Grief in Adult Life*, London, Tavistock.

PARKINSON, S.R., LINDHOLM, J.M. and URELL, T. (1980) 'Ageing, dichotic memory and digit span', *Journal of Gerontology*, **35**, pp. 87–95.

PENFOLD, P.S. and WALKER, G.A. (1984) *Women and the Psychiatric Paradox*, Milton Keynes, Open University Press.

PERETZ, J.A. and CUMMINGS, J.L. (1988) 'Subcortical dementia', in HOLDEN, U. (Ed.) *Neuropsychology and Ageing*, Croom Helm, London.

PERSSON, G. (1980) 'Sexuality in a 70-year-old urban population', *Journal of Psychosomatic Research*, **24**, pp. 335–42.

PETERSON, J.A. (1980) 'Social-psychological aspects of death and dying and mental health', in BIRREN, J.E. and SLOANE, R.B. (Eds) *Handbook of Mental Health and Aging*, Englewood Cliffs, NJ, Prentice-Hall.

PFEIFFER, E. (1969) 'Sexual behaviour in old age', in BUSSE, E.W. and PFEIFFER, E. (Eds) *Behaviour and Adaptation in Late Life*, Boston, Little, Brown.

PFEIFFER, E. and DAVIS, G.C. (1972) 'Determinants of sexual behaviour in middle and old age', *Journal of the American Geriatrics Society*, **20**, pp. 151–8.

PFEIFFER, E., VERWOERD, T.A. and WANG, H.S. (1969) 'The natural history of sexual behaviour in a biologically advantaged group of aged individuals', *Journal of Gerontology*, **24**, pp. 193–8.

PIROZZOLO, F.J., HANSCH, E.C., MORTIMER, D.A., WEBSTER D.D. and KUSKOWSKI, M.A. (1982) 'Dementia in Parkinson's disease. A neuropsychological analysis', *Brain and Cognition*, **1**, pp. 71–83.

PITT, B. (1982) *Psychogeriatrics: An Introduction to the Psychiatry of Old Age*, Edinburgh, Churchill Livingstone.

PITT, B. (1987) 'Delirium and dementia', in PITT, B. (Ed.) *Dementia*, Edinburgh, Churchill Livingstone.

PLOPPER, M. (1990) 'Evaluation and treatment of depression', in KEMP, B., BRUMMEL-SMITH, K. and RAMSDELL, J.W. (Eds) *Geriatric Rehabilitation*, Boston, College-Hill Press.

POST, F. (1962) 'The Significance of Affective Symptoms in Old Age', Maudsley Monograph, **10**, London, Oxford University Press.

POST, F. (1966) *Persistent Persecutory States in the Elderly*, London, Pergamon.

POST, F. (1972) 'The management and nature of depressive illnesses in late life', *British Journal of Psychiatry*, **121**, pp. 393–404.

POST, F. (1980) 'Paranoid, schizophrenia-like, and schizophrenic states in the aged', in BIRREN, J.E. and SLOANE, R.B. (Eds) *Handbook of Mental Health and Aging*, Englewood Cliffs, NJ, Prentice-Hall.

POWERS, E.A., KEITH, P. and GOUDY, W.H. (1975) 'Family relationships and friendships', in ATCHLEY, R.C. (Ed.) *Environment and the Rural Aged*, Washington, DC, Gerontological Society.

PROHASKA, T.R., PARHAM, I.A. and TEITELMAN, J. (1984) 'Age differences in attributions to causality: Implications for intellectual assessment', *Experimental Aging Research*, **10**, pp. 111–117.

RABBITT, P. (1965) 'An age decrement in the ability to ignore irrelevant information', *Journal of Gerontology*, **20**, pp. 233–8.

RABBITT, P. (1968) 'Age and the use of structure in transmitted information', in TALLAND, G.A. (Ed.) *Human Aging and Behaviour*, New York, Academic Press.

RABBITT, P. (1977) 'Changes in problem-solving ability in old age', in BIRREN, J.E. and SCHAIE, K.W. (Eds) *Handbook of the Psychology of Ageing*, 1st edn, New York, Van Nostrand Reinhold.

RABBITT, P. (1980) 'A fresh look at changes in reaction times in old age', in STEIN, D. (Ed.) *The Psychobiology of Ageing: Problems and Perspectives*, New York, Elsevier/North Holland.

RABBITT, P. (1988) 'Social psychology, neurosciences and cognitive psychology need each other; (and gerontology needs all three of them)', *The Psychologist*, **1**, 12, pp. 500–6.

RABINS, P.V. and FOLSTEIN, M. (1982) 'Delirium and dementia: Diagnostic criteria and fatality rates', *British Journal of Psychiatry*, **140**, pp. 149–53.

RAGAN, P.K. and WALES, J.B. (1980) 'Age stratification and the life course', in BIRREN, J.E. and SLOANE, R.B. (Eds) *Handbook of Mental Health and Aging*, Englewood Cliffs, NJ, Prentice-Hall.

RAKOWSKI, W. (1984) 'Methodological considerations for research on late life future temporal perspective', *International Journal of Aging and Human Development*, **19**, pp. 25–40.

REDING, M., HAYCOX, J. and BLASS, J. (1985) 'Depression in patients referred to a dementia clinic: A three-year prospective study', *Archives of Neurology*, **42**, pp. 894–6.

REICHARD, S., LIVSON, F. and PETERSON, P.G. (1962) *Ageing and Personality: A Study of Seventy Eight Older Men*, New York, John Wiley and Sons.

REID, D.W., HAAS, G. and HAWKINS, D. (1977) 'Locus of desired control and positive self-concept of the elderly', *Journal of Gerontology*, **32**, pp. 441–50.

REIFLER, B.V., LARSON, E. and HANLEY, R. (1982) 'Co-existence of cognitive impairment and depression in geriatric outpatients', *American Journal of Psychiatry*, **139**, pp. 623–6.

REIFLER, B.V. and TERI, L. (1986) 'Rehabilitation and Alzheimer's disease', in BRODY, S.J. and RUFF, G.E. (Eds) *Aging and Rehabilitation: Advances in the State of the Art*, New York, Springer.

REISBERG, B., FERRIS, S.H., DeLEON, M.J. and CROOKS, T. (1982) 'The global deterioration scale for assessment of primary degenerative dementia', *American Journal of Psychiatry*, **139**, pp. 1136–9.

RILEY, M.W. (1976) 'Age strata in social systems', in BINSTOCK, R.H. and SHANAS, E. (Eds) *Handbook of Aging and the Social Sciences*, New York, Van Nostrand Reinhold.

RILEY, M. and FONER, A. (1969) *Aging and Society*, **II**, New York, Russell Sage Foundation.

ROBINSON, R.G., STARR, L.B. and PRICE, T.R. (1984) 'A two year longitudinal study of post-stroke mood disorders: Prevalence and duration at six months follow-up', *British Journal of Psychiatry*, **144**, 256–62.

ROSOW, I. (1969) *Social Integration of the Aged*, New York, The Free Press.

ROSOW, I. (1974) *Socialization to Old Age*, Berkeley, CA, University of California Press.

ROTH, M. (1955) 'The natural history of mental disorders in old age', *Journal of Mental Science*, **102**, pp. 281–301.

ROTTER, J.B. (1966) 'Generalised expectancies for internal versus external control of reinforcement', Psychological Monographs, **80** (1, Whole No.), 609.

ROYAL COLLEGE OF PHYSICIANS (1981) 'Organic mental impairment in the elderly', *Journal of the Royal College of Physicians*, London, **15**, pp. 141–7.

RYFF, C.D. and HEINCKE, S.G. (1983) 'Subjective organisation of personality in adulthood and aging', *Journal of Personality and Social Psychology*, **44**, pp. 807–16.

SAINSBURY, P. (1955) *Suicide in London*, London, Chapman and Hall Ltd.

SALTHOUSE, T.A. (1988) 'The role of processing resources in cognitive ageing', in HOWE, M.L. and BRAINERD, C.J. (Eds) *Cognitive Development in Adulthood: Progress in Cognitive Development Research*, New York, Springer-Verlag.

SALTHOUSE, T.A., KAUSLER, D.H. and SAULTS, J.S. (1988) 'Utilization of path-analytic procedures to investigate the role of processing resources in cognitive aging', *Psychology and Aging*, **3**, pp. 158–66.

SANFORD, J.R.A. (1975) 'Tolerance of debility in elderly dependants by supporters at home: Its significance for hospital practice', *British Medical Journal*, **iii**, pp. 471–3.

SAVAGE, R.D. BRITTON, P.G., BOLTON, N. and HALL, E.H. (1973) *'Intellectual Functioning in the Aged*, London, Methuen.

SCHAIE, K.W. (1958) 'Rigidity-flexibility and intelligence: A cross-sectional study of the adult life span from 20 to 70', Psychological Monographs, **72**, 462 (Whole No. 9).

SCHAIE, K.W. (1967) 'Age changes and age differences', *Gerontologist*, **7**, pp. 128–32.

SCHAIE, K.W. (1980) 'Intelligence and problem-solving', in BIRREN, J.E. and SLOANE, R.B. (Eds) *Handbook of Mental Health and Aging*, Englewood Cliffs, NJ, Prentice-Hall.

SCHAIE, K.W. (1983) 'The Seattle Longitudinal Study: A twenty-one year exploration of psychometric intelligence in adulthood', in SCHAIE, K.W. (Ed.) *Longitudinal Studies of Adult Psychological Development*, New York, Guilford.

SCHAIE, K.W. (1990) 'Intellectual development in adulthood', in BIRREN, J.E. and SCHAIE, K.W. (Eds) *Handbook of the Psychology of Aging*, 3rd edn, London, Academic Press.

SCHAIE, K.W. (1989) 'Late life potential and cohort differences in mental abilities', in PERLMUTTER, M. (Ed.) *Late Life Potential*, Washington, DC, Gerontological Society of America.

SCHAIE, K.W. and LABOUVIE-VIEF, G. (1974) 'Generational versus ontogenetic components of change in adult cognitive behaviour: A fourteen year cross-sequential study', *Developmental Psychology*, **10**, pp. 305–20.

SCHAIE, K.W. and PARHAM, I.A. (1976) 'Stability of adult personality traits. Facts or fable?' *Journal of Personality and Social Psychology*, **34**, pp. 146–58.

SCHAIE, K.W. and WILLIS, S.L. (1986) 'Can intellectual decline in the elderly be reversed?' *Developmental Psychology*, **22**, pp. 223–32.

SCHONFIELD, D. (1980) 'Learning, memory and aging', in BIRREN, J.E. and SLOANE, R.B. (Eds) *Handbook of Mental Health and Aging*, Englewood Cliffs, NJ, Prentice-Hall.

SCHONFIELD, D., TRUEMAN, V. and KLINE, D. (1972) 'Recognition tests of dichotic listening and the age variable', *Journal of Gerontology*, **27**, pp. 487–93.

SCHROOTS, J.J.F. and BIRREN, J.E. (1990) 'Concepts of time and aging in science', in BIRREN, J.E. and SCHAIE, K.W. (Eds) *Handbook of the Psychology of Aging*, 3rd edn, London, Academic Press.

SEELBACH, W.C. and SAUER, W.J. (1977) 'Filial responsibility expectations and morale among aged parents', *Gerontologist*, **17**, pp. 492–9.

SELIGMAN, M. (1975) *Helplessness: On Depression, Development and Death*, San Francisco, W.H. Freeman.

SHANAS, E. (1968) 'A note on restriction of life space: Attitudes of age cohorts', *Journal of Health and Social Behaviour*, **9**, pp. 86–90.

SHANAS, E., TOWNSEND, P., WEDDERBURN, D. FRIIS, H., MILHAJ, P. and STEHOUWER, J. (1968) *Old People in Three Industrial Societies*, London, Routledge and Kegan Paul.

SHEPPARD, H.L. (1976) 'Work and retirement', in BINSTOCK, R.H. and SHANAS, E. (Eds) *Handbook of Aging and the Social Sciences*, New York, Van Nostrand.

SHERMAN, E. (1981) *Counseling the Aging. An Integrative Approach*, New York, The Free Press.

SHNEIDMAN, E.S. (1973) 'Suicide notes', *Psychiatry*, **36**, pp. 379–94.

SIEGLER, I.C. (1980) 'The psychology of adult development and ageing', in BUSSE, E.W. and BLAZER, D.G. (Eds) *Handbook of Geriatric Psychiatry*, New York, Van Nostrand Reinhold.

SIEGLER, I.C. and BOTWINICK, J. (1979) 'A long-term longitudinal study of the ability of older adults — the matter of selective subject attrition, *Journal of Gerontology*, **34**, pp. 242–8.

SIEGLER, I.C. and GATZ, M. (1985) 'Age patterns in locus of control', in PALMORE, E., BUSSE, E.W., MADDOX, G.L., NOWLIN, J.B. and SIEGLER, I.C. (Eds) *Normal Ageing*, **II**, Durham, NC, Duke University Press.

SIEGLER, I.C., GEORGE, L.K. and OKUN, M.A. (1979) 'Cross-sequential analysis of personality', *Developmental Psychology*, **15**, pp. 350–1.

SIMON, A. (1980) 'The neuroses, personality disorders, alcoholism, drug use and misuse, and crime in the aged', in BIRREN, J.E. and SLOANE, R.B. (Eds) *Handbook of Mental Health and Aging*, Englewood Cliffs, NJ, Prentice-Hall.

SIMONTON, D.K. (1988) 'Age and outstanding achievement: What do we know after over a century of research?' *Psychological Bulletin*, **104**, pp. 251–67.

SIMONTON, D.K. (1990) 'Creativity and wisdom in aging', in BIRREN, J.E. and SCHAIE, K.W. (Eds) *Handbook of the Psychology of Aging*, 3rd edn, London, Academic Press.

SIMPSON, I.H., BLACK, K. and McKINNEY, J. (1966) 'Work and retirement', in SIMPSON, I.H. and McKINNEY, J.C. (Eds) *Social Aspects of Aging*, Durham, NC, Duke University Press.

SIMPSON, S., WOODS, R.T. and BRITTON, P.G. (1981) 'Depression and engagement in a residential home for the elderly', *Behaviour Research and Therapy*, **19**, pp. 435–8.

SINEX, F.M. and MERRIL, C.R. (1982) 'Alzheimer's disease, Down's syndrome and aging', *Annals of the New York Academy of Sciences*, **396**, pp. 39–53.

SINGLETON, W.T. (1955) 'Age and performance timing on simple skills', in *Old Age in the Modern World*, Report 3rd Congress, International Association of Gerontology, London, 1954, Edinburgh, Livingstone.

SINNOTT, J.D. (1986) 'Sex roles and aging. Theory and research from a systems perspective', *Contributions to Human Development*, **15**, New York, Karger.

SLOANE, R.B. (1980) 'Organic brain syndrome', in BIRREN, J.E. and SLOANE, R.B. (Eds) *Handbook of Mental Health and Aging*, Englewood Cliffs, NJ, Prentice-Hall.

SMITH, J.S. and KILOH, L.G. (1981) 'The investigation of dementia: Results in 200 consecutive admissions', *Lancet*, 11 April, pp. 824–7.

SMITH, R.G. and MINDHAM, R.H.S. (1987) 'Dementia in disorders of movement', in PITT, B. (Ed.) *Dementia*, Edinburgh, Churchill-Livingstone.

SOCIAL TRENDS (1989) No. 19, Central Statistical Office, London, HMSO.

SOLEM, P.E. (1976) 'Paid work after retirement age and mortality', in *Retirement: Norwegian Experiences*, Oslo, Norwegian Institute of Gerontology.

SONTAG, S. (1978) 'The double standard of ageing', in CARVER, V. and LIDDIARD, P. (Eds) *An Ageing Population*, Sevenoaks, Kent, Hodder and Stoughton.

SPEARMAN, C. (1904) 'General intelligence': Objectively determined and measured', *American Journal of Psychology*, **15**, pp. 201–92.

SPEARMAN, C. (1927) *The Abilities of Man*, London, Macmillan and Co.

STENBACK, A. (1980) 'Depression and suicidal behaviour in old age', in BIRREN, J.E. and SLOANE, R.B. (Eds) *Handbook of Mental Health and Aging*, Englewood Cliffs, NJ, Prentice-Hall.

STERNBERG, R.J. (1985) 'Implicit theories of intelligence, creativity, and wisdom', *Journal of Personality and Social Psychology*, **49**, pp. 607–77.

STEVENSON, O. (1981) 'Caring and dependency', in HOBMAN, D. (Ed.) *The Impact of Ageing*, London, Croom Helm.

STOKES, G. (1983) 'Work, unemployment and leisure', *Leisure Studies*, **2**, pp. 269–86.

STOKES, G. (1990a) 'Work, unemployment and mental health', in COCHRANE, R. and CARROLL, D. (Eds) *Psychology and Social Issues*, London, The Falmer Press.

STOKES, G. (1990b) 'The management of aggression', in STOKES, G. and GOUDIE, F. (Eds) *Working with Dementia*, Bicester, Oxon., Winslow Press.

STOKES, G. and ALLEN, B. (1990) 'Seeking and explanation', in STOKES, G. and GOUDIE, F. (Eds) *Working with Dementia*, Bicester, Oxon., Winslow Press.

STOKES, G. and HOLDEN, U.P. (1990) 'Dementia: Causes and clinical syndromes', in STOKES, G. and GOUDIE, F. (Eds) *Working with Dementia*, Bicester, Oxon., Winslow Press.

STONE, J.L. and NORRIS, A.H. (1966) 'Activities and attitudes of participants in the Baltimore Longitudinal Study', *Journal of Gerontology*, **21**, pp. 575–80.

STREIB, G.F. and SCHNEIDER, J.J. (1971) *Retirement in American Society*, Ithaca, NY, Cambridge University Press.

STREIB, G.F. and THOMPSON, W. (1965) 'The older person in a family context', in SHANAS, E. and STREIB, G.F. (Eds) *Social Structure and the Family: Generational Relationships*, Englewood Cliffs, NJ, Prentice-Hall.

SUNDERLAND, A., WATTS, K., BADDELEY, A.D. and HARRIS, J.E. (1986) 'Subjective memory assessment and test performance in elderly adults', *Journal of Gerontology*, **41**, pp. 376–84.

SUSSMAN, M.S. (1965) 'Relationships of adult children with their parents in the United States', in SHANAS, E. and STREIB, G. (Eds) *Social Structure and the Family: Generational Relationships*, Englewood Cliffs, NJ, Prentice-Hall.

TAULBEE, L.R. and FOLSOM, J.C. (1966) 'Reality orientation for geriatric patients', *Hospital and Community Psychiatry*, **17**, pp. 133–5.

TAYLOR, R. and FORD, G. (1983) 'Inequalities in old age: An examination of age, sex and class differences in a sample of community elderly', *Ageing and Society*, **4**, pp. 183–208.

THOMAE, H. (1976) *Patterns of Aging*, Basle, Karger.

THOMAE, H. (1980) 'Personality and adjustment to aging', in BIRREN, J.E. and SLOANE, R.B. (Eds) *Handbook of Mental Health and Aging*, Englewood Cliffs, NJ, Prentice-Hall.

THOMAE, H., MATHEY, F.J. and KNORR, F. (1977) *Verhaltensweisen und Einstellungen alterer Menschen im Strassenverkehr Schriftenreihe des Bundesministers für Jugend, Familie und Gesundheit*, Bd.50, Bonn-Bad Godesberg.

THOMPSON, C. and WEST, P. (1984) 'The public appeal of sheltered housing', *Ageing and Society*, **4**, pp. 305–26.

THOMPSON, G.B. (1973) 'Work versus leisure roles: An investigation of morale among employed and retired men', in BELL B.D. and PALMORE, E. (Eds) *Contemporary Social Gerontology*, Springfield, IL, Charles C. Thomas.

THURSTONE, L.L. (1938) *Primary Mental Abilities*, Chicago, University of Chicago Press.

TOBIN, S.S. and ETIGSON, E. (1968) 'Effects of stress on earliest memory', *Archives of General Psychiatry*, **19**, pp. 435–44.

TOMLINSON, B.E., BLESSED, G. and ROTH, M. (1970) 'Observations on the brains of demented old people', *Journal of Neurological Science*, **11**, pp. 205–42.

TOWNSEND, P. (1963) *The Family Life of Old People*, Harmondsworth, Penguin.

TROLL, L.E. (1982) *Continuations: Adult Development and Aging*, Monterey, CA, Brooks/Cole.

U'REN, R.C. (1987) 'Introduction', in PITT, B. (Ed.) *Dementia*, Edinburgh, Churchill Livingstone.

VANITY FAIR (1991) 'Has Margaret Thatcher blown it?', June.

VERWOERDT, A., PFEIFFER, E. and WANG, J.S. (1969a) 'Sexual behaviour in senescence. Changes in sexual activity and interest of aging men and women', *Journal of Geriatric Psychiatry*, **2**, pp. 163–80.

VERWOERDT, A., PFEIFFER, E. and WANG, J.S. (1969b) 'Sexual behaviour in senescence II. Patterns of sexual activity and interest', *Geriatrics*, **24**, pp. 137–54.

VICTOR, C.R. (1989) 'Income inequality in later life', in JEFFERYS, M. (Ed.) *Growing Old in the Twentieth Century*, Routledge, London.

VINICK, B. (1978) 'Remarriage in old age', *Family Coordinator*, **27**, pp. 359–63.

WADE, J.P.H. and HACHINSKI, V.C. (1987) 'Multi-infarct dementia', in PITT, B. (Ed.) *Dementia*, Edinburgh, Churchill Livingstone.

WALLER, W. (1938) *The Family: A Dynamic Interpretation*, New York, Dryden.

WALSH, D.A. (1982) 'The development of visual information processes in adulthood and old age', in CRAIK, F.I.M. and TREHUB, S. (Eds) *Ageing and Cognitive Processes*, New York, Plenum Press.

WALSH, D.A. and THOMPSON, L.W. (1978) 'Age differences in visual sensory memory', *Journal of Gerontology*, **33**, pp. 383–7.

WARREN, D.I. (1981) *Helping Networks: How People Cope with Problems in the Urban Community*, Notre Dame, IN, University of Notre Dame.

WARRINGTON, E.K. and SANDERS, H.I. (1971) 'The fate of old memories', *Quarterly Journal of Experimental Psychology*, **24**, pp. 432–42.

WECHSLER, D. (1955) 'Manual for the Wechsler Adult Intelligence Scale', *Psychological Corporation*, New York.

WECHSLER, D. (1958) *The Measurement and Appraisal of Adult Intelligence*, Williams and Wilkins, Baltimore.

WEISMAN, A.D. (1972) 'Common fallacies about dying patients', in WEISMAN, A.D. (Ed.) *Dying and Denying: A Psychiatric Study of Terminality*, New York, Behavioural Publications.

WELFORD, A.T. (1958) *Ageing and Human Skill*, Oxford University Press, London.

WELFORD, A.T. (1977a) 'Motor performance', in BIRREN, J.E. and SCHAIE, K.W. (Eds) *Handbook of the Psychology of Ageing*, 1st edn, New York, Van Nostrand Reinhold.

WELFORD, A.T. (1977b) 'Serial reaction times, continuity of task, single-channel effects and age', in DORNIC, S. (Ed.) *Attention and Performance*, **VI**, Hillsdale, NJ, Erlbaum.

WELFORD, A.T. (1980) 'Sensory, perceptual, and motor processes in older adults', in BIRREN, J.E. and SLOANE, R.B. (Eds) Englewood Cliffs, NJ, Prentice-Hall.

WENGER, G.C. (1984) *The Supportive Network: Coping with Old Age*, London, Allen and Unwin.

WENGER, G.C. (1986) 'A longitudinal study of changes and adaptations in the support networks of Welsh elderly over 75', *Journal of Cross-Cultural Gerontology*, **1**, 3, pp. 277–304.

WENGER, G.C. (1989) 'Support networks in old age: Constructing a typology', in JEFFERYS, M. (Ed.) *Growing Old in the Twentieth Century*, London, Routledge and Kegan Paul.

WILKIE, F. and EISDORFER, C. (1971) 'Intelligence and blood pressure in the aged', *Science*, **172**, pp. 959–62.

WILLIAMSON, J., STOKOE, I.H., GRAY, S., FISHER, M., SMITH, A., McGHEE, A. and STEPHENSON, E. (1964) 'Old people at home: Their unreported needs', *Lancet*, 23 May, pp. 1117–20.

WILLIS, S.L. (1985) 'Towards an educational psychology of the adult learner: Cognitive and intellectual bases', in BIRREN, J.E. and SCHAIE, K.W. (Eds) *Handbook of the Psychology of Aging*, 2nd edn, New York, Van Nostrand Reinhold.

WILLIS, S.L. (1989) 'Improvement with cognitive training: Which dogs learn what tricks?', in POON, L.W. (Ed.) *Everyday Cognition in Adult and Late Life*, New York, Cambridge University Press.

WILSON, B.A. (1989) 'Designing memory therapy programs', in POON, L.W., RUBIN, D.C. and WILSON, B.A. (Eds) *Everyday Cognition in Adulthood and Old Age*, New York, Cambridge University Press.

WINGFIELD, A., STINE, E.A.L., LAHAR, C.J. and ABERDEEN, J.S. (1988) 'Does the capacity of working memory change with age?' *Experimental Aging Research*, **14**, pp. 103–7.

WOLK, S. and KURTZ, I. (1975) 'Positive adjustment and involvement during aging and expectancy for internal control', *Journal of Consulting and Clinical Psychology*, **43**, pp. 173–8.

WOODS, R.T. and BRITTON, P.G. (1985) *Clinical Psychology with the Elderly*, London, Croom Helm.

WORSLEY, P., FITZHENRY, R., MITCHELL, J.C., MORGAN, D.H.J., PONS, V., ROBERTS, B., SHARROCK, W.W. and WARD, R. (1970) *Introducing Sociology*, Harmondsworth, Penguin Books Ltd.

WRIGHT, R.E. (1981) 'Ageing, divided attention, and processing capacity', *Journal of Gerontology*, **36**, pp. 605–14.

WROE, D.C.L. (1973) 'The elderly', *Social Trends*, **4**, pp. 23–33.

ZACKS, R.T. (1982) 'Encoding strategies used by young and elderly adults in a keeping track task', *Journal of Gerontology*, **37**, pp. 203–11.

ZEMORE, R. and EAMES, N. (1979) 'Psychic and somatic symptoms of depression among young adults, institutionalised aged and non-institutionalised aged', *Journal of Gerontology*, **34**, 5, pp. 716–22.

Index

DATE DUE